AF412113

Europeanisation and new patterns of governance in Ireland

Manchester University Press

Europeanisation and new patterns of governance in Ireland

Nicholas Rees, Bríd Quinn, Bernadette Connaughton

Manchester University Press

Manchester and New York

distributed exclusively in the USA by Palgrave

Published by Manchester University Press
Oxford Road, Manchester M13 9NR, UK
and Room 400, 175 Fifth Avenue, New York, NY 10010, USA
www.manchesteruniversitypress.co.uk

Distributed in the United States exclusively by
Palgrave Macmillan, 175 Fifth Avenue, New York,
NY 10010, USA

Distributed in Canada exclusively by
UBC Press, University of British Columbia, 2029 West Mall,
Vancouver, BC, Canada V6T 1Z2

British Library Cataloguing-in-Publication Data
A catalogue record for this book is available from the British Library

Library of Congress Cataloging-in-Publication Data applied for

ISBN 978 0 7190 7620 6 *hardback*

First published 2009

18 17 16 15 14 13 12 11 10 09   10 9 8 7 6 5 4 3 2 1

Typeset in Minion
by Florence Production Ltd, Stoodleigh, Devon
Printed in Great Britain
by TJ International, Padstow, Cornwall

Contents

List of figures and tables

List of contributors

Nicholas Rees is Professor of Politics and Head of the Department of Politics and History, Liverpool Hope University. His teaching and research interests include: EU institutions and policy-making, Ireland and the EU, EU external relations, regional integration, international relations and UN peacekeeping. He is co-author of *The Poor Relation: Irish Foreign Policy Towards the Third World* (Gill and Macmillan, 1993), *United Nations Peacekeeping in the Post-Cold War Era* (Frank Cass, 2005), *EU Enlargement and Multi-level Governance in Public Policy-making* (Ashgate, 2006).

Bríd Quinn lectures in Public Administration and Politics in the Department of Politics and Public Administration, University of Limerick. Her research interests include: EU regional policy; governance; renewal of local democracy; partnership; comparative local government and public management reform. She has contributed to a range of books and journals, most recently to the *International Journal of Public Sector Management* (2008), *Tensions between Local Governance and Local Democracy* (Reed Elsevier, 2007), *EU Enlargement and Multi-level Governance in Public Policy-making* (Ashgate, 2006) and the *Jahrbuch des Foderalismus* (2005).

Bernadette Connaughton lectures in Public Administration in the Department of Politics and Public Administration, University of Limerick. Her teaching and research interests include: environmental policy and administration, the impact of EU policy-making on national administrative systems, and political-administrative reform in a comparative perspective. Her publications include journal articles in *Public Administration, Regional and Federal Studies, Irish Political Studies* and the book *Politico-administrative Dilemma: Traditional Problems and New Solutions* (NISPAcee, 2006), co-edited with B. Guy Peters and Georg Sootla.

Preface and acknowledgements

In the fifty years or so since publication of the first Programme for Economic Expansion, and particularly during the 'celtic tiger' years, the pace of Ireland's economic, social and political development has intrigued analysts. A leading role in this transformation is commonly ascribed to Europeanisation, with the European Union being credited as the instigator, facilitator and dictator of change. But is this the only explanation? This book challenges the usually unquestioning acceptance of the EU's dominant role in effecting change. It contends that domestic structural and cultural features as well as global developments must also be considered as major determinants of change.

The book has its genesis in research carried out during the EU 5th Framework ADAPT project, Adapting to EU Multi-level Governance: Regional and Environmental Policy in Cohesion and CEE countries. Analysis of the adaptation and adjustments evident in the governance of the regional and in understanding the environmental spheres prompted further questions and debates about the impact of Europeanisation. As observers of political and administrative development in Ireland, the authors were engrossed by the interplay of internal and external catalysts of change and sought to explore the nuances of Ireland's vicarious relationship with the EU. We believe the study provides a topical and perceptive exploration which will be of interest to both scholars and policy actors seeking to understand Ireland's transformation and the EU's contribution to that transformation.

We are grateful to our Greek, Portuguese, Hungarian and Polish partners in the ADAPT project whose questions and observations inspired this study. In researching the material for the book we benefited from the insights of academics, administrators, activists and analysts, through formal interviews and social conversations. We acknowledge their contribution and respect the wishes of those who sought anonymity. Our thanks also go to the team at Manchester University Press for their advice and assistance. In addition, our colleagues at the University of Limerick and Liverpool Hope University provided help which was much appreciated. We want to express thanks to our families whose support and encouragement enabled us to bring our book project to fruition.

Nicholas Rees, Bríd Quinn and Bernadette Connaughton

Abbreviations and Irish terms

Abbreviations

CAP	Common Agricultural Policy
CBF	Córas Beoistoic agus Feola
COPA	Comité des Organisations Professionnelles Agricoles
COREPER	Committee of Permanent Representatives
COSAC	Conference of European Affairs Committees
CFSP	Common Foreign and Security Policy
CSF	Community Support Framework
DAF	Department of Agriculture and Food
DFP	Department of Finance and Personnel, Northern Ireland
EAGGF	European Agricultural Guidance Guarantee Fund
ECB	European Central Bank
ECJ	European Court of Justice
ECU	European Currency Unit
EFTA	European Free Trade Association
EMS	European Monetary System
EMU	Economic and Monetary Union
EP	European Parliament
EPA	Environmental Protection Agency
EPC	European Political Cooperation
EPCU	European policy and coordination unit
EPU	European Political Union
ERDF	European Regional Development Fund
ERM	Exchange Rate Mechanism
ESDP	European Security and Defence Policy
ESF	European Social Fund
ETUC	European Trade Union Confederation
FÁS	National Training Authority
FDI	Foreign Direct Investment
FSAI	Food Safety Association of Ireland

GAA	Gaelic Athletic Association
GATT	General Agreement on Tariffs and Trade
GDP	gross domestic product
GFA	Good Friday Agreement
GNP	gross national product
GVA	gross value added
IBEC	Irish Business and Employers' Confederation
ICMSA	Irish Creamery Milk Suppliers' Association
ICTU	Irish Congress of Trade Unions
IDA	Industrial Development Authority
IFA	Irish Farmer's Association
ILO	International Labour Organisation
IMF	International Monetary Fund
MEP	Member of the European Parliament
MNC	multi-national corporation
MTR	mid-term review
NATO	North Atlantic Treaty Organisation
NDP	National Development Plan
NFA	National Farmers' Association
NEPI	New Environmental Policy Instrument
NESC	National Economic and Social Council
NESF	National Economic and Social Forum
NGOS	Non-governmental Organisations
NIEC	National Industrial Economic Council
NPM	New Public Management
NSRF	national strategic reference framework
NUTS	Nomenclature of Territorial Units for Statistics
OECD	Organisation for Economic Cooperation and Development
OEE	Office of Environmental Enforcement
OMC	Open Method of Coordination
ONEIB	Office of the Northern Ireland Executive in Brussels
PfP	Partnership for Peace
PNR	Programme for National Recovery
PPP	public private partnerships
RDO	Regional Development Organisations
REPS	Rural Environment Protection Scheme
SEA	Single European Act
SEUBP	Special EU Programme Body
SMI	Strategic Management Initiative
SPC	Strategic Policy Committee
SPS	Single Payment Scheme
SSBs	State sponsored bodies

TASC	Think-tank for Action in Social Change
TEU	Treaty on European Union
UN	United Nations
UNEP	United Nations Environmental Programme
UNICE	Union of Industrial and Employers' Confederations of Europe
WCED	World Commission on Environment and Development
WEU	Western European Union
WTO	World Trade Organisation

Irish terms

Aer Lingus	Air fleet Aer Loingeas
An Bord Pleanála	Planning board
An Taisce	National Trust for Ireland
Bunreacht na hÉireann	Constitution of Ireland
Dáil Éireann	Lower house of parliament
Fianna Fáil	Soldiers of Ireland
Fine Gael	Irish race
Forfás	National policy and advisory board for enterprise, trade, science, technology and innovation
Garda Síochána na hÉireann	Peace guard of Ireland
Gardái	Guards
Oireachtas	Irish parliament (both houses)
Seanad Éireann	Senate (upper house of parliament)
Tánaiste	Deputy Prime Minister
Taoiseach	Prime Minister
Teachta Dála	Member of Dáil Éireann

1

Ireland and the European Union

Nicholas Rees, Bríd Quinn and Bernadette Connaughton

Introduction: examining Europeanisation in Ireland

Politicians, diplomats and policy-makers consider Ireland's economic and political development as an unparalleled success story with the state long ranked as one of the top performing economies in Europe. It was only in late 2007 that Ireland's economic growth faltered in the light of escalating oil prices, a downturn in global markets and a drop-off in domestic consumption and production. However, its performance over almost two decades has been remarkable even when measured against large economies such as Germany and France. It has also outstripped the performance of other cohesion states, such as Portugal, Spain and Greece and is considered an example to be emulated among new EU member states, as evidenced by the many parliamentary, economic and political officials who have visited Ireland.

Ireland moved from being amongst the poorest members in 1973 to one of the richest EU member states by 2006. More recently, Ireland's place in Europe is being redefined in the light of the global economic turmoil which witnessed oil prices doubling in the year up to April 2008. This creates not only domestic pressures but creates a paradox for Irish policy-makers as they seek to maintain Ireland's economic position, while remaining supportive of those new member states which have yet to climb out of relative poverty (Holmes, 2005). Irish diplomats have been past masters at reconciling such contradictions and have usually found pragmatic 'Irish' solutions to 'Irish' problems (Laffan and Tannam, 1998; Laffan, 2006). What is less well understood is that Ireland's early experience with EU membership was problematic on a range of economic, social and political fronts. Ireland was not an instant success story following membership in the 1970s, while the 1980s were characterised by a period of economic stagnation, with high unemployment and little economic growth. Ireland was literally the poor relation during this period and it is only since the mid-1990s that the state has made significant economic progress.

Ireland's economic and political relationship with Europe has been changing, particularly because of its changed economic circumstances. It is not that Ireland has become increasingly anti-European; rather, the Irish public are not convinced that a further deepening of European integration will be beneficial to Ireland and are distant from EU developments. Furthermore, as the outcome of the first Nice referendum in 2001 and the lead-up to and outcome of the referendum on the Lisbon Treaty in June 2008 highlighted, many among the Irish public had little knowledge about the treaty, despite all the media coverage and the various party campaigns, and were fearful that they might be voting for something that might adversely affect them. Ireland is by no means atypical in this sense, as successive Eurobarometer surveys suggest that such trends are evident throughout Europe. Public apathy and evidence of antipathy towards further European integration is apparent even in the new member states, while the French and Dutch publics' rejection of the Constitutional Treaty in 2005 indicates disquiet in older EU member states. In many countries, citizens are more interested in seeing the EU as contributing to a rise in the standard of living and the creation of more jobs. Europeans are also concerned about the effects of globalisation, which is seen as a threat to European jobs.

Hence, the impact of Europe on its member states can have both positive and negative consequences. Economies that are dependent on high levels of trade are particularly vulnerable to external forces, whether European or global. Ireland, because of its open economy, has been susceptible to external pressures thus making it an interesting case to examine in terms of the impact of Europeanisation. Europeanisation is used to describe and explain the extent of change in national politics. Such change is believed to be brought about by participating in and implementing EU policies which the member states shape themselves. The challenge in research terms is to develop a theoretical and methodological framework for understanding the impact Europeanisation has had on Ireland. Fundamental to this endeavour is a consideration of how well the Irish case is understood and a realisation that much of the literature on the 'celtic tiger' does not adequately explore the relationship between EU membership and Ireland's domestic economic, political and social development.

In most analyses of Ireland's success, Europeanisation is regarded as having been a primary factor. Consequently, in this study the dependent variable is Europeanisation, or more precisely the impact of Europeanisation on Ireland. Although purporting that such a relationship exists, and that it is essential to understanding how Ireland has changed, relatively few studies of Ireland have defined Europeanisation or systematically considered how it can be examined (Tonra, 2001). A wealth of literature, however, does exist on the concept of Europeanisation. This provides a rich framework and, as a starting point for this study, it is explored in chapter 2. This literature highlights the need to examine the impact of the European Union on its member states and uses the term 'Europeanisation' to describe and explain the changes resulting from participation in EU structures, policies and processes. Because of its comprehensiveness, Radaelli's definition has been selected as a key element of the conceptual basis for this book. This explication suggests that 'Europeanisation refers to the processes of (a) construction (b) diffusion and (c) institutionalisation of formal and informal rules, procedures, policy paradigms, styles, "ways of doing things" and shared beliefs and norms which are first defined and consolidated in the making of EU decisions and then incorporated in the logic of domestic discourse, identities, political structures, and public policies' (2003: 30). There are, of course, a range of other definitions some of which are discussed in chapter two. The main emphasis in these explanations is on how, or to what extent, has EU membership and participation changed domestic policies and institutions.

Cognisant of these dimensions of Europeanisation, the objective of the present study is to systematically explore the impact Europeanisation has had on selected policy domains. The range of case studies selected, namely, the economy, regional development, agricultural and rural policy, environmental policy and foreign relations encompasses the key sectors of change. Each of the cases examined is located in its historical context with the focus on the domestic arrangements which prevailed prior to EU membership, particularly, the institutional and policy arrangements. It is hypothesised that following EU membership, and over time, different policy areas are subjected to varying adaptational pressures, reflecting differing levels of EU policy influence and involvement. In some instances, European pressures are clearly a catalyst for change, given that member states are required to adopt EU policies. In other areas the pressures have been less apparent, perhaps reflecting the EU's more limited policy involvement, or the fact that limited change is required. In each instance the impact of Europeanisation on existing institutional arrangements is examined and the degree of adaptation and change assessed. Closely related to the impact of Europeanisation on institutional adaptation is its impact on policy content and patterns of governance, key themes in this study.

Historical and political dimensions prior to EEC membership

To understand the impact of Europeanisation on Ireland it is important to locate the analysis in the historical context of the development of the modern Irish state. The immediate aftermath of Irish independence in 1922 did not herald major change and, until the 1960s, Ireland remained an isolated island on the periphery of Europe. In its first four decades of sovereignty, rather than following the European model of development or actively engaging in international affairs, the new state remained not merely geographically linked but also economically and politically linked to Britain. In effect, Ireland's progress was closely tied to that of Britain, and its neighbour continued to exert a strong influence on many facets of Irish life. The state remained largely aloof from international politics, albeit joining the United Nations in 1955. Neutrality in World War II was regarded as both a practical policy choice and a symbol of Irish sovereignty (Girvin, 2006; Falkner and Laffan, 2005; Finnegan, 2001). Ireland was not an active early supporter of European integration, and while the state did join a number of European and international organisations in the post-war period, it used such organisations to assert its independence and sovereignty (Coakley *et al.*, 1997).

Politically, independence did not precipitate transition problems as Ireland inherited a well-established set of structures based on the British model. The new Irish administration exhibited conservative cultural norms and wholly absorbed the organisation and principles of its predecessor. Domestic politics revolved mostly around the realm of the centrist civil war parties Fianna Fáil and Fine Gael. In terms of economy, Ireland was predominantly agricultural and had yet to experience the rigours of an industrial revolution. The state missed out on the strong growth witnessed in other European economies during the post-war expansion. The need for access to wider markets, lack of industry, high unemployment, sustained emigration and the declining condition of public finance prompted a shift in government thinking in the 1950s. Instrumental to this change from a rhetorical tradition of protectionist 'self sufficiency' to liberalisation was the publication of T. K. Whitaker's *Economic Development* in 1958 and the leadership of Taoiseach Séan Lemass. The perception that the Irish economy could only prosper if it were fully open to the European and wider international market transformed policy-making strategy and provided the rationale for the application for EEC membership.

Three economic programmes were implemented prior to EEC membership. They utilised state aids and tax concessions to attract foreign companies to Ireland. As a result the 1960s heralded a decade of unparalleled growth and change in the Irish economy and Europe became a focal point of government policy. The decision to seek membership was therefore bound up with the decision to open the economy in the search for prosperity and welfare (Laffan and O'Donnell, 1998: 156). The reassessment of the domestic economic paradigm is also reflected in concerns over the isolation of Ireland from the discussions to move towards closer economic integration in Western Europe and the eventual formation of the European Free Trade Association (EFTA) in 1958 (Falkner and Laffan, 2005: 211).

Ireland made its first application to join the EEC in July 1961. The driving motive behind the application was principally economic (Laffan, 2003; Maher, 1986). The common agricultural policy would provide expanded markets for Irish farmers while free access to markets for exporters would guarantee that foreign direct investment would flow into Ireland from non-EEC countries.

Symbolic factors also mattered since forging relations with Europe diminished the primacy of the link with Britain and positioned Anglo-Irish relations against the multilateral backdrop of the EEC. The issue of neutrality featured on the agenda, but any perceived threats to Irish neutrality were minimised in the debate. The task facing the government was to illustrate that the Irish position was *sui generis* and did not correspond to those of Sweden, Switzerland or Austria in that its non-involvement in military alliances did not preclude full commitment to the political aims of the Community (Maher, 1986: 141).

In the initial negotiations reservations about Ireland's commitment to the political aims of the Community did arise given its non-membership of the North Atlantic Treaty Organisation (NATO) and doubts were also expressed over the underdeveloped state of the economy (Finnegan, 2001). Despite setbacks caused by the fractious French–British relationship regarding Britain's application, EEC membership remained an objective. Meanwhile, the shift from 'dependence to interdependence' in the emergence of international governance (Laffan and O'Donnell, 1998) continued with Ireland joining the International Monetary Fund (IMF) and the General Agreement on Tariffs and Trade (GATT) by 1967. Trade links with Britain were also strengthened under the Anglo-Irish Free Trade Agreements signed in 1965. In 1969 de Gaulle's departure and replacement with Pompidou marked a transition whereby Ireland's application was revived and negotiations began in 1970.

Ireland's entry into the EEC

Following the treaty of accession in 1972, Ireland became a member of the EEC on 1 January 1973. Although EEC membership was moulded by the expectation of economic benefits, it was apparent by 1970 that membership would entail implications of a political and social character. Membership altered the relationship between the executive and parliament (Oireachtas) as the latter no longer had the sole law-making power. This required an amendment to the Irish Constitution that formed part of the 1972 referendum. A necessary preliminary to formal ratification was the publication of a white paper entitled 'The Accession of Ireland to the European Communities'. This provided a detailed account of the terms for Ireland's accession. But it also contained an assessment of the implications of accession and its constitutional and legal ramifications. Subsequently, the government concluded that the national interest and welfare would best be served by joining the enlarged community. Little attention was paid to how European affairs would be managed after membership since the white paper contained no systematic discussion of the possible implications of membership for policy-making procedures. However, considering the underdeveloped economy and inward looking perspective it is not difficult to adduce that EU membership had a profound impact on the internationalisation of public policy and was a significant factor in the modernisation and industrialisation of economy and society.

Surprisingly, the diminution in sovereignty did not become a major issue in the referendum campaign preceding accession as was the case in Denmark or Britain who also joined in 1973. Before the constitutional referendum Article 29.6 stated: 'no international agreement shall be part of the domestic law of the state save as may be determined by the Oireachtas'. The European Communities Act 1972 provided that, 'The Treaties governing the EC and the existing and future acts adopted by the institutions of those Communities shall be binding on the state and shall be part of the domestic law thereof.' This heralded a major change in Irish administrative law; but was not the subject of particular interest during the referendum campaign. The amendment to Article 29 of the Constitution permitted Irish membership of the EC and provides that the Constitution cannot be invoked to nullify European law or any national law required by membership.

Economic issues continued to be the main focus of the debate over EEC membership with European integration regarded by the Irish political and economic elite and society as a positive sum game (Laffan, 2003). The two major parties Fianna Fáil and Fine Gael together polled 80 per cent of the first preferences in the election prior to the referendum and urged a 'yes' vote. A turnout of 71 per cent voted 83 per cent in favour of membership on 10 May 1972. The Labour party and Sinn Féin had campaigned against membership but Labour accepted the outcome when it went into government with Fine Gael in 1973. The broad political consensus was assisted by the fact that membership in 1973 preceded the growth in the European regulatory framework and the institutionalisation of the 1980s and 1990s. Until direct elections to the European Parliament in 1979 Irish MEPs were selected from the Dáil and served under a dual mandate. Fine Gael was more pro-active in its engagement with the European Parliament and aligned its members to the Christian Democrats whereas Fianna Fáil's strategy was more reactive with it siding with the French Gaullists. Being a small state the objective of the government and other institutional actors was to participate positively in the Community as opposed to engaging as a strategic architect of European integration.

In the early years of membership government attention was focused on issues of key interest to Ireland – agriculture, distributive policies, budget and market access. In general, political actors remained concerned with short-term national issues and public attitudes were largely influenced by the immediate direct economic and social benefits membership could bring. This was an era when GDP per capita levels were merely 58 per cent of the EU average and it would be two more decades before the economic benefits of membership would be compellingly evident (Falkner and Laffan, 2005; Laffan and O'Donnell, 1998). The impact of accession on the legal and social fabric of the state, however, was immediately evident with the application of European law. One early example concerns the guarantee of equal pay for men and women for equal work as detailed in the equal pay directive, a guarantee which initially met with resistance from the Irish government.

Government and governance in Ireland: responding to internal and external influences

The decision to join the European Community marked a significant turning point in the development of the Irish state as it changed the context in which Irish politicians and officials functioned. The community that Ireland joined in 1973 was very different from the European Union of today. In 1973 it was a fledgeling economic community, largely focused on developing a common market, free movement of goods, labour, people and services, and a limited number of policy areas such as agriculture, and it comprised only nine states, compared to twenty-seven in 2008. Therefore, Ireland's development since membership has been occurring in tandem with that of the European Union, an entity which has changed in significant ways since the 1970s. There is, then, a complex relationship between the deepening and widening of European integration and the EU's impact on Ireland's development. The context in which the European Union and its member states function has been evolving and changing, reflecting EU treaty changes and enlargement, the evolution of the modern welfare state system in western Europe, and its response to globalisation. By implication, this means any understanding based on a study of Europeanisation is likely to involve a simplification of a complex process.

The changing character and policy repertoire of the European Union has significant implications for the way in which its member states go about their daily business. Over time, a complex system of multi-level governance which involves an array of national and European level actors in the policy process has emerged. A reawakening of interest in integration theory during the 1990s reflected developments in the European Union. The Single European Act (with its emphasis on completing the internal market) and the Maastricht Treaty on European Union (with its increased involvement of the EU in a range of new policy areas in which competences were shared with the member states) led to a shift in interpretative approaches with such developments being interpreted using a governance lens. As an approach, governance and the study of multi-level governance, offers an alternative to the meta-level or grand theories of integration (Hooghe and Marks 2001; Majone 1996; Peters, 1994, Marks, 1993). It also provides the basis for a more systematic study from a comparative perspective, utilising, as it does, the tools of political science and public policy analysis, thereby allowing for comparison with other systems in Europe and elsewhere (Hix, 2005; Scharpf, 1999). Governance models help in conceptualising and examining the relationship between the EU, its institutions and the member states.

Research on the Irish case has often focused on the institutional and policy adaptation of the state to the requirements arising from the development of new EU policy competences (Laffan and Tannam, 1998; Tonra, 2001; Flynn, 2004; Adshead, 2005; Rees *et al.*, 2006; Laffan, 2006; O'Mahony, 2007). The focus tends to be predominantly on how Irish institutions have adapted their structures, processes and operating procedures to comply with European rules, norms, expectations and practices. Much of the evidence available in studies on EU structural funds, agricultural policy and social affairs suggest that Ireland has pragmatically adapted to Europe or, at least, is perceived by the Commission as being compliant (Barry, Bradley and Hannan; 2001; National Economic and Social Council (NESC); 1989). Arguably the costs of not adapting to Europe would have been high and would have severely damaged the Irish economy, dependent as it was, during much of the 1970s and 1980s on financial subsidies from Europe. In other areas such as environmental policy, taxation, justice and home affairs and foreign policy the state has more vigorously defended national interests. Europeanisation is, therefore, not a unidirectional force, as might be inferred from much of the discussion in the literature. Member states do have an opportunity to influence, shape and at times block European policy at the negotiation stage in the Committee of Permanent Representatives (COREPER), the Council of Ministers and in European summit meetings.

Aside from external forces, such as Europeanisation and globalisation, Ireland's development also needs to be understood in terms of internal forces that have shaped the polity and economy. In this study we place a considerable emphasis on examining domestic structures and policy preferences as important to understanding Europeanisation. In the 1960s Ireland emerged from a period of protectionism and economic isolation that had characterised the 1940s and 1950s, and successive governments sought through their economic policies to promote inward investment. Ireland's membership of the EC in 1973 coincided with a world oil crisis and a breakdown of the international monetary system. Ireland continued to prosper as result of a mix of national incentives, aimed at attracting in foreign investment, and through the transfer of European subsidies to the economy. But international recession in the 1980s highlighted both the internal weaknesses of the economy and its vulnerability to international change. Ireland's traditional industries, in areas such as textiles, clothing, footwear, chemicals and engineering, were exposed to international market forces, leading to import penetration and the demise of many of these domestic industries. By the mid-1980s Ireland faced stagnation, rising taxes, high unemployment, mounting debts and net out-migration. In order to address these problems, the government of the day adopted a new social partnership arrangement. The partnership approach provided a critical means for managing Ireland economic development and is seen by many as core to understanding Ireland's economic success.

This summary suggests that while Europeanisation has impacted on government and governance in Ireland, it only partly explains the change and the developments that have taken place in the Irish state in recent years. In order to understand institutional change and adaptation in the Irish case, it is necessary to examine the interplay between external and internal influences that have shaped the polity. Therefore, this study focuses on both Europeanisation and domestic mediating structures such as political parties, interest groups and public opinion, as well as formal institutions, structures and policy processes. The research also seeks to ascertain whether there is evidence of new patterns of governance in the Irish case; a possible effect of Europeanisation, but also a consequence of social partnership and the socio-political transformation which Ireland has undergone. The kernel of the investigation is the complex interplay between the domestic and external influences which framed and nurtured Ireland's enigmatic transformation. The remainder of the study explores different aspects of this interplay and uncovers a perplexing narrative of continuity and change.

Organisation of the book

The study is organised around ten chapters. This, the first chapter, depicted the context and outlined the hypotheses which prompted the study. Chapter 2 considers whether Europeanisation has been a catalyst for change. A theoretical framework for understanding the effects of Europeanisation on Ireland is provided in this chapter. Drawing on the wide theoretical and substantive literature on Europeanisation, the chapter interrogates these conceptualisations and relates them to the Irish case. It is argued that Europeanisation has influenced changes in Irish policy-making and imple-mentation but domestic forces have mediated the impact of Europeanisation. Using insights from historical and social institutionalism, this chapter explores the relationship between Europe and the Irish political system. It examines the way in which key variables (namely, institutions, policies, intergovernmental relations, political parties and cultural values) have been affected to differing degrees.

Chapter 3 examines the mediating forces and the domestic polity. The chapter looks at the underpinnings of Irish society, considering the role of culture, values and attitudes as important in understanding the degree to which Europeanisation impacts on Ireland. The effects of Europeanisation have been filtered by Ireland's complex history, distinctive political culture, social norms, nationalistic penchants and strongly centralised political-administrative structure as well as its geographical and population size. This chapter analyses the way in which these factors have moderated the Europeanisation process. Following this, chapter 4 discusses the political institutions and administrative adaptation. The impact of Europeanisation on Ireland's national and sub-national institutions and systems of public administration and public policy is examined. Key themes include: the principal institutional structures of government and the impact of Europe on the organisation of policy-making; examination of the major adjustments to Europe in response to pressures for change; evidence of institutional innovation and new sub-national structures, as well as the impact on the organisation of public administration and the policy process (design, content, outcomes and implementation).

The first case study, chapter 5, considers the development of the Irish economy and Europe. This chapter uses the evolution of Ireland's economic policy as a test case for Europeanisation. By exploring the significant moves from protectionism (in the early decades of the new state) to partnership (since the 1980s) and Ireland's adaptation to the strictures of the single market, the single currency and increasing global pressures, this chapter illustrates the degree to which Europe frames Ireland's economic policy choices and highlights the importance of domestic mediating forces. Chapter 6 focuses on regional policy and politics by examining the impact of Europeanisation on regionalism and territorial politics and the pragmatic manner in which Ireland has adapted to European opportunities and requirements. It also explores how regional policy in Northern Ireland has been influenced by Europeanisation and how North-South cooperation has been fostered in this policy area. The chapter examines existing sub-national structures, institutions and policy-making as well as Irish attitudes to regional policy. It investigates the impact of Europe on sub-national government, the changes arising from EU membership, including new structures and patterns of governance, the impact on central–local relations, local participation in governance and cross-border collaboration.

Chapter 7 looks at the politics of environmental policy. The impact of Europeanisation on Irish environmental policy is considered, by first looking at Ireland's existing environmental policy framework, institutional structures and attitudes to environmental issues. The chapter then examines the impact of European legislation on Ireland, focusing on institutional and policy changes, as well as opposition to change. Particular case studies are used to highlight the range of environmental problems Ireland has faced and how public and private actors have responded to these challenges.

The following chapter examines agricultural issues, which have tended to dominate Ireland's involvement within the EU. This chapter maps the changing position of agriculture within Ireland's economy and society and the adaptational pressures arising from European policy changes. It traces the influence of these policies and the significant financial transfers on Irish agricultural policy and practices as well as the social consequences of such change. The chapter also explores the emergence of rural development policies as a feature of changing agricultural policy at both national and European levels.

Ireland's foreign relations especially its place and role in international affairs provides the focus for chapter 9. Involvement in the EU has had a considerable influence on both the formulation and conduct of Ireland's foreign policy. This chapter uses foreign policy as a case study to illustrate how an established policy area was fundamentally affected and shaped by Europeanisation. By examining the evolution of Ireland's foreign policy and the adaptation of its substance and conduct, the chapter suggests how Ireland's engagement with the EU has influenced its political development and challenged the traditional stance on issues such as military neutrality. It is argued that this is a case where Irish political leaders, largely from Fianna Fáil and Fine Gael, and the civil service, mainly from the Department of Foreign Affairs, utilised Europeanisation to refocus Irish foreign policy inside Europe.

The concluding chapter considers the institutional learning and adaptation to Europe which has occurred in Ireland. The chapter assesses the main institutional and policy changes which have arisen out of Europeanisation, while highlighting the limits of such change and stressing the importance of the pre-existing institutional and social structures. The chapter includes a comparison of the contrasting policy areas – established and nascent – with a view to establishing the impact of Europeanisation and deducing under what conditions adaptation and learning are most likely to occur. The chapter concludes by suggesting Europeanisation has a limited explanatory value, which can only account some of the time for why and how change occurs at the domestic level, although it helps to highlight the complex interplay between European, global and domestic pressures for change, adaptation and learning.

The study expands our understanding of the remarkable phenomenon of Ireland's development, especially following EEC membership up to the present day. The different and contrasting case studies serve to provide an extensive comparative assessment of the impact of Europeanisation and the multifarious manner in which it is mediated through domestic factors. Analysis of the varying degrees of change and adaptation within the specific policy spheres helps to codify and explain the conditions under which successful adaptation and learning are likely to take place. It makes a further contribution by extrapolating from the specificities of the Irish experience insights which have a general application for explaining the impact of Europeanisation and globalisation on polity, policy and politics in other EU member states.

2

Europeanisation: a catalyst for change

Nicholas Rees and Bernadette Connaughton

Introduction

Europeanisation has emerged as a relatively new yet significant area in the study of European integration. It represents a shift in conceptualising developments in the European Union and presents opportunities for structuring and analysing the impact of the EU on the polity, politics and policies of member states. Europeanisation is critical to our understanding of transformations of the national system, improvements in institutional capacity and success or failure in the implementation of EU public policy (Paraskevopoulos, 2006). It shifts the methods by which we study the EU and its member states towards a focus on policy processes and outcomes – specifically raising questions about the impact of the EU on member states. This is reflected in the burgeoning academic literature on the theme since the 1990s which includes case studies (Featherstone and Radaelli, 2003; Heritier *et al.*, 2001), single and multiple country studies (Bache and Jordan, 2006) and investigations of specific policies (Giuliani, 2004; Jordan and Liefferink, 2004; Thatcher, 2004).

This chapter explores the conceptual underpinnings of Europeanisation and considers the approaches developed in the academic literature. The task is not without challenges since the field is not represented by a singularly agreed definition or explanatory framework. There have also been a number of distinct shifts in the way the concept is used, from an early focus on policy convergence to studying causality, especially policy style, content and discourse, and then onto to examining Europeanisation as a two-way policy process, focusing particularly on learning. It remains problematic to bring together the different layers of analysis, as the European integration process continues to create new multi-level politics that in turn recalibrates how domestic actors respond to integration (Bulmer and Lequesne, 2005). The review leads to the formulation of a methodology and framework of analysis for the assessment of change impelled by EU membership, a framework which will later be applied to the Irish polity, politics and selected policies. The chapter concludes that a comprehensive understanding of Europeanisation enables us to map new patterns and modes of governance, which contribute to our understanding of dynamic political systems.

Europeanisation: a contested concept?

Significance

There can be little question that the EU has transformed European governance (Bulmer and Lequesne, 2005) and that Europeanisation has been firmly established within the lexicon of academic study. It is a valuable yet contested concept that is shaping the research agenda by focusing on how European integration and European policy-making affect member states. Despite this, Europeanisation remains a phenomenon that does not have a single and precise definition and is used in different ways to describe a variety of experiences and processes of change involving the EU and its member states. This complexity has prompted scholars to refer to Europeanisation as a concept too unwieldly for organisation or more a problem than a solution (Graziano and Vink, 2007; Featherstone and Radaelli, 2003; Olsen, 2002; Kassim *et al.*, 2000) while others contest its importance as a phenomenon (Haverland, 2006).

The significance of Europeanisation may in part be explained by the increasing salience of the EU for its member states. This is reflected in developments during the 1990s and onwards: the Single European Market, Economic and Monetary Union (EMU), increasing regulation, enlargement and CFSP. Such developments indicate that Europeanisation is not just confined to defined policy domains since the EU has also impacted on political processes and behaviour, intergovernmental relations and domestic opportunity structures for national and sub-national actors. In broad terms effects can be exhibited for all levels of a traditional political regime: polity, politics and policies (Börzel and Risse, 2003).

This has prompted scholars from the fields of international relations, comparative politics and public administration to engage in assessing outcomes and searching for 'the cause in search of an effect' (Goetz, 2000). Many studies have focused on domestic political institutions: executives, parliaments and judiciary; specific public policy areas (Bugdahn, 2005), while a few studies have considered the impact of Europeanisation on parties, interest groups, and citizen attitudes to Europe (Goetz and Hix, 2001; Ladrech, 2002). Some scholars portray the EU as a multi-level system of governance characterised by networks (Kohler-Koch, 2000; Marks, 1996) and others as a fusion of national and EU administrations (Rometsch and Wessels, 1996). There are also arguments claiming that the EU has led to domestic transformation and debates on the fundamental nature of existing state structures even prompting constitutional reform (Toonen, 1992: 110–11). However, other scholars are more sceptical, and while accepting Europeanisation has impacted on the member states, perceive the member states as far more resilient to change then might be assumed (Goetz and Hix, 2000; Bulmer and Burch, 1998). It is also argued that Europeanisation has averted the demise of the state by strengthening national governments (Milward, 1992).

Europeanisation: a generation shift in EU studies

Hix and Goetz have described the literature on Europeanisation as 'still fairly inchoate' within an emergent field of inquiry (2001: 14–15). Whereas Bulmer and Radaelli (2005: 339) suggest that use of the term facilitates a 'rebranding' of existing research themes. It is evident that attention to the domestic level of politics did not emerge until the coining of the term 'Europeanisation' in the EU studies vernacular during the late 1990s. Although much earlier research focused on the search for composite theories and approaches to the study of European integration, a 'first generation' analysis is associated with the literature from the 1970s and 1980s on EC/EU policy-making. From this perspective the impact of the EU was typically approached from a top-down standpoint in terms of a vertical relationship between EU and national levels (Lenschow, 2006: 56–57; Adshead, 2005: 159), with general expectation of convergence in cross-national arrangements over time. Studies by Wallace *et al.* (1977, 1983) and Bulmer's (1983) article on domestic politics and EC policy-making, however, reflect a turn in scholarship towards the inter-relations between EU and national levels. Bulmer (1983: 350) stressed the importance of links between domestic politics and the European Community and sought to explain how the former may have a vital impact on the policy-making output of the EC. Moreover, EU developments over time have broadened the spectrum of analysis and re-oriented attention to the variegated relationships between member states and EU. Despite suggestions that Europeanisation may be a fad or fashionable term at one level, it does denote a shift beyond categorising the EU to what has been referred to as a post-ontological stage, which focuses more on understanding the policy process and outcomes (Featherstone, 2003: 3–5). This is central to the research in this volume which examines the impact of Europe on the Irish domestic policy process and policy outcomes.

Searching for a definition: second-generation studies

The range of definitions used to refer to Europeanisation reflects the multiplicity of understandings of the concept in second generation studies. Few writers have sought to define its precise meaning and since Europeanisation is not a theory but a phenomenon that needs to be explained (Bulmer, 2007) this has resulted in a maze of explanations. Proponents of Europeanisation, such as Radaelli, have raised concerns about how the concept is used, pointing out that concepts which are not well defined lead to confusion (2000: 2). Radaelli also raises the issue of 'concept stretching', whereby a concept that is used to explain too many things becomes meaningless. This is echoed in other critiques such as that of Kassim (2000) who maintains that the assortment of ways to describe different phenomena has diluted the utility of the concept. This means that boundaries need to be established in order for the concept to have some explanatory power.

Most definitions, however, focus on Europeanisation as a process and one in which there is a 'transformation' or, perhaps, more accurately, a change in the policy-making processes and outcomes in the member states arising out of participation in European-level institutions and policy-making. The assumption is that change in the domestic polity is a response to adaptational pressures, although the degree of causality is often disputed. In such accounts, Europeanisation is not treated as a dependent variable but, rather, as a process leading to 'still unspecified outcomes' (Lenschow, 2006: 57). Featherstone's (2003) typology of many of these studies suggests that the focus of much of the work on Europeanisation can be classified into four categories: Europeanisation as a historic phenomenon; transnational cultural diffusion of norms, ideas, identities and patterns of behaviour; institutional adaptation (public administration, parliaments, non-governmental actors, sub-national governance, networks); and adaptation of policy and policy processes. Table 2.1 juxtaposes several definitions advocated by scholars, illustrating the different uses to which the concept is put.

Table 2.1 Definitions of Europeanisation

- 'Europeanisation is an incremental process re-orienting the direction and shape of politics to the degree that EC political and economic dynamics become part of the organisational logic of national politics and policy-making' (Ladrech, 1994: 69).
- 'A process whereby domestic policy arenas become increasingly subject to European policy-making' (Börzel, 1999: 574).
- 'The emergence and development at the European level of distinct structures of governance, that is, of political, legal and social institutions associated with problem solving that formalise interactions among the actors, and of policy networks specialising in the creation of authoritative European rules' (Risse *et al.*, 2001: 3).
- 'Sets of structures, cognitive frameworks, and processes operating at or below the level of the Member States in the overlapping realms of polity, economy and society that derive, whether directly or indirectly from European integration, are ubiquitous.' (Anderson, 2002: 796).
- 'Processes of (a) construction (b) diffusion and (c) institutionalisation of formal and informal rules, procedures, policy paradigms, styles, "ways of doing things" and shared beliefs and norms which are first defined and consolidated in the making of EU decisions and then incorporated in the logic of domestic discourse, identities, political structures and public policies'. (Radaeli, 2003: 30, also used by Bulmer and Radaelli, 2005).
- 'the domestic adaptation to European regional integration' (Vink and Graziano, 2007: 7–8).

These definitions exhibit varying views as to whether Europeanisation is a top-down process (Risse *et al.*, 2001; Ladrech, 1994), a bottom-up, state to state process (Radaelli, 2004) or a round-about process involving national to EU to national processes (Bulmer and Radaelli, 2005). Falkner *et al.* (2005: 11) identify Europeanisation phenomena operating on at least three levels: EU development of policies or policy networks (Risse *et al.*, 2001); reactions in domestic systems to top down influence from EU level (Radaelli, 2000; Ladrech, 1994); indication of changes at the national level induced by transnational influences (Kohler-Koch, 2000). In addition some scholars hold the broad view that it reflects the sum of all these notions (Börzel, 1999). In embarking upon a study of Europeanisation the starting point is the domestic level with subsequent identification of the effects and pressures stimulated by the diffusion of European integration.

Contrary to other views, Olsen (2002: 1) suggests that the diversity of definitions is acceptable in a new area of study, as 'it eventually may help us to give better accounts of the emergence, development and impacts of a European, institutionally ordered system of governance'. Olsen distinguishes five possible faces (or model-building puzzles) of Europeanisation, including: as changes in external territorial boundaries; as the development of institutions of governance at the European level; as central penetration of national and sub-national systems of governance; as exporting forms of political organisation and governance that are typical and distinct for Europe beyond the European state; and as a political project aiming at a unified and political stronger Europe. He examines each in turn with a view to identifying the constituent parts, as well as highlighting the possible validity of a range of different conceptual frameworks (Olsen, 2002). The focus in this volume is largely on the third approach to Europeanisation, which concentrates on changes in domestic institutions of governance and politics and looks at empirical cases of the impact of the EU on its Member States. Olsen suggests that domestic systems can be seen as adapting on the basis of experiential learning and competitive selection. In the case of experiential learning, institutional change is understood as being the product of different actor understandings and interpretations of alternate forms of domestic organisation and governance. In contrast, changes under conditions of competitive selection are seen as a product of contextual imperatives with change required for survival. However, Olsen suggests that adaptation will not be perfect and that there will be differential responses and patterns of adaptation because of the nature of the EU as an unevenly developed polity and because states encompass varied institutional histories, resources and capabilities as well as different state and nation building processes.

The issue of causality: second-generation studies – mark II

Many of the early studies, such as Ladrech's on Europeanisation in France (1994), focused on how member-state actors redefined their interests and changed their behaviour in response to EU membership (Olsen, 1996). They examined how states adjusted to integration and to the EU pressure for change and domestic adaptation. In the first phase of these studies European integration was the independent variable explaining domestic change. The more recent second-generation studies have moved onto more complex multi-causal explanations which focus on the internal dynamics of the policy process, policy change and adaptation and learning in the member states (Laffan, 2006; Paraskevopoulos *et al.*, 2006; Adshead, 2005; Giuliani, 2004; Featherstone and Radaelli, 2003). Such approaches draw on comparative politics and public administration to conceptualise the policy process, thereby methodologically enriching the study of Europeanisation, as well as providing further case studies for analysis. This contrasts with the earlier emphasis on examining the EU as the cause of domestic change, with research aimed at testing that hypothesis. The focus was on examining the pressures for adaptation. By contrast, second-generation studies have suggested that it is Europeanisation which needs to be explained. As Radaelli suggests, Europeanisation is the problem that needs to be explained and is not in itself the explanation (2006: 60). He contends that to understand change, a range of intervening variables (mediating forces), such as domestic factors (interest formations, veto points and culture) need to be examined. This would suggest that research should investigate not only whether the EU matters, but also the degree to which it does matter (Haverland, 2006: 136). The study undertaken in this book contributes at this level by focusing on the domestic mediating forces and pre-existing domestic structures.

Radaelli (2006: 67) suggests that Europeanisation occurs when the *logic of domestic political actors changes*, change both in the sense of responses to EU pressures and in the sense of other usages of Europe that do not presuppose pressure. Europeanisation is a process of composite sequences and time patterns and, therefore, is not seen either as a bottom-up or top down process, but as a complex process in which causality is no longer the focus of attention but wherein Europeanisation is perceived as a discursive process. Such an approach helps to explain why many of the empirical studies, including some of the comparative cross-country and cross-sector analyses, have provided inconclusive evidence that the EU causes domestic change. A study of telecom and electrical liberalisation in Spain and Portugal, by Jordana, Levi-Faur and Puig (2006) suggests that there is a weak causal link between national policy change and European-level pressures for change. This outcome is also apparent for some of the country cases discussed in Jordan and Liefferink's (2004) comparative study of the Europeanisation of environmental policy. Bulmer and Burch (2000), while viewing Europeanisation of public policies as a two-way process, conclude that both local and national level forces are at work affecting the direction of causality. Therefore, in studying Europeanisation it is difficult to identify precisely the changes it has wrought at the domestic level since change may occur independently of the EU, yet, be attributed to it.

Aside from EU pressures for change, globalisation has also been a phenomenon which some authors consider to have eroded the traditional domestic political authority of states and resulted in rapid technological, social and political changes (Pierre, 2000). International competitiveness factors have also led to a fundamental shift from interventionist to regulatory state (Majone, 1996). The development of new public management and the diminishing role of the state in the provision of public goods have also resulted in governance transformation. To isolate the impact of Europeanisation may therefore be problematic and scholars have been challenged to distinguish the effects of Europeanisation from those of globalisation in particular (Olsen, 2002; Schneider, 2001; Hennis, 2001). Schneider, in a study of the telecommunications sectors in Britain, Italy and France notes that:

> In all three countries, there was a 'misfit' between the proposed EU directives and the existing telecommunications monopolies. However, both France and Germany began to liberalise their telecommunications markets in response to global deregulation pressures. Thus, their liberalisation efforts were made parallel to – and at times, in advance of – the emerging European policies. (2001: 61)

His study also highlights domestic political factors, as well as European and global pressures for change. In relation to the current study of Ireland, the importance of understanding the ongoing process associated with modernisation of the economy and society is critical to understanding the impact of Europe. Ireland as a small open polity is highly vulnerable and sensitive to international changes, such as financial crises, trade and foreign direct investment patterns.

Europeanisation: convergence versus a differential impact?

A further problematique addressed by scholars is whether Europeanisation leads to greater convergence or continuing differentiation among member states' domestic arrangements. Many early studies expected Europeanisation to lead to greater convergence, with member states adopting common approaches to public policy (Dimitrova and Steunenberg, 2000; Ladrech, 1994) and institutional practices (Meny *et al.*, 1996). It was assumed that Europeanisation impacts in the same way on all member states leading to a 'convergence towards strengthening, weakening or transformation of the nation state' (Börzel, 1999: 574). In the study by Héritier *et al.* (2001)

Europeanisation is discernible in the 'differential' impact of European requirements on domestic policies. There has been no metamorphosis within any of the national systems and certainly no significant convergence towards a common institutional model homogenising the various domestic structures of the states. This is borne out in the majority of later studies which depict a lack of convergence. Rather, Europe has a variegated effect on the member states and this is what needs to be examined and explained (Jordan and Liefferink, 2004; Börzel and Risse, 2000; Börzel, 1999; Harmsen, 1999; Knill, 1998).

What this demonstrates is that the domestic impact of Europe depends on the level of adaptational pressures on domestic institutions and the degree to which mediating factors facilitate or inhibit change. There has been a greater focus on understanding national differences and the differing responses of the member states to EU policies. For example, Knill's study of the impact of the EU on national administrations illustrates how cultural factors and state tradition can be important in shaping the way in which European legislation is received at the national level (Knill, 2001). The research undertaken by Börzel (2002) has particularly highlighted the need to understand the mechanisms and means by which policy is both 'uploaded' and 'downloaded'. Other scholars have focused on the complex nature of multi-level systems of governance and the existence of hierarchical and vertical policy networks (Paraskevopoulos *et al.*, 2006; Kohler-Koch, 2000, 2003).

There is also disagreement in the literature over the impact of Europe on federal and unitary member-state systems. Member states such as Germany, Belgium, Italy and Spain have constitutional arrangements that grant sub-national government partial or exclusive legislative authority in certain policy domains, thereby curbing central government's flexibility and influence. Schmidt (1999, 2006) argues that unitary systems face greater pressures to adapt because of differences of institutional fit. By, contrast Börzel (1999: 580) suggests that federal and regionalised systems face higher pressures to adapt and that institutional change is more likely to occur in these systems than in unitary or weakly decentralised member states. These perspectives highlight the importance of understanding the nature of the political system, including its historical, constitutional and cultural make-up as well as factors like administrative capacity, the role of national parliaments, degree of public support and resources. It is clear that such factors moderate the impact of Europeanisation and 'the core features of the democratic polity in Europe have proven quite resilient in the face of integration pressures' (Anderson, 2002: 795). In short, diversity persists among the core domestic structures of governance in member states despite increasing contact between EU and national models. Yet established national arrangements, though resistant, are generally flexible enough to cope with change at the European level.

Theoretical approaches and insights: explaining domestic change

Second-generation studies have utilised theoretical approaches in order to understand how Europeanisation processes affect the member states. The literature is, however, dominated with reference to new institutionalism. Thus, the study of institutions remains central to Europeanisation scholarship since all types of governance are embedded in institutional webs that shape and constrain political action (March and Olsen, 1989). Institutions form part of the 'black box', turning politics to policy, defining norms and routinising values. New institutionalist perspectives interpret the development of national EU policy-making systems as a specific case of institutional change or reform (Harmsen, 1999). The theoretical perspectives presented in the literature include: interest-based rational choice and game behaviour; institutionalism and historically shaped patterns of development; and, finally, constructivism, whose proponents emphasise social constructions of action, culture and identity, as well as ideas and discourse (Schmidt and Radaelli, 2004: 183).

In a broader context these studies can also be located in the theoretical discussions that have been concerned with the study of European integration, although the post-ontological focus of Europeanisation has been on more specific research questions that are concerned with the impact of the EU on the member states (Radaelli, 2000: 5). Intergovernmentalism (Hoffmann, 1982) and, more recently, new institutionalism, focus on the member states as the main drivers of integration. The main focus of much of this research has been on explaining the processes and dynamics of European integration, especially the outcome of EU level reforms as the product of member state bargaining and negotiation (i.e. liberal intergovernmentalism à la Moravcsik, 1991). In a number of instances these studies highlight how political elites in the member states used EU reforms as a means of leveraging change at home and even strengthening the role of the state. Examples include Italy (SEA, EMU) and Portugal (accession), where the EU was used to progress domestic reforms. In this context, some proponents of intergovernmentalism viewed Europeanisation as enhancing the role of national governments as gatekeepers relative to other domestic actors.

By contrast, those scholars associated with neo-functionalism (Haas, 1958) and more recently, multi-level governance and policy networks (Hooghe and Marks, 2003; Sandholtz, 1996; Caporaso, 1996; Kohler-Koch, 1996; Marks, 1996) focus on particular groups of interests, particularly supranational interests that favour further integration, which is complementary to political and economic interests. In this context the EU is perceived as an autonomous and independent actor in its own right, able to exert its own influence over the member states. Such studies focus particularly on institution building at a European level. The EU is therefore seen as a significant influence, although not the sole source of influence over changes in the member states. Scholars often note the influence of Europe on the development of federalism in Belgium, devolution in the UK and decentralisation in Italy, as illustrative of the impact of Europe on the distribution of political power in some member states. Proponents of multi-level governance highlight the interdependence and interaction of the differing levels of government in Europe, as opposed to suggesting any one level has more power over another (Kohler-Koch, 1996). Such studies have focused on the interactions that occur between local, regional, national and European-level actors in this multi-level system of governance with regard to public policy.

Other studies focus not solely on institutions and policies, but have followed a largely constructivist turn, with a focus on discourse and ideational factors as means of constructing Europe (Hay and Rosamond, 2002). Schmidt and Radaelli (2004: 184) examine discourse as 'a set of policy ideas and values, and in terms of its usage, as a process focused on policy formulation and communication'. They classify their approach as a variant of institutionalism – discursive institutionalism – and suggest that what they are interested in examining is when such discourse acts as a causal factor to exert an influence on policy change (Radaelli, 2006: 65). Alternatively, some research explores European policy values and policy paradigms, as how these are internalised at the domestic level (Checkel, 2001). The emphasis in these types of studies is on the link between institutional analysis and policy learning.

Interest-based rational choice

Explanations from this perspective assume that actors have a hierarchical fixed set of preferences and act in a goal-orientated and instrumentalist manner. Under such assumptions actors aim to engage with others with a view to maximising their individual gain from such strategic interactions. In such a context institutions may be seen as either impediments of change or as opportunity structures.

Knill and Lehmkuhl (2002; 1999) take a top-down approach to understanding how Europe matters by examining the *mechanisms* of Europeanisation in relation to three ideal types of European policy-making. These include 'positive integration', where the member state has to change and become compliant in response to EU obligations (e.g. environmental policy), 'negative integration' where the EU alters the domestic opportunity structures and a state has to respond (e.g. the rules regarding the single market) and finally, framing integration where EU policy alters the beliefs and expectations of domestic actors (leading to a change of preferences and strategies). Positive integration is particularly applicable to 'goodness of fit' explanations that focus on the degree of policy fit between European and national policy. A moderate misfit is hypothesised as leading to policy change, whereas in instances where there are high levels of misfit it may be difficult to achieve policy change. In cases where there is clear-cut European policy and it is downloaded to the member states changes may well occur. However, such explanations may only apply in a limited number of cases where the member state is receptive to such policy change and may already be in a process of change. In such cases proponents of change may use European-level developments to justify change and may be easily moved forward in instances where there is an absence of a strong veto player. In areas of negative integration, it may be more difficult to distinguish the effects of Europeanisation, given that policy is not being downloaded to the member states and change is dependent on regulatory competition along horizontal lines. In these instances states are in competition with one another and it may be difficult to distinguish the effects of Europeanisation from global and national forces.

More recently, Mastenbroek and van Keulen (2006) have adopted a preference-based account of Europeanisation whereby they suggest that the focus should be on the preferences of the member states in relation to the issue under discussion. This suggests that the member states seek to change the existing domestic policy via EU legislation. Such an approach focuses attention on the early stages of policy formation (negotiations), as well as the transposition of policy and the findings of the empirical research suggest that policy preference accounts may help to explain policy implementation failure.

Institutionalism

In developing an explanation around Europeanisation, 'new' institutionalism provides an important source of ideas and a basis for understanding domestic change in the member states. New institutionalism acknowledges a variety of economic and societal influences on policy outcomes. Its various approaches provide different insights into how institutions shape the way decision-making takes place. Historical institutionalism emphasises that 'history matters' since change is 'path dependent' and new institutional configurations will be conditioned by the existing system's trajectory. Once in place, the features of a system's trajectory will perpetuate itself and limit alterations brought about by external change. The approach of rational choice institutionalism underscores the role of institutions in shaping policy preferences and outcomes. Sociological institutionalism underlines the significance of cultural explanations based on an understanding of culture as shared attitudes or values. Hence, institutions encompass not only formal rules but informal rules, routines and conventions. The present study draws on a mix of rational choice institutionalism, historical institutionalism and sociological institutionalism.

As noted, many of the studies that focus on Europeanisation do so by means of institutionalism: that is, they focus on existing institutional frameworks, norms and processes in order to understand the EU's impact on its member states (Radaelli, 2003; Börzel, 2002a, 2002b, 2001; Schmidt, 2002; Héritier *et al.*, 2001; Knill, 2001; Risse, *et al.*, 2001; Olsen, 1996). A number of such studies take a top-down approach by assessing the impact that EU institutions' decision-making procedures and rules have upon different state policy-making processes. There are studies, however, that also examine the linkages between the levels (Marks *et al.*, 1996). Cowles *et al.* (2001) examine the EU from the perspective of historical institutionalism on different levels: institution building at the EU level, impact of EU on member states and effects of globalisation. The authors comment on 'domestic adaptation with national colours' (*ibid.*: 1). Consequently, to account for variations in the impact of European developments on member states, one must endeavour to explain the varying responses and robustness of domestic institutions against this pressure. The pre-existing institutions and broad values inherent clearly condition adaptation and raise the question whether Europeanisation has as considerable an impact as some scholars suggest. For example, Olsen (2002: 23) contends that 'Institutions should not be expected to change easily and fast except under extraordinary conditions.' Anderson suggests that domestic institutions may prove more resilient than is sometimes assumed, reflecting what he terms the stickiness of institutions and their general resistance to transformation (2002: 800). It takes a significant incident to produce a critical juncture or punctuate the pre-existing equilibrium. Thus, the European influences are mediated through the existing institutional structure and traditions that characterise the national system.

Rational institutionalists view Europe as providing opportunities and constraints on their actions. It is assumed that behaviour is driven by strategic calculation rather than by impersonal historical or sociological forces. Europe may provide additional legal and political resources to enable actors to govern, while constraining some actors. A resource-dependent relationship assumes actors are rational and goal-oriented and know what they want. Based on such assumptions there will be winners and losers in the domestic polity. This is likely to be affected by two sets of mediating factors: multiple veto players and facilitative formal institutions. In relation to multiple veto points some scholars (Héritier, 2001; Haverland, 2000) suggest that in systems with a large number of players and where power is widely dispersed, it is more difficult to make changes in response to Europeanisation. Governments may be blocked by domestic opposition that prefers an alternative or the status quo. Regarding facilitative formal institutions it may be questioned whether domestic players exploit European opportunities in order to bring about change. The outcome will depend on whether local actors have the capacity to act.

The focus of much of this literature is on the *goodness of fit* between European policies and domestic institutions and policies (Bulmer and Lequesne, 2005; Falkner, 2003; Knill, 2001; Börzel and Risse, 2000; Knill and Lenschow, 1998). It is argued that domestic change will be determined by a congruence or 'goodness of fit' between Europeanisation and domestic equivalents. In other words the closer the 'fit' between European policy and the domestic policy the fewer pressures for adaptation with less impact or change necessary to existing policy. Alternatively, 'misfits' occur in instances where EU policy requires significant pressures for change and where states may oppose such change. It is assumed that such change is mediated through a range of domestic factors including political elites, institutional veto points and organisational culture and learning. This is likely where adaptational pressure is deemed moderate as domestic change is unlikely to occur if Europeanisation confronts entrenched administrative traditions. Knill (2001), in his study of national administrations and the impact of EU environmental policy in Germany and the UK, argued that it made a crucial difference whether European policies challenge core institutional patterns of national administrative traditions or only required adjustments within the institutional core.

Risse *et al.* (2001) employ a three-step model of Europeanisation (later elaborated upon by Börzel and Risse, 2003). This identifies that misfit and adaptational pressure are a necessary but insufficient condition for change. Rather, the likelihood of domestic change (and successful adaptation) is explained by a set of mediating factors (as noted above). The literature has identified two broadly different mediating logics of domestic institutional and policy change in response to Europeanisation: the rational choice and the sociological (see Paraskevopoulos, 2006; Börzel and Risse, 2003). The 'logic of consequentialism' affects the opportunities and constraints of actors within institutions. It points to the role of redistribution of resources and subsequently differential empowerment of actors at the domestic level. Second, the 'logic of appropriateness' is underpinned by a sociological institutionalist perspective. It posits that institutions affect the behaviour of their actors and that they internalise the norms of the institution and develops identities associated with the institution.

Börzel (2005) focuses on *what* changes and the *mechanisms* by which change is brought about. In her review of literature she identifies institutional compliance, judicial review; and regulatory competition (Knill and Lehmkuhl, 1999), whereby the EU prescribed a particular model, changing the domestic opportunity structures and policy frames and altering the beliefs of domestic actors. She suggests that each of these approaches draws on rationalist institutionalism and sociological institutionalism in order to understand the causal mechanisms of domestic change. Both approaches assume the differential impact of Europe on its member states which is explained by the 'goodness of fit' between European and national policies, institutions and processes and the existence of mediating factors that filter that impact. There is, then, in many instances likely to be a certain level of misfit. Börzel observes that, 'The lower the compatibility between European and domestic processes, policies and institutions, the higher is the adaptational pressure Europe exerts on the member states' (2005: 50).

However, the idea that misfit constitutes a necessary condition for change has become contested in the literature (Thatcher, 2004; Héritier and Knill, 2001; Haverland, 2000; Knill and Lehmkuhl, 1999). Even where EU prerequisites match domestic preferences, Europeanisation may facilitate pre-existing domestic strategies for reform through exploitation by domestic interests who are motivated to change. Although the model by Risse *et al.* (2001) concedes that adaptational pressure can only produce domestic change if agents react to them, it cannot account for the fact that change may be initiated by them in the absence of adaptational pressure. In such an instance, Europe may provide the context for domestic change, but may not be the source of adaptational pressures. Despite this many scholars accept that misfits do occur, but have argued this only happens in policy areas that are concerned with regulating the market as opposed to those areas in which there is significant latitude for member-state action, such as those governed by the Open Method of Coordination (Knill and Lehmkuhl, 1999). Others contend that the changing nature of the EU and the domestic polity obviate the easy identification of such misfits and that member states may pursue their own policies regardless of EU requirements or even seek changes at the European level. The goodness of fit approach assumes that there is a clear European policy, which can be fully understood at the domestic level, and within which domestic actors are able to express particular preferences. Bulmer and Burch (2006), for example, argue that the impact of EU policies at the domestic level may be understood differently and may even be disputed by political elites. 'Put another way, Europeanisation will not always be an external reality that can be mediated or adjusted to by domestic actors' (Bulmer and Burch, 2006: 391). Others, such as Falkner (2003), highlight the need to distinguish different types of misfits: policy misfits, legal misfits, political and/or polity misfits as well as the size of the misfits and costs (also see Haverland, 2003).

As noted earlier, Europeanisation cannot be conceptualised in terms of one direction. The member states may also seek to shape EU decision-making (Kassim *et al.*, 2000). Börzel (2005, 2002) has sought to link both the bottom-up and top-down aspects of Europeanisation by focusing on the role of member state governments as the intermediaries in this process of transmission. The focus in this instance was on national executives and how they shape Europeanisation and adapt to it (i.e. adjustment of preferences). Her 2002 study examined how national governments sought to upload national policies to the European level thereby reducing the potential adaptation costs at a later stage in the implementation process, as well as other associated costs to different domestic client groups. The strategies that member states may pursue in trying to shape European policy include pace-setting, foot-dragging and fence-sitting (see Börzel and Risse, 2003).

Social constructivists and sociological institutionalists

By contrast, sociological institutionalists focus on the degree to which domestic actors are likely to be socialised into European norms and roles via persuasion and social learning and hence redefine their interests and identities (Checkel, 1999). Europeanisation exposes the member-state actors to the impact of supranational influences and its incremental logic fits well with learning and socialisation processes, as well as the thick interpretation of institutions (Paraskevopoulos, 2006). The platform for socialisation is provided by the EU where domestic actors such as civil servants and politicians may exchange ideas and models between each other. In turn these actors or elites may project the European discourse into domestic debate and seek to shape domestic perceptions. Therefore if there is a misfit it may not lead to change – domestic actors may resist change regardless of pressures for adaptation. The degree of change may depend on the existence of norm entrepreneurs through the existence of epistemic communities with shared beliefs and values (Radaelli, 1997) and a cooperative political culture which facilitates change.

Scholars, such as Checkel (1999: 546), suggest that social constructivist approaches which build on sociological institutionalism can be used to understand aspects of Europeanisation, including those elements concerned with social learning and normative diffusion. Such a perspective provides a counterview to that of rational-choice theorists in that it suggests that it 'is not just about agents with fixed preferences who interact via strategic exchange' (Checkel, 1999: 548), but sees actors' identities/preferences as socially constructed. The institutional density of a system may have powerful sociali-sation effects on national actors. Again, the emphasis on thick institutionalism as evident in sociological approaches to understanding institutions suggests that actor identities and preferences are shaped by the logic of organisations as argued by March and Olsen (1989). Bulmer and Burch (2006: 405) suggests that if Europeanisation can be socially constructed by individuals then more attention needs to be paid to the role of agency, as opposed to focusing on institutions, as has been the case in many new institutionalist studies.

Others, such as Schmidt and Radaelli (2004), suggest that a focus on discourse serves to bridge the gap between institutional and actor centred approaches. However, as they note, the empirical analysis of discourse is not an easy task and it may be difficult to establish what accounts for change. They conclude that discourse is never the sole factor that explains policy change, but, rather, suggest that it needs to be considered as a *mediating factor.*

For them, the main mediating factors that influence policy change include:

- policy problems that establish the need for change (international and EU pressures);
- policy legacies that may/may not fit proposed policy solutions;
- policy preferences that may/may not change in light of the problems and proposed solutions;
- political-institutional capacity of actors to respond to the problems through new policy initiatives even if these reverse policy legacies and preferences;
- the discourse that serves to enhance capacity by altering perceptions of problems and legacies and by influencing preferences (*ibid.*, 2004: 186).

The value of this approach is that it places considerable emphasis on understanding the domestic polity, policy and politics as key to understanding change.

Towards a conceptual framework?

Scholars of Europeanisation have not only provided theoretical insights but have identified crucial factors which determine the impact of Europeanisation. As Giuliani concludes, 'the focus of Europeanisation research has therefore progressively moved towards a more specific analysis of conditions, factors and mechanisms for adaptation and change' (2003: 11). Radaelli (2000) suggests that what is being Europeanised and, therefore, what needs to be examined are: (1) the domestic political structures including political institutions, public administration, intergovernmental relations, the legal structure, structures of representation and cognitive and normative structures (2) public policy, and (3) outcomes: inertia, absorption, transformation and retrenchment. Bulmer and Lequesne (2005: 13) use a slightly simpler approach to Radaelli in that they focus on polity (institutions and patterns of government), politics (including political parties and interest groups) and policy. A similar typology is used in Lenschow (2006: 61) in which the possible dimensions of change are outlined in Table 2.2.

Through examining these dimensions it is possible to ascertain the depth of change that occurs as a result of Europeanisation. Although the role of national governments in the transformation of the domestic governance structure is crucial, studies indicate that the formation of preferences and coalitions at the domestic level cannot be seen as being confined within the central state level, but, rather, should include the intra-state and state–society relations

Table 2.2 Dimensions of domestic change

Polity	*Politics*	*Policy*
Government–parliament relations	Party and electoral politics	Norms and goals
Administrative structures	Interest intermediation	Policy instruments and style
Judicial structures	Patterns of contestation	
Intergovernmental relations	Public opinion	Standards
		Resources
		Organisational structures
		Actor networks

Source: Adapted from Lenschow (2006).

(Lenschow, 1999). Furthermore, to understand the complexity of the policy-making process in any one area it has been found necessary to focus on the issue of networks, policy networks and policy communities. The development of such phenomena is linked to the nature of the polity, reflecting differing national political traditions and patterns of interest intermediation, as well as micro-policy variations (Schmidt, 2006). Characteristics of the member states such as statist, corporatist, unitary or federal are therefore significant. Some analyses imply that polities and politics are more resilient to change (Radaelli, 2004; Anderson, 2002), whereas sectoral domestic policy areas are more fundamentally altered (Jordan and Liefferink, 2004). It has also been shown that Europeanisation may lead to facilitated coordination, wherein change is brought about through learning based on the Open Method of Coordination (OMC), soft laws and policy transfer. Radaelli, citing the literature on policy transfer, notes that 'it also requires robust networks of stakeholders that facilitate the adoption of new policies at home, a strong civil society, and administrative-political capability to consciously modify, edit and adapt foreign experience to national circumstances' (2006: 71).

Thus, it is likely that any EU decision will have a different impact in each member state allowing for differing mediating factors (as defined by Schmidt and Radaelli, 2004). Differences also emerge within and between policy areas. The attempt by Bulmer and Radaelli (2005) to link policy types to different default explanations is useful because it distinguishes four patterns of governance in the European Union (see Table 2.3), which are each associated with a particular policy area and which provide some guidance for researchers. This approach suggests that it is likely that the impact of Europeanisation will be stronger in those areas in which the EU is the dominant player, and in which governance is exercised through a hierarchy.

The pre-existing domestic institutions and patterns of activity are viewed as critical to understanding the domestic response to European pressures to adapt.

Table 2.3 Governance, policy and the mechanisms of Europeanisation

Mode of governance	*Type of policy*	*Analytical core*	*Main mechanism*	*Examples of policy area*	*Default explanation*
Governance by negotiation	Any of those below	Formation of EU policy	Vertical – uploading	Varies across policy areas	
Governance by hierarchy	Positive integration	Market correcting rules: EU policy templates	Vertical – downloading of policy templates	Aspects of social policy, environmental policy, regional policy, CAP, EMU	Goodness of fit
Governance by hierarchy	Negative integration	Market-making rules: absence of policy templates	Horizontal	Competition policy, single market, telecommunication, energy, corporate governance, etc.	Regulatory competition
Facilitated coordination	Coordina-tion	Soft law, OMC, policy exchange	Horizontal	Foreign policy, aspects of employment policy; social inclusion, Schengen, justice and home affairs	Learning

Source: Adapted from Bulmer and Radaelli (2005).

In some policy areas, and particular instances, it is suggested that adaptational pressures exist and are likely to affect domestic behaviours. How domestic actors respond is likely to be shaped by actors' preferences and the degree of policy fit, as suggested in the literature that examined policy fits/misfits in Europeanisation. In other policy areas, European adaptational pressures may be less, although this does not necessarily mean that domestic change will not occur, since policy change may be based on the desire of national elites to adopt a common position and approach to an international issue. By implication, adaptational pressures need to be more broadly considered as coming from different directions (global, European, domestic) and representing differing policy requirements and actor preferences as outlined in Table 2.3, where different mechanisms and default explanations are posited. This suggests that change, where it does occur, may be the product of these differing adaptational pressures and actor preferences and opportunity structures. There may also be instances where European adaptational pressures are high, but no change occurs, perhaps as a result of resistance to change. In effect, this means that it is important to examine the mediating forces (or intervening variables) in the member state. Pre-existing structures and the varying role of domestic actors are likely to be the key to understanding policy change, whatever the sphere.

Analysing Ireland's adaptation

Previous sections have shown that Europeanisation is measured by many scholars on the basis of the depth of change that occurs. The studies referred to above examine the intensity, specificity and perviousness of Europeanisation and the various factors which mediate it. The research in this volume focuses on a comparison of different policy areas in one state, Ireland, and the degree to which these policy areas changed over time and reflect new patterns of governance. Europeanisation is interpreted as the process by which EU policy-making affects domestic structures *and* the processes by which domestic structures (polity, politics and policies) adapt to Europe (Caporaso, 2007; Paraskevopoulos, 2006; Börzel and Risse, 2003).

The objective of the research in the volume is to acquire a comprehensive overview of Ireland's relationship with the EU. The case studies provide a means of examining the domestic institutional structures (including formal and informal institutions) and policy adaptation in each area, with the objective of understanding where and how European pressures for adaptation are mediated through domestic institutional structures (Risse *et al.*, 2001: 9–12). Risse *et al.* (2001: 9–12) define such mediating structures as: multiple veto points, mediating formal institutions, political and organisational cultures, differential empowerment of actors, and learning.

The pre-existing pattern of domestic activity such as traditions, formal institutions, policies and culture are important in terms of learning and adaptation. It is assumed that such domestic factors may either facilitate or block change, depending on the type of change being proposed and/or undertaken. The studies cited suggest that Europeanisation can have asymmetrical impact on policy, polity and politics. Contrasting evidence and differential adaptation is anticipated in view of the cases selected. For example, considerable 'downloading' of policy has occurred in the environmental field, whereas in agriculture Ireland has been pro-active in 'uploading' policy preferences. The outcomes of these two-way processes on the domestic level will be discussed in the substantive policy chapters, illustrating differing adaptative pressures. Institutional and policy adaptation is likely to vary across the policy areas, reflecting both the different adaptational pressures and pre-existing domestic structures and patterns of interest intermediation.

Governance rather than the almost obsolete 'government' reflects the multiplicity of actors, institutions and relationships involved in the process of governing (Paraskevopoulos, 2006: 3). The objective of the sectoral analyses is to identify the role of actors (agents of change) and the range of public and private actors involved in the policy process and to assess whether they form dense or loose policy networks. In particular, the investigation seeks to determine the extent to which each policy is contested, fought over and subjected to competing political views thereby resulting in domestic adaptational pressures. Thus, adaptation to Europeanisation may have both direct and indirect effects on the nature and practice of government in Ireland, fostering the emergence of new patterns of governance and interest intermediation. The case studies illustrate the multiplicity of actors, institutions and relationships involved in the process of governing and show how EU impact is moderated by underlying domestic social and institutional considerations. New patterns of governance become apparent in the development of new structures, networks and partnerships resulting from adaptation to multi-level governance approaches. The different and contrasting case studies illustrate the diversity of the governing process.

The selected policy areas – agriculture, economy, environment, foreign affairs and regional – provide sufficient variety to ensure an extensive assessment of the impact of Europeanisation relative to other factors that may have prompted change. The case studies examine the development at a macro-level of policy in each area over time. Each case study focuses on indicators of change, such as policy statements, new regulations and procedures, with a view to examining the purported reasons for change. The objective in each case is to map the changes that have occurred by focusing on the mediating factors concerned, such as domestic discourse, actors and formal structures, with a view to understanding the stated reasons for change and whether these are attributable to Europeanisation,

Given the variegated character of Europeanisation and the different types of policies discussed it is difficult to present a single analytical framework. However, in each case study we use the distinction between polity, politics and policies to identify three dimensions along which the domestic change and new patterns of governance can be assessed drawing on new institutionalist approaches to Europeanisation (Figure 2.1).

As noted above (Table 2.3) the policy areas have been selected with a view to examining spheres in which Europeanisation may vary in accordance with different patterns of governance. In the first case study, the EU has led to fundamental change in domestic economic policy, thus analysis of economic adaptation reveals the pervasive influence of the EU. The environmental policy case study illustrates the difficulty of adapting to the European regulatory framework. As Ireland's economic growth has accelerated, environmental

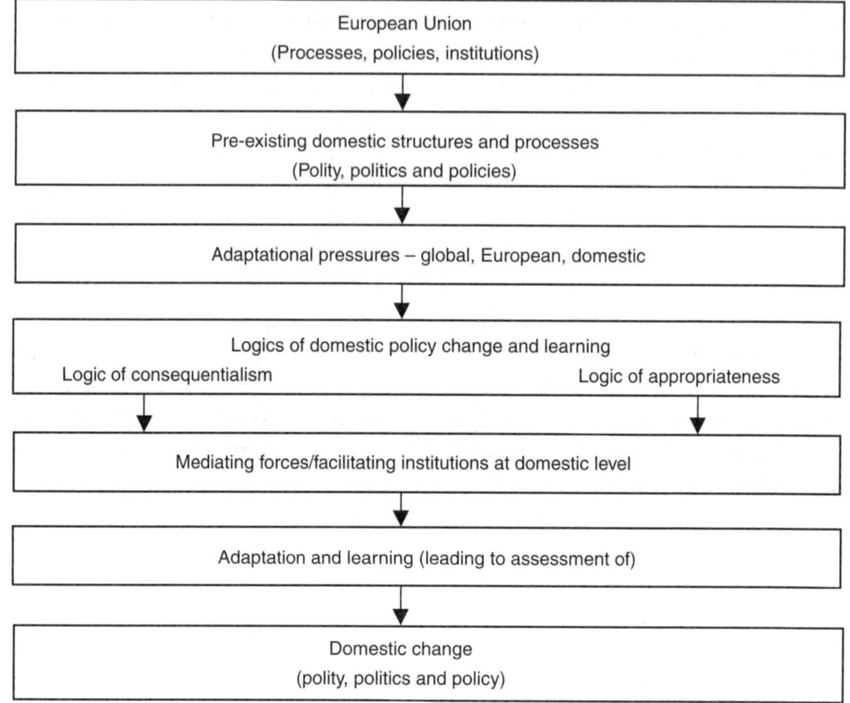

Figure 2.1 Europeanisation and the process of domestic change
Source: Adapted from Borzel and Risse (2003)

issues have become more important, reflecting the impact of economic development and a growing awareness that Ireland's environment is being challenged. This sphere illustrates the tension between national economic priorities and environmental concerns as well as the problems encountered in trying to comply with EU demands. The regional policy case demonstrates the ability of the state to adapt in a pragmatic manner to European policy obligations and opportunities. Economic prosperity has challenged the state to address regional disparities, especially in areas that have not benefited economically from the 'celtic tiger', leading to new attempts at local and regional innovation, spatial planning and institution building. In this arena, new patterns of governance have emerged that engage not only public actors, but also private and civil society actors, resulting in a range of sub-national partnerships.

Agriculture has traditionally been the cornerstone of Ireland's economic development. The change from an agrarian to a post-modern industrialised society has been circumscribed by developments within the EU and Ireland has exerted strong influence during negotiations of EU agricultural policy. This policy sphere illustrates the changing adaptational pressures as domestic and European circumstances and priorities have altered. Again, Ireland's distinctive foreign policy approach has been modified significantly as a result of Europeanisation. The development of the EU's Common Foreign and Security Policy (CFSP), European Security and Defence Policy (ESDP) and Common Commercial Policy has led to a questioning and re-scoping of Ireland's role in international affairs. The mechanisms of foreign policy have also been changed with a greater emphasis on 'democratisation' of the process and incorporation of a broader array of institutional and non-governmental actors. This case study illustrates varying dimensions of Europeanisation, highlighting the challenges of policy adaptation and the impact on Ireland's foreign policy outlook and focus.

Collectively, the case studies weave an image of dynamic interaction between domestic, European and global forces resulting in political, economic and social adaptation. In order to depict the context in which this change occurred the analysis commences with the identification of core features of the Irish polity (chapter 3) and an overview of the political-administrative system, including its adaptation to the EU (chapter 4). These chapters identify the mediating forces (formal and informal institutions, veto points/players) contingent to understanding change (and lack of change) in the Irish polity, politics and policies.

3

Mediating forces and the domestic polity

Brid Quinn and Bernadette Connaughton

Introduction

The effects of Europeanisation have been filtered by Ireland's complex history, distinctive political and social culture, nationalistic penchants and strongly centralised political-administrative structures. This chapter outlines the key elements of Irish political and social culture and analyses the way in which these factors have moderated the Europeanisation process. It looks at the under-pinnings of Irish society, considering the role of culture, values and attitudes in determining the degree to which Europeanisation impacts on Ireland.

Nationalism, the focus of this chapter's first section, has in various guises continued to be a defining characteristic at both the personal and state levels and has affected and been affected by the Europeanisation process. The issue of public attitudes towards the EU is an increasingly salient one following Ireland's rejection of the Lisbon Treaty in June 2008. Over many years of membership, Irish public attitudes towards the EU have generally been very positive (Holmes, 2005) but there are intimations that rejection of the Nice and Lisbon Treaties signalled a marked shift in the Irish mind-set and outlook towards Europe. This chapter includes an analysis of the way in which Irish elites and the general public have regarded the EU and how attitudes have altered over time. In most societies policy-making is strongly influenced by electoral competition incorporating the priorities of political parties. However, this is not the case in Ireland because the Irish party system differs from the patterns and structures of mass politics evident elsewhere in Europe. Consequently, Europeanisation has had little influence on the development and actions of political parties in Ireland. This is not true with regard to interest groups as there has been significant change in interest representation, reflecting both the perceived significance of the Brussels arena of politics and the range of EU-influenced policy changes. The final section of the chapter outlines the mutation of interest representation within an increasingly Europeanised Ireland. Thus, the chapter serves to identify and elaborate core features of the Irish polity which mediate the impact of Europeanisation.

Irish nationalism and European identity

Collins and Cradden assert that:

> For Ireland, nationalism is the dominant ideology. It binds diverse individuals into 'a people', acts as a motive for economic, cultural and sporting achievement, and provides a source of genuine pride and sympathy. The nation has become the highest affiliation and obligation of the individual, and through it a significant part of personal identity is formed. (1991: 154)

Nationalism has been a defining feature of Ireland's history. The desire for Irish independence in the late nineteenth and early twentieth centuries was founded on both political and cultural nationalism. There was a prevailing belief that being Irish was irreconcilable with being ruled from England and that sovereignty was necessary to underpin Irish identity. For a society whose identity was culturally referenced, political independence was perceived as vital. The early years of the independent state witnessed concerted efforts to forge a common identity, impute a common culture, diminish diversity and realise an 'imagined community' (Garvin, 2004; O'Carroll, 2002). While a distinction between civic nationalism and ethnic nationalism is frequently made by sociologists and political scientists, in Ireland the ethnic dimensions (such as language and religious beliefs) combined with the political and territorial dimensions of civic nationalism to create a particular Irish national identity. From the 1930s to the 1950s economic, foreign and social policies promoted isolationism and self-sufficiency and reinforced a nationalism that advocated cultural monochromism, social homogeneity and political solidarity. A Catholic outlook, a Gaelic perspective and a belief in the uniqueness of Ireland were elements of the distinctive national identity supported by and supportive of the state. The 1937 Constitution gave normative effect to these core values of Irish national identity (Coakley, 2005a; Girvin, 2002). The Catholic Church, a dominant force in the educational, social and moral as well as religious spheres was given special status in the Irish Constitution. The GAA (Gaelic Athletic Association), which promoted Irish games, was strongly supported by political and community leaders. A national radio station, Radio Éireann, was established by the state in 1926 and was expected 'to contribute to the project of building the Irish state and nation' (Kelly and Rolston, 1995: 565). Similarly, the original national television channel, when launched in 1961 was regarded as an instrument of public policy, with President de Valera lauding the new service as a means of building the character of the nation while also expressing concern about its potential to lead, through demoralisation, to decadence and dissolution. More recently an Irish language radio station (Radio na Gaeltachta) and television channel (originally Telifís na Gaeilge, now TG 4) were established and continue to enjoy state sponsorship. Children who receive their full first- and second-level education in Ireland are compelled to study

Irish while fluency in Irish is still a requisite for some public-sector jobs. All these dimensions of state-supported nationalism served to underpin a narrow version of nationalism.

The 1960s saw significant change in both the economic and socio-political dimensions. Mass education (free second-level education was made available from 1966), increased affluence, improved communications and foreign travel contributed to a detraditionalisation of Ireland and promoted a diversity of views and experiences. Since then Ireland has become more politically and socially eclectic. As a result of all these changes the conceptualisations and uses of nationalism have evolved, an evolution encapsulated in Coakley's comment that the performance of Sinn Féin in recent local and general elections derived from identification of the party with 'social radicalism rather than funda-mentalist nationalism' (2005a: 66). Similarly, Fahey *et al.* highlight changing interpretations of identity with ethnic elements lagging behind civic features – only 13 per cent of those surveyed in the Irish Republic saw the ability to speak Irish as 'very important' to Irish identity (2005a: 69). However, there continues a great pride in being Irish and a strong attachment to the nation and its symbols. The 1995 International Social Survey Programme provides data on national identity. Of those surveyed in Ireland 53.8 per cent *felt very close to Ireland* while only 45.5 per cent of the total survey population held that view. The significance of history as an element of national identity was also underscored by the survey. Collective myths and shared memories are perceived as important elements of national identity and 53.2 per cent of Irish respondents were *very proud of their history* compared with 33.5 per cent of the entire survey population. Eurobarometer trend files show that pride in national identity in the Republic has increased from 59 per cent in 1982 to 70 per cent in 2003, with a sharp increase in pride in identity among young people (Fahey *et al.*, 2005). These data show the ongoing significance of national identity.

The evolution of national identity within the Irish Republic has taken place against the backdrop of conflict in Northern Ireland, a situation which has strongly influenced it. Girvin distinguishes between conservative nationalism and expansionist nationalism 'that insisted on Irish unity as the continuing objective of nationalism' (2002: 201). Although the Constitution, in Articles two and three (deleted following a referendum in 1998) asserted a claim to the six counties of Northern Ireland, the major political parties did little to end partition. Only the militant republicans sought to change the situation and their skewed version of nationalism gained limited public support. The communities on both sides of the border led distinctive lifestyles and there were significant attitudinal gaps and widely varying tenets of nationalism. However, the Good Friday Agreement of 1998 saw 94 per cent of voters in the south and 71 per cent of voters in the north supporting self-determination in Northern Ireland. Since then there is greater evidence of a desire for solidarity and peaceful co-existence in Northern Ireland and increased collaboration between local communities and state agencies on both sides of the border – an accommodation of nationalisms is gradually evolving.

Ireland's national identity has been internationally influenced. In both historical (Dunkerley, 2000) and contemporary[1] references America has been used as a referent but it is the European dimension which has wrought the greatest influence. As the then Taoiseach asserted,

> Ireland belongs to Europe by history, tradition and sentiment no less than by geography. Our destiny is bound up with that of Europe and our outlook and our way of life have for fifteen centuries been moulded by the Christian ideals and the intellectual and cultural values on which European civilisation rests. Our people have always tended to look to Europe for inspiration, guidance and encouragement. (Séan Lemass, 1962)

For Irish people 'Europe' has always been, and still is, an enabling symbol. Throughout Ireland's turbulent history mainland Europe was perceived as a source of hope, help and high ideals. Ideas from France fanned the revolutionary fever of the United Irishmen at the end of the eighteenth century while the Romanticism and Nationalism of nineteenth-century Germany fostered the cultural nationalism which shaped Ireland's development in the early part of the twentieth century. It is also true to say that Ireland has made a significant contribution to the culture and history of Europe over the centuries, through her missionaries, writers and musicians. Hence, the Irish–European relationship has always been a mutually beneficial one and it is not therefore surprising to find that in the 1972 referendum on membership of the European Community 83.1 per cent of the electorate voted 'yes'. The journey towards membership had been long and arduous. While much of the pre-entry debate centred on economic, political, industrial and neutrality considerations, concerns were also expressed about the continuation of a distinctive Irish identity and the upholding of sovereignty. However, from the time of accession Ireland has demonstrated a positive attitude towards Europe as will be demonstrated. The ways in which EU membership provided Ireland with opportunities to act as an important player in community policy-making has helped Ireland develop a self-confident identity that is not dependent on the UK. Some aspects of Ireland's nationalism such as the emphasis on neutrality have led to dissonance with regard to the EU's foreign policy. Similarly, attempts to achieve tax harmonisation between member states as well as proposals for expansion of social regulation have generated opposition from Irish political parties. Trade unions, political parties and some sectoral and interest groups have opposed aspects of membership at various times with Holmes (2005) assessing that in terms of aims, actors and forums, ongoing evidence of Oberreuter's 'competitive opposition' can be traced in Ireland.

As a member of the EU, Ireland's identity is constructed through openness rather than through the isolationism that shaped it in the past.

Culture and values as mediating forces

Chapter 1 sketched the enormous social and cultural changes experienced in Ireland in recent years. This section explores how culture and values acted as mediating forces, distilling the impact of Europeanisation and affecting the political and administrative outcomes. Ireland's comparatively late industrial development and the persistence of an agrarian lifestyle meant that the country developed at a different pace and in a different way from other European states and a relatively homogenous society existed until recently. The persistence of such a homogenous society meant that basic values and beliefs were shared and there was little evidence of the strong class cleavages evident in other societies. Although distinctions existed between 'strong' and 'small' farmers and 'small' and 'big' businesses, social roles were ascribed and there was little social mobility. Irish society was less socially stratified than that of the UK or France, for example. Because of this homogeneity, state and society were co-terminous and there was a strong equivalence between state, society and the Catholic congregation. Girvin describes pre-1950s Ireland as a place where 'puritan patriots and priests had tried gamely to preserve and reproduce a certain social type, pious, familial, loyal to the native acres, culturally ingrown and obedient to clerical guidance in matters moral and intellectual' (2004: 145). Cichowski (2000) identifies the major social structures in Ireland as the Catholic Church, the family, the education system and the workplace and judges that these contributed to the homogeneity of Irish society and the prevalence of authoritarian structures and deferential attitudes which, until recently, were determining elements of Irish societal culture. Family values were paramount; family structures were patriarchal and inter-generational family roles were clear and immutable.

The development of Ireland's education system has reflected and influenced the country's cultural, social and political evolution. Education and learning have always been cherished in Ireland, whether in the monastic settlements of the Golden Age or the hedge schools of the eighteenth century. Although the British state apparatus financed schools from the middle of the nineteenth century, the churches insisted on a denominational approach with the Catholic Church being the dominant force. Following independence, the state-funded schools were church-owned and managed, reinforcing a denominational approach and most secondary schools saw their purpose as preparing young people for their role as priests or nuns – accordingly the curriculum emphasised the classics rather than the sciences. The contribution of the churches to education in Ireland was invaluable with regard to resources and expertise but often stultifying with regard to educational experience. Access to second- and third-level education was quite limited until the introduction of free secondary education in 1966 because few families could afford the fees or carry the loss of potential earnings from their teenage children. Thus, because of its structural limitations and obstacles to mass participation, the education system served to reinforce a culture of obedience, conformity, dependence and limited intellectual stimulation. Cichowski's third determining structure, the workplace, was probably less influential in Ireland than elsewhere, because of the continuing agrarian practices and slow industrialisation of Ireland. Nevertheless, workplace practices also served to reinforce hierarchical attitudes and behaviours and discourage initiative and entrepreneurship.

The strongest influence on Ireland's societal culture was the Catholic Church. Not only did the Church influence the attitudes and behaviour of individuals and instil a sense of community but it also issued pronouncements on social issues and played a dominant role in policy-making and resource allocation. The Catholic Church also made an important societal contribution, being the main providers of educational and hospital services from the 1830s until the 1980s. Until 1972 the Irish Constitution accorded a special position to the Catholic Church and the rights delineated in Articles 40–4 of the Irish constitution reflected Catholic social teaching on education, property and the family. The interlinking of church and state reinforced the homogeneity of Irish society since, until the mid-1990s much public policy and legislation in Ireland reflected the ethos of the authoritative Catholic Church. It was only in 1979 that the sale of contraceptives was restrictively legalised and in 1995 the Constitution was amended in order to allow divorce but the referendum was passed by a tiny majority, reflecting the continuation of conservative values. Since then the church's socio-political influence has waned.

Gender relations mirror the values and attitudes pertaining in society and Europeanisation has been a catalyst for changed gender relations in Ireland. Traditionally, gender relations in Ireland were characterised by a hegemonic masculinity and social and economic subordination of the female. Prior to the 1965 Succession Act a married woman could be completely disinherited by her husband. Until 1973 women had to retire from most public service employment after marriage and anomalies based on gender and dependency-classification continued to restrict married women's access to social security payments until recently. While, since the 1970s, the influence of the European Community is evident in the enactment of legislation aimed at eliminating discrimination, the enforcement of equal pay legislation (despite national government's desire for derogation), a heightened awareness of equality issues and a number of positive actions. In 1971 women accounted for only 26 per cent of the labour force, with married women constituting only 3.5 per cent of the total labour force (Doyle, 1999). A report published towards the end of 2007 shows that women accounted for 42.4 per cent of persons aged over fifteen in employment (Central Statistics Office (CSO), 2007: 15). Such change has led to an improvement in the position of women in Ireland although they continue to be under-represented in local, national and European political fora.

Political institutions and practices reflect the culture in which they are situated and sustained – this is as true of Ireland's current political institutions as it was of the institutions and practices created after independence. Ireland's development as a state saw the emergence of a distinctive political culture characterised by a strong belief in democracy and public allegiance to the political system as well as traits such as paternalism, clientelism, personalism, authoritarianism, and contradictory trends of centralism and localism (see Hayward and MacCarthaigh, 2007; Coakley, 2005a; Garvin, 2004; Tovey and Share, 2005). The belief in democracy and support for the system continues as evidenced by survey data and Ireland's comparatively high voter turn-out patterns. An assessment of democracy in Ireland found that 70 per cent of respondents are satisfied or quite satisfied with the way democracy is developing (Hughes *et al.*, 2007). Results from a 2005 democratic audit depict a strongly egalitarian concept of democracy with almost 40 per cent regarding 'a more equal society' as the most important feature of democracy (Think-tank for Action on Social Change (TASC), 2005: 7). The European Values survey found that 10 per cent of Republic of Ireland questionees were very satisfied with how democracy was developing in the country – this compared with a figure of 4 per cent for the rest of Europe (Fahey *et al.*, 2005: 196). Irish people also rated their system of governance more positively with 36 per cent giving the system a rating of 7 or higher whereas only 22 per cent of those surveyed in the rest of Europe gave a similar rating. Although the authoritarianism and paternalism have diminished somewhat in the light of personal and societal modernisation, clientelism and personalism prevail. The clientelist approach fostered easy access to politicians and public servants and allowed for informality in administrative and political practices. The proportional representation-single transferable vote (PR-STV), multi-seat constituency system supports a personalist approach as politicians seek to retain popular support and ensure re-election. Despite abolition in 2004 of the dual local and national mandate, TDs still tend to focus on local issues (which raise their local profile) rather than national policy issues. The democratic audit found that 61 per cent of those questioned saw 'representing constituency and local interests' as the single most important duty of a TD (TASC, 2005: 15). Furthermore, the absence of a highly developed welfare system and social democratic approach to governance helped reinforce a culture of patronage and brokerage as politicians are perceived to be able to 'fix' or overcome the inadequacies of the system. The strong sense of community which has always been evident in Ireland and the high levels of voluntary activism have also served to reinforce the personalist approach by placing the politician in the role of local promoter. This localism exists side by side with strong centralist tendencies. Peter John states that although local government within a dual system enjoys autonomy, it is, 'the creature of statute and has little protection from re-organisation and centralisation' (2001: 32). This is the case in Ireland where formal relations between local authorities and central government are highly regulated and the regional level is seriously underdeveloped.

These dimensions of political culture mediated the impact of Europeanisation. The centralised approach meant that national government retained a strong role in the allocation and implementation of EU interventions, such as the Structural Funds. Even when responding to pressure from Brussels to involve sub-national actors, central government created regional structures which were hollow and superficial. The personalist/clientelist dimensions of Irish political culture made administrative adjustment to EU requirements easier because of the easy interaction between public actors. The pragmatic and opportunistic tendencies which had characterised Ireland's political development continued after accession to the EU with Ireland responding to all available funding opportunities. This adaptive culture proved positive in the sphere of evaluation, for example. Ireland did not have a strong culture of evaluation of policies but as obligations were imposed by Brussels, the Irish administration developed systems such as the HERMAN model which are now regarded as examples of best practice. The strong community spirit which was always a key element of Irish political culture meant that EU programmes such as LEADER (Liaisions entre Actions pour le Development Européen Rurale) could be easily and successfully implemented. Thus, the adaptive political culture facilitated aspects of Europeanisation while the EU's support, particularly for local development, 'pump-primed the economic experimentation and local innovation that stimulated the emergence of a more responsive and entrepreneurial governance milieu' (Kitchin and Bartley, 2007: 11).

In attempting to outline the manner in which Ireland's culture and values mediated the influence of Europeanisation, it is important to remember that the first thirty years of EU membership were also a time of unprecedented social change in Ireland. An eminent sociologist contended in 2000 that 'Irish society has changed more in the past twenty-five years than at any other time in its history' (Ryan, 2000: 55). International media broadened people's frames of reference; a significantly higher proportion of the population engaged in second- and third-level education and became more articulate and less subservient; new family structures became commonplace and sexual attitudes and behaviour changed; more Irish people travelled abroad, comparatively greater employment opportunities emerged and with them greater affluence, consumerism and increased social mobility. These changes also led to a desire for political and social pluralism. Patterns of people movement altered hugely.

Economic difficulties in Ireland had always resulted in mass emigration (particularly, post-Famine, in the 1950s and in the 1980s) but since the 1990s there is significant immigration made up of returning Irish emigrants and immigrants from all over the world seeking employment and citizenship in Ireland. Consequently, Ireland's mono-cultural society has changed to a more multi-cultural and cosmopolitan society although there is occasional evidence of racial prejudice and mild xenophobia. Thus, during the period of Europeanisation, attitudes and values have changed but not all the changes can be attributed to the Europeanisation process.

Halligan suggests that, at the time of entry to the EEC, a latter day de Tocqueville would have noted two features of Irish society 'a rural ethos and a monolithic culture based on Catholicism' (2000: 24). All has changed. It was only in 1971 that more than half the Irish population was found to be living in settlements of more than 1,500 people. By contrast, Tovey and Share claim that 'in contemporary Ireland, to be urban has become the cultural norm, even if it is still not the material reality for much of the population' (2005: 346). The 2006 census showed that approximately 61 per cent of the population were living in urban areas (CSO, 2006). The changes that have taken place in Ireland have not only attenuated the influence of the church on state and society but embedded a hybrid culture of cosmopolitanism, individualism, secularisation, religious pluralism, moral situationalism, political fickleness and a unique combination of globalism and localism. What has emerged is an internationalised culture reflecting European and wider global influences. O'Donnell, in summing up the social and political change evident in Ireland, contends that 'Europe is not so much the cause of these transformations as their context' (2000: 212).

Attitudes to Europe: changing over time?

In conjunction with strong national and European identity, Irish levels of support for membership and policies have been consistently high. Irish people are enthusiastic advocates of the EU with recorded support peaking in 1997 at the level of 82 per cent (Eurobarometer 68, 2007). Irish governments have participated constructively in the EU system and while not instrumental in the architectural design of EU policies, the Irish position is consensual and as '*communautaire* as possible within the limits of national preference' (Laffan, 2004: 125). This sustained affirmation markedly contrasts with the trend in reduction in support recorded across the EU during the 1990s. As a whole this has only marginally improved, and while attitudes in countries like Luxembourg and the Netherlands remain staunchly supportive, they are relatively low in several new EU member states from Central and Eastern Europe.

Although the commentary above paints a picture of a broadly positive outlook to the EU in Ireland there is evidence that public attitudes have adjusted over time. In particular, the rejection of the Nice Treaty in the referendum in June 2001 possibly signals a marked shift in the Irish mind-set towards Europe which is now further entrenched by the solid No vote in the Lisbon Treaty referendum in June 2008. This may imply that despite remaining a committed EU member, Ireland is likely to prove to be an increasingly awkward one as well (Holmes, 2005: 76) and that there is little evidence to suggest that the Irish public has 'internalised the European experience' in the same way the elites have (Coakley, 2005b: 110).

Eurobarometer 68 (autumn 2007) reports that 74 per cent of Irish people surveyed believed membership to be a good thing, whereas 87 per cent acknowledged the benefits that Ireland has accrued since accession. A positive image of the EU and high levels of support are related to knowledge and conditioned by education and occupation. Of interest is that while a mere 8 per cent believed EU membership to be a bad thing, high levels of indifference were recorded at 43 per cent. Although Irish people continue to be broadly supportive of EU membership they are also tentative about further integration. This is compounded by a distinct lack of public engagement in the substance of issues like a Constitution for Europe. It is these undecided and ambivalent citizens that pose a significant challenge to political elites who must engage and inform the public of the benefits of further European cooperation. The Irish case is not unique in this regard since a substantial portion of the European public are both uninformed and indifferent to the details and process of integration (European Commission, 2008; Niedermayer and Sinnott, 1995). Such evidence gleaned from both Commission initiated surveys and academic research on public attitudes raises fundamental questions about the legitimacy of the EU and its relations with the citizens of Europe.

Since the Irish constitution can only be amended by referendum, any substantive departure from EU treaties must be submitted to the Irish electorate in a new referendum. In taking stock of the previous ratifications of treaty change, it is apparent that the support for membership in May 1972 remained relatively consistent in both the SEA in 1987 and the TEU in 1992. As Table 3.1 illustrates, the referendum on the Amsterdam Treaty in May 1998 marked a change whereby support dipped to 62 per cent of voters in favour in a turnout of 56.2 per cent. This period marks a consolidation of the No bloc in Irish EU referendums.

It may be speculated that a change in attitudes is linked to a change in Irish perceptions of the EU. For the first twenty-five years of membership the Community was viewed as a predominantly economic entity with considerable emphasis placed on the agriculture and cohesion policies, of which Ireland has been a major beneficiary. The debate has now broadened with more attention

Table 3.1 European referendums in Ireland

Date	Topic	Yes (%)	No (%)	Turn-out (%)
1972	Membership	83.1	16.9	70.9
1987	Single European Act	69.6	30.1	44.1
1992	Maastricht Treaty	69.1	30.1	57.3
1998	Treaty of Amsterdam	61.7	38.3	56.2
2001	Treaty of Nice	46.1	53.9	34.8
2002	Treaty of Nice	62.9	37.1	49.5
2008	Treaty of Lisbon	46.6	53.4	53.1

Source: Adapted from Holmes (2005).

on political dimensions such as the impacts of enlargement and an evolving foreign and security policy. Observers, such as Hayward (2003: 129), register the consistency in the size of the yes and the no constituencies in referendums throughout Irish membership. They suggest that change is also explained by the inability of the politicians to mobilise opinions into votes and their capacity to carry the democratic mandate for European integration. This point is illustrated by the result of Nice 1 on 7 June 2001 whereby 53.9 per cent of the electorate voted no in a turnout of 34.8 per cent, thus confirming abstention and ambivalence towards a deepening of the EU project. The government clearly overlooked the information deficit which existed amongst the electorate and disregarded the degree of contention associated with the issues since only an ineffective three week campaign was run.[2] Added to this was what may be interpreted as dissident comments by high-profile ministers or comments that were interpreted by the more volatile middle-class voters as anti-EU. In 2000 the Minister for Finance Charlie McCreevy rebuked the European Commission's criticism of elements of the Irish government's budgetary strategy. This followed an earlier speech by the Tánaiste Mary Harney where she spoke of her support for a Europe of independent states and not a United States of Europe which could be harmful to Ireland's economic success. That we are closer to 'Boston or Berlin' became an infamous sound-bite that would haunt the government. Another area that was highlighted by Ministers was the threat to Irish identity and tradition which was construed as resonating with the Eurosceptic's arguments. The Minister for Arts, Heritage, Gaeltacht and the Islands, Síle de Valera, complained in a speech delivered in Boston that legislation agreed in Brussels impinged upon identity and culture. In short voters received a number of mixed signals from senior figures in the mainstream political parties.

The *post hoc* evaluation of Nice 1 required the political establishment to reflect on the disconnection of the public with EU institutions and the need to demonstrate that capacities exist for national politicians to scrutinise EU legislation. The referendum results also highlighted the need to improve public knowledge and understanding about Europe. Accordingly, a cross-party National Forum on Europe was established. Laffan sums up the anomaly of the Nice 1 referendum in her comment that it 'exposed a disjuncture between Ireland's highly internationalised economy and localised politics' (Laffan, 2004: 131). Following a far more rigorous campaign, the second Nice referendum in Ireland was passed with a turnout of 49.7 per cent, almost 15 per cent greater than in its predecessor but low enough to confirm public apathy for European affairs. The Nice experience demonstrated two consequential outcomes. On the one hand, despite solid support for EU membership amongst the Irish, European decision-making is perceived as a matter for the government and bureaucracy as opposed to the active engagement of the electorate. On the other hand, Nice awakened the political establishment to the fact that a greater scepticism existed within Irish public opinion in respect to Ireland's long-term relationship with Europe. This deepening cynicism towards Europe may have shaped the government's decision not to opt for parliamentary ratification or test the constitutionality of the Lisbon Treaty before the Supreme Court. If a referendum was inevitable, any perceived attempts to circumvent the electorate from decision-making would have played into the hand of the No bloc. Yet despite this caution and the lessons from Nice the government and the main opposition parties ran a rather lack-lustre campaign and failed to mobilise the proportion of 'soft' support for Ireland's participation in further integration. This contrasted with the effective organisation and vigorous campaign mounted by the No side.[3] The rejection of the Lisbon Treaty has delivered a serious jolt to the political class in Ireland and precipitated crisis since EU leaders indicated an unwillingness to re-open negotiations on the Treaty, the ratification of which has become more complicated in other EU member states.

Political parties as mediating forces?

Despite the significant impact of the EU on government and policy-making process and the changes in society, it is more difficult to identify European influence on the Irish party system. The party framework in Ireland is different from most European systems since it does not fit into the more widely applicable models of conservatives, christian democrats, socialists and liberals (Collins *et al.*, 2007; Mair and Weeks, 2005). Irish political party ideologies grew from national and constitutional issues rather than the social basis which underpinned party ideologies elsewhere. Consequently, Irish political parties were less susceptible to the effects of European integration. The party groupings that emerged in the 1920s bore little resemblance to the arrangement before independence as the division of the country into two separate states had largely removed the main cultural cleavage between the Protestant Unionists and the Catholic Nationalists. The major issue after independence in 1922 was the Anglo-Irish Treaty and it was precisely the 'national question' and consequent split in Sinn Féin that polarised Irish politics and largely produced and formed the basis of appeal and commitment to the two major political parties – Fianna Fáil (soldiers of Ireland) and Fine Gael (Irish race), with their stances on Northern Ireland being their most distinguishing policy difference.[4] Although it has been asserted, that the EU could emerge as a new cleavage between Fianna Fáil and Fine Gael (Gilland Lutz, 2003: 55), there is limited evidence of this to date.

In the fifty years following the establishment of the state, Fianna Fáil evolved into the largest and most eclectic party, drawing its support from all sections of society. It was the dominant force in Irish politics until 1989 when the party had to enter coalition for the first time. The Labour Party, established in 1912, never quite fitted into the dominant patterns imposed upon Irish politics by the two largest parties (Chubb, 1992: 91) and given the predominantly rural society of the Republic of Ireland its alliance of trade unionism and socialism was initially depreciated by the loss of the industrialised area of Belfast and its environs. The pervasiveness of Catholic values also contributed to the absence of a liberal party. The establishment of the Progressive Democrats (PDs) in 1985 with their aim to 'break the mould of Irish politics' and provide a real alternative to civil war parties has to some extent filled that gap. The PDs have exerted their influence relative to electoral strength through partnership in several coalition governments with Fianna Fáil. Their dismal performance in the 2007 national elections, however, diminished the PDs' standing relative to the other parties when they lost six of eight Dáil seats, including that of party leader, Michael McDowell.[5]

Overall, the number of Irish political parties has grown and the PR by STV, in multi-member constituencies facilitates the electoral opportunities for small parties and independents to win seats. Farrell (1999: 44) indicates that changes in Irish party competition during the 1990s matched comparative trends in western Europe in that increased electoral volatility enabled smaller parties to emerge. Smaller parties represented in Dáil Éireann include Sinn Féin, the Green Party, and several independents. Many independent Teachtaí Dála (Dáil deputies, TDs) use specific issues, for example the state of the health service, as their electoral platform which may signal a declining electoral attachment to parties. Since 1989 there has been a succession of coalition governments and this has altered the nature and perception of coalition government and the complexity of post-election bargaining whereby small parties exert greater leverage and Independents may hold the balance of power.[6] These coalition governments have contributed to the 'erosion of the majoritarian nature of governing that had characterised Irish politics' (MacCarthaigh, 2005: 87).

Since the 1970s, civil war politics has faded into the background and alignment to political parties is now more on the basis of loyalty and economic factors. Table 3.2 illustrates the range of parties attracting first-preference votes in the 2007 general election. Commentators refer to the Irish party system as unique (Hughes *et al.*, 2007; Gilland, 2002; Farrell, 1999; Laver and Hunt, 1992) because ideological differences between left and right are not marked and Ireland records the lowest level of electoral support for left-wing parties in Europe (Mair and Weeks, 2005: 136). Following the poor electoral showing in the 1997 general election, the Democratic Left party merged with Labour to form one Labour Party serving as the platform for politics left of the centre. In addition, the Green Party has a clear ideological left-wing position reflected in policies that call for social redistribution and economic reform in tandem with the promotion of environmental consciousness. The principal political parties, Fianna Fáil and Fine Gael, are both centre-right parties. It has been observed, however, that Fianna Fáil in particular has had little trouble re-inventing itself as a party of the centre right or centre left and making the necessary policy concessions as the exigencies of coalition demand (Gilland Lutz 2003: 43). Reflecting on the political culture discussed here, by and large, the main Irish parties tend to be run on personalist lines. Consequently, internal disputes have focused largely on personalities rather than on policies, and the emphasis tends to be on securing office as opposed to developing alternative policies (Connaughton, 2005: 249). The persistence of personalist and personality politics is likely to be a factor in the low impact of Europe on party policies and priorities. Heretofore, it has been difficult to sustain debate on European issues because national and local politics tend to dominate. However, the inclusion of the Green Party in the government that followed the May 2007 election resulted in increased attention to the debate on the European Reform Treaty because of inter-party and intra-party differences.

Table 3.2 General election results, 2007

Party	First preference votes	%	Seats
Fianna Fáil	858,565	41.6	78
Fine Gael	564,428	27.3	51
Labour Party	209,175	10.1	20
Green Party-Comhaontas Glas	96,936	4.7	6
Independent	106,719	5.2	5
Sinn Féin	143,410	6.9	4
Progressive Democrats	56,396	2.7	2
Others	30,181	1.5	0

Source: www.irlgov.ie. Voter turnout in the general election (24 May 2007) was 67 per cent.

This would seem to confirm the assertion of Gilland (2002) that if smaller parties, such as the Green Party or Sinn Féin, became part of a coalition government this would test policy towards Europe. The referendum on the Lisbon Treaty 2008 provided such a test.

As noted in chapter 1, accession to the EEC did not precipitate any divisive splits within Irish political parties. There has been a gradual but reluctant acceptance of EU membership across the political spectrum (Holmes, 2005; Laffan, 2003). Despite this, the advent of coalition governments has propelled smaller parties to tactically articulate points of difference, particularly during campaigns, in order to highlight their identity. In some instances, however, it has also muted them in order to maintain relations with the larger coalition partner(s). For example, Democratic Left opposed the Treaty on European Union in opposition but supported the Treaty of Amsterdam while in government as part of the 'rainbow coalition'. Parties which have become associated with opposition to the current structures of the EU are the Green Party and Sinn Féin. Holmes (2005: 83) asserts that the existence of such parties on the fringes of the political establishment has encouraged them to adopt a far more competitive stance in dealing with European issues and with a focus on criticisms of specific areas of European cooperation, rather than placidly joining in the pro-European consensus. For example, during the Nice Treaty referendums the Green Party highlighted the potential impact on Irish neutrality and voiced concern at whether the proposed institutional changes would be fair to the accession states of Central and Eastern Europe. This challenge to the consensus of the mainstream political parties altered for the Lisbon Treaty campaign in 2008. As second party in the governing coalition, the Green Party did not advocate an explicit party position but its ministers did present an unequivocal support for the Treaty. On a more general level the clientelist nature of Irish constituency politics and weakness of the committee system in the Oireachtas continues to militate against a more pro-active political involvement in EU affairs which remain largely an executive function (see chapter 4).

Given the Irish party system's lack of fit with the patterns and structures of mass politics evident elsewhere in Europe it is not surprising that Irish political parties have adopted an à la carte approach to their respective political groupings in the European Parliament (EP). Fine Gael appears to be the most pro-European party and cleverly aligned itself to the Christian Democrats (European People's Party) prior to accession. The Labour Party is part of the Socialist group whereas Fianna Fáil presents itself as the least Europeanised party in terms of its involvement in a grouping with the French Gaullists whose forces are split along pro- and anti-European lines in the European electoral arena. Given the fault-lines of Irish politics it is not surprising that the two centre-right parties felt the necessity to join different groups in the EP.

European elections, however, remain subsidiary to national elections both in terms of turn-out and interest with national political parties serving as the main gatekeepers within the European electoral arena, seeking to monopolise access and dominate the agenda (Mair, 2001). Of the thirteen MEPs elected in 2004, two are independents and one Sinn Fein which would mirror trends in national elections; whereas the Green Party lost its two seats and the Progressive Democrats did not run a candidate. The lack of development of a European-level party system protects the national party system from spill-over effects and national party systems have had the capacity to resist the impact of Europeanisation (*ibid.*: 38). Therefore in terms of the development of debate and an effective arena to thrash out European affairs, referendums have become the principal instrument for contestation of European issues.

Interest groups and the Europeanisation processes

While historical and constitutional factors have had a greater impact than Europe on the development of Irish political parties, Europeanisation has wrought significant change in interest representation, reflecting policy and processual changes and the increasing influence of the Brussels arena of politics. Though the central role of government remains obvious, organised interest groups are a significant mediating force internally and externally in Ireland's experience of EU membership. They also have considerable influence on domestic change given their participation in the national agreements that have framed public policy since the 1980s. The political context within which interest groups operated prior to membership was one in which governments had a virtual monopoly in proposing policy legislation and almost complete control of the activities and output of the Oireachtas (Chubb, 1992: 121). In contrast to the mainstream political parties, the trade union movement was initially lukewarm towards EEC membership. As a result of government rather than market forces, interest groups participated fully in the process whereby Ireland made the transition from a protected economy to one where interdependence with other economies was assumed (Murphy, 2003: 105). The establishment of forums such as NIEC (the National Industrial and Economic Council) in 1963 and NESC (the National Economic and Social Council) in 1973 prompted a shift in the nature of public decision-making towards a broadly 'European style proto-corporatist social democracy' (Murphy, 2005; 2003).

From 1973, economic interests that were most affected by European policies (IBEC and agricultural interests) mobilised and established a presence in Brussels to exert influence on Commission proposals and lobby on EU affairs. Organisations such as ICTU, IBEC and agricultural interests are well integrated into the policy-making process in Ireland and have extensive involvement within Brussels umbrella groups such as UNICE, ETUC and COPA.

Participation is not limited to economic interests but to other sectoral and cause-centred interest groups such as environmentalists, local authorities, anti-poverty groups and community groups which have benefited significantly from various EU programmes. As O'Donnell indicates such groups are drawn into trans-national politics by EU finance and the deliberate creation of networks by the Commission whereby 'validation by the Commission can be an important resource in dealing with the government at home' (2000: 195). Policy networks are not necessarily open and the Irish agricultural policy network has developed into an effective and stable network which is capable of limiting access to outsiders (Evans and Coen, 2003: chapter 6).[7]

Following a brief return to collective bargaining and non-intervention by the state in the late 1970s and early 1980s, the tripartite approach became firmly anchored within Irish economic governance from 1987 onwards through the medium of 'social partnership'. Table 3.3 outlines the various agreements and their duration. Hardiman (2002: 7) argues that social partnership since the 1980s refers to a process of consultation between government and the principal organisations representing employers, trade unions and the farmers.

The Programme for National Recovery (PNR) 1987 marked the beginning of successive agreements and social partnership has widened to include community and voluntary sectors in the so-called social pillar. The making and implementation of these agreements show how closely employers' associations and unions have become involved not only in public policy-making but also in its administration (Chubb 1992: 128). It should be acknowledged, however, that the government is not a neutral referee in this process since it has a serious stake in relation to public service pay and conditions. Today social partnership and 'partnership governance' operates in many forums – both sectoral and issue based – at the national, regional, sectoral and firm levels. But while there has been considerable consensus that social partnership has been an essential factor in a sustained period of economic growth, there is evidence that an uneven sectoral distribution placed a strain on the 'one size fits all' pay norm

Table 3.3 Social partnership agreements

Programme	*Duration*
Programme for National Recovery	1987–90
Programme for Economic and Social Progress	1991–93
Programme for Competitiveness and Work	1994–96
Partnership 2000	1997–99
Programme for Prosperity and Fairness	2000–2
Sustaining Progress	2003–5
Towards 2016	2006–16

(Hardiman, 2002: 18) which has led to long and complex negotiations in the formation of agreements since 2000. There has also been a tendency for each successive agreement to cover a wider and more diverse range of policies including infrastructure, the environment, poverty, health and equality. In addition, it is evident social partnership has not lived up to its image of social inclusiveness with some commentators going so far as to claim it is a 'myth' and that a critical examination of the functioning of social partnership and the 'celtic tiger' presents a picture of increasing inequalities (Allen, 2000). Although some groups are not engaged in the process, the institutionalisation of interest-group activity in social partnership is interpreted as a new form of governance. For House and McGrath (2004: 29) Irish social partnership goes beyond continental corporatism in several important ways since it is more inclusive, covering a large array of social interests, more strategic and more firmly institutionalised. The embeddedness of social partnership in the policy-making culture is being tested by changing economic circumstances. Nevertheless, as Murphy comments Ireland may now be more generally placed in 'the mainstream of West European politics in relation to interest group influence which has witnessed a blurring of the distinction between corporatist and pluralist models of group behaviour' (2005: 379–80).

Conclusions

Referring to the European Union, Cox asserted that 'policy but not yet politics has been Europeanised' (2003: 19). This assessment also seems true of the Irish case. Features such as the prevalence of positive attitudes towards Europe, the relative homogeneity of Irish society, the absence of customary ideological cleavages between political parties, the open but clientelist political culture, the adaptability of the Irish public administration all moderated the impact of Europeanisation and diminished the potential for conflict. The congruence of the EU's social and regional policies with the issues surrounding uneven economic development and personal and societal modernisation which were pertinent in Ireland meant that the requirements of Europeanisation frequently chimed with Irish needs and priorities. Frequently, the focus was on what Ireland could gain from Europe rather than on Ireland's position and role in Europe. In responding to European policy requirements domestic mediating forces sought to minimise the disruption to existing processes and policies while aiming for a sufficient degree of compliance. To date, Ireland's outlook on Europe has been positive but recent developments presage a more vacillating relationship. Becoming a net contributor rather than a net beneficiary is likely to remove some of Europe's gloss from the public perception. The increasing emphasis within the EU on political rather than economic issues is likely to provoke questioning attitudes and engender controversy. The growing complexity of EU issues may serve to distance the public – the negative results of the Nice 2001 and Lisbon 2008 referendums are symptomatic of such alienation. The reluctance of Ireland's political parties to initiate or engage in serious debate on European issues, their lack of pro-activity on EU policy issues and their continuing focus on domestic issues demonstrate a certain indifference and imperviousness to Europeanisation. Involvement in the EU has further expanded and endorsed the role of interest groups in the policy process but the resultant professionalisation of lobbying etc. raises questions of democracy, representativeness and accountability. Thus, the indicators would seem to point to a less predictable Irish stand on Europe in the future.

Notes

1   In the aftermath of the first Nice referendum in 2001, the then Tánaiste suggested that the Irish policy model was actually closer to that of 'Boston than Berlin'.
2   Ironically the main opposition parties were in favour of the treaty, as were the principal business associations, farmers and trade unions. The dissension highlighted the threat to neutrality, the lack of parliamentary scrutiny of Ireland's EU policy and the growing legislative role of the union.
3   The 'no' bloc included Sinn Féin, Socialist Party, Communist Party of Ireland, several MEPs including independent Kathy Sinnott, activist groups and platforms such as the National Platform, Cóir, prominent personalities and business elite and Libertas, a group led by businessman Declan Ganley.
4   Both Fianna Fáil and Fine Gael represent farmers. As well as the policy gulf between them on the national question, Fine Gael and Fianna Fáil were initially separated by intellectual/social barriers, urban and rural.
5   A special conference in November 2008 voted to disband the Progressive Democrat party as it was no longer perceived as being 'politically viable'.
6   The Fianna Fáil–Progressive Democrats government 1997–2002 was reliant on three independent TDs in order to secure a majority in the Dáil. From 2002 to 2007 the Fianna Fáil party was just three seats short of majority but chose to enter government with the Progressive Democrats as opposed to relying on independents for support. In 2008 Fianna Fáil entered a third term in office with the Green Party and the Progressive Democrats.
7   Many senior policy members of the IFA have formerly worked in Brussels.

4

Political institutions and administrative adaptation

Bernadette Connaughton

Introduction

Ireland is regarded as one of the most centralised liberal democracies (Lijphart, 1999). Its unitary political system is characterised by a strong central executive with subordinate local authorities answerable to and financially dependent on the centre. In 1922 the new state absorbed rather than transformed the principal features of government and administration. The parliament, government and public administration were all consciously modelled on British institutions. The endurance of Westminster institutions was an asset since it brought stability and the benefit of experience to the newly independent state. Despite external and internal pressures for reform in the following decades, the institutional framework and administrative practice were largely unchanged when Ireland acceded to the EEC in 1973. As a result both EU membership and economic and social modernisation presented a catalyst for adjustment of domestic policy-making processes and institutional innovation.

Membership of such a complex political system as the EU confronts governments with particularly testing challenges (Kassim, 2003; Laffan, 2001) and participation in its policy-making process is extremely demanding. Studies on the impact of the EU on national structure emphasise that there is little evidence of Europeanisation leading to a convergence between member states but rather national systems have retained their distinctive structures and operating procedures (Wessels *et al.*, 2003; Harmsen, 1999; Page and Wouters, 1995). The impacts of European integration are deemed to be mediated by pre-existing inter- and intra-institutional features and power balances in the member states (Kassim, 2005). It has been claimed that this is true of the Irish case where institutional change has been described as 'pragmatic adaptation' (Rees, Quinn and Connaughton, 2006; 2004) and 'gradual incremental adjustment' (Laffan and O'Mahony, 2007).

This chapter discusses the adaptation of the political-administrative framework in Ireland and the impact of Europeanisation on domestic policy processes. It is asserted that the central tenets of the political-administrative framework have not fundamentally changed and trends evident in other member states are apparent, such as executive dominance and a more passive role for parliament.[1] For Ireland, a relatively small administration and informal policy style facilitated adaptation to the EU policy process. Policy-making structures and processes were nudged into change but with a distinct element of 'path dependency'. Developments in EU governance, international trends in public management and the belated modernisation personified by the 'celtic tiger' era have wrought changes in inter-institutional relations and in a formalisation of policy arrangements that hitherto did not exist. It will be ascertained whether the nature and extent of these changes over time led to a realignment of the institutional machinery and administrative practice.

Architectural features of the political-administrative system

The evolution of political institutions and the governmental system between 1922 and 1973 was characterised by state consolidation and the establishment of democratic institutions, nationalist activism and a transition from protectionism to a more outward looking economy and society. Although British influence predominantly shaped the institutional framework, there were some significant constitutional departures (Collins *et al.*, 2007; Gallagher, 2005; Elgie and Stapleton, 2003). For example, *Bunreacht na hÉireann*, 1937 (replacing the constitution of the Irish Free State in 1922) is a written Constitution. The proportional representation, single transferable vote (PR-STV) electoral system, provisions for referendums on both laws and constitutional amendments and judicial review of the constitution also denote features that digress from British tradition (Gallagher, 2005: 73–4).

Articles 12–33 of *Bunreacht na hÉireann* deal with political institutions and provide that the Oireachtas (Parliament) shall consist of two houses: *Dáil Éireann* (lower house) and *Seanad Éireann* (upper house), a *President*, together with the government and independent court system. Dáil Éireann, born out of armed rebellion and civil war, has 166 seats and is by far the most authoritative part of the Oireachtas. It is able to introduce any type of legislation, it elects the *Taoiseach* and government and they remain responsible to it alone. The role of Seanad Éireann is defined in line with other Westminister model second chambers in that it has no substantive power or influence. Since inauguration the Seanad's role in the legislative process has been restricted in terms of its ability to stop, discuss and amend legislation, as its amendments may be ignored by the Dáil.

However, in following the model of the British parliament the Irish system failed to develop effective scrutiny procedures to hold government adequately to account. The methods introduced by the Oireachtas – debates, questions and committees – to deal with the policy proposals of government were those evolved by British parliaments characterised as debating assemblies in the nineteenth century (Malone, 2007; Gallagher, 2005). Its poor organisation and rather archaic procedures resulted in weak performance further compounded by the clientelistic features of Irish politics and the preoccupation with local affairs. As a result it became accepted that the main activity of the average *Teachta Dála* (TD) was to go about 'persecuting civil servants' (Chubb, 1992) rather than devoting their time into developing capacities as legislators. A second feature that produced a Dáil with relatively little policy effect is that the Irish system is characterised by strong party government. Given the strength of party discipline, the Dáil has been viewed by many commentators as developing into little more than a 'rubber stamp' (Malone, 2007; Chubb, 1992). Bills are prepared in government departments, agreed in Cabinet, and then presented to the Dáil for approval. As a result, though given absolute power in the Constitution to make laws, in reality the Dáil has very little power vis à vis government.

The *Taoiseach* is the head of government and he/she nominates the other members of government. The *President* is the guardian of the rights of the Irish people and guardian of the Constitution. The role of President is largely viewed as a secondary political office devoid of expectations of political leadership (Elgie and Fitzgerald, 2005). But despite the ceremonial ethos of the role he/she is the only office holder directly elected by all citizens of the state. The Taoiseach, as the head of the executive has consistently been a powerful actor. The government is not directly elected by the people; rather, it is chosen by the Dáil through the election of a Taoiseach and the approval of his choice of ministers.[2] In practice no item can be tabled at Cabinet meetings without the Taoiseach's approval. Decision-making processes are affected by collective responsibility and through the doctrine of ministerial responsibility where ministers are the political heads of fifteen departments of state. Cabinet discussions are strictly confidential under the constitution and decisions are recorded in the minutes only by the secretary general to the government.

As the administrative machinery of the new state was not recreated, a senior civil service steeped in British tradition was inherited (Collins *et al.*, 2007; Chubb, 1992). Continuity of personnel was marked by continuity of procedure. Senior civil servants were debarred from engaging in any form of political activity and the Irish system remained one of the least politicised in comparison to other European states. However, certain weaknesses inherent in the British system were also inherited. The generalist pattern of recruitment, although underpinned by open competition from 1923, was prolonged and was perceived to lead to the 'cult of the amateur' being enshrined within the administration (Lee, 1989: 93). Likewise, another maxim of British civil service was 'clear sight over short distances' and this also became a hallmark of the Irish bureaucracy (Barrington, 1980: 31). One aspect where the Irish civil service departed from its UK counterparts was the class background from which recruits were drawn. The Irish service was largely composed of young men educated in the Christian Brothers' ethos whose families could not afford third-level education (Chubb, 1992). This cohort was deemed to be deeply conservative and non-innovative, progressing slowly through the ranks on the basis of seniority rather than performance.

The legal basis for the civil service was provided for in the Ministers and Secretaries Act (1924). The act designated the minister in charge of each department a 'corporation sole' and has had a fundamental impact on the way the administrative system performs. From a legal point of view, the civil service were seen to play a subservient role with parliamentary control of the service, indirect in nature, occurring through the ministers and the government. As a result, a risk averse culture prevailed in order to ensure the minister was not embarrassed by the performance of his/her department. Managerial accountability remained weak, dealt with internally within the departmental hierarchy with civil servants rarely held publicly to account for their actions/inactions (Connaughton, 2006). As a result, ministers' limited time to shape policy became further diluted because incumbents were burdened with administrative details presented by the 'permanent government'. In terms of organisation a sectoral approach to departments dominated resulting in weak horizontal coordination.

A strong central executive contrasted with the erosion of the powers of local government. Following partition and independence the new Irish state moved swiftly to curtail the powers of local authorities in an alleged sacrifice of democracy to combat anarchy and eliminate corruption (Callanan, 2004; Haslam, 2003). The democratic government provided for at county level in the Local Government (Ireland) Act 1898 endured and the administrative frameworks established by that act were largely retained (O'Broin, 2006: 158). This provided for a single-tier urban and two-tier rural government structure. Local authorities possessed a limited range of functions in comparison to continental European administration and the Irish system remained locked in a creation of Victorian Britain and nineteenth-century legislation adapted for Ireland. The authorities had to be able to adduce legal authority for their actions[3] and crucially a high level of tax centralisation made local government weak and dependent on the government departments for resources.

In the decades following independence the chief innovations in local government included the introduction of the Local Appointments Commission (1926) whereby allocating appointment to paid positions was removed from the remit of elected representatives. The tradition of the dual mandate, however, reinforced clientelism as politicians endeavoured to ensure their election to national office by looking after their local voters (Quinn, 2003: 455). Other developments of note include the Local Government (Planning and

Development) Acts from 1963 which underpinned physical planning as a mandatory function of local government and the transfer of health and welfare services to health boards in 1970. A principal innovation and concomitant intensification of bureaucratic centralisation was the introduction of the manager system, pioneered in Cork in 1929 and applied in other counties through the County Management Act 1940. Each local authority therefore comprised two key components – the elected councillors and a Manager. The managerial system distinguished between functions reserved to the elected councillors and executive functions performed by the city/county manager who has played a key role in the initiation and implementation of policies. This did not, however, reflect the way in which business was actually carried out (Dooney and O'Toole, 1998) but reform was not attended to for decades and it was only following a referendum in 1999 that a constitutional provision for local government was included in *Bunreacht na hÉireann.*

A further section of the institutional architecture was the development of commercial and non-commercial state-sponsored bodies (SSBs) as instruments for development.[4] On independence the new Irish state was faced with serious economic challenges and infrastructural deficits. The first major commercial public enterprise development commenced with the establishment of the Electricity Supply Board (ESB) in 1927. In the era of protectionism between the 1930s and late 1950s a number of SSBs were established in a drive towards self-sufficiency in agriculture, industry, investment and production e.g. Irish Sugar Company (1933), Aer Lingus (1936), Industrial Development Authority (IDA) (1950). The demise of protectionism led to the creation of new types of state agencies directed to export marketing and attraction of foreign direct investment e.g. Shannon Development (1959). It was asserted that the rigidity of the civil service system was considered unsuitable for the running of such commercial operations (Dooney and O'Toole, 1998). Their organisation took the form of ministers being placed at one remove from these bodies, namely that ministers were responsible for policy but not for the detail of operations. Although established for practical reasons they emerged unsystematically and led to another tier of administrative bodies in addition to government departments and local authorities.

What can be inferred from this overview is that in the years following the establishment of the state continuity rather than change reflected the development of the core political-administrative framework, which would have implications for EEC membership. A strong sense of institutional pride characterised government departments which 'viewed themselves as a reservoir of brainpower which existed nowhere else in Irish society outside of academia' (Garvin, 2004: 227). Although this was a national asset, the nature of the relationship that developed between politicians and civil service had the effect of enabling the public service to be largely its own keeper with respect to reform. As a consequence the civil service resisted change and proposals for reform (Chubb, 1992; Barrington, 1980). The Oireachtas developed along a trajectory that mirrored the demise of the legislature in other liberal democracies. Its oversight mechanisms were weak and legislators were predominantly resident in their constituencies in order to prioritise constituency work. Holding government to account fell largely to members of opposition parties in their scrutiny and criticism of government proposals and performance reflective of the British style of adversarial politics. Outside of the principal institutions of government and the central bureaucracy numerous administrative demarcations were created in spheres such as health, tourism and regional development. This evolved into an unwieldy and poorly coordinated network of agencies both within and between the network of local authorities and has prompted descriptions of a 'jungle of administrative areas' (Chubb, 1992) that was inefficient and unfathomable to the ordinary citizen. But reform, change and modernisation were necessary. The socio-economic growth and change occurring in the wake of the Secretary of the Department of Finance, T. K. Whitaker's, economic plans from 1958 onwards rapidly overtook an institutional framework poorly adapted to cope with the tasks now demanded of it. Government responsibility for developing and steering the economy necessitated the creation of policy-making units in departments. In 1969 Ireland's EEC application was revived and from June 1970 the energies of a core of officials in Finance, Foreign Affairs and key line departments were consumed in the accession negotiations. Prior to this the Irish administration did not have to deal internationally with anything more elaborate than the Council of Europe and the United Nations although some departments, namely agriculture, would have developed some international competence through trade. Community membership in 1973 thus placed a heavy burden on the Irish public sector for which it was relatively unprepared as, paradoxically, accession posed a greater challenge to the system than did the emergence of the independent state.

Adaptational pressures: global, European and domestic

In examining the adaptation pressures facing Ireland, it has been suggested that a unitary state faces fewer adaptational pressures from the EU than federal states or those where sub-national government has more autonomy (Börzel, 2002). Membership of other international organisations such as the World Trade Organisation (WTO), International Labour Organisation (ILO), also places varying constraints on policy determination. Since the late 1970s, a myriad of reform pressures has affected states, impelling a variety of reforms and a questioning of institutional structures and administrative performance. These pressures included economic, financial and technological change, the so-called managerial revolution and a rapidly changing political environment.[5] The forces of globalisation have impacted upon the way states organise their institutional framework to respond to expanding communication, mobility, liberalisation, deregulation, transnational governance besides European integration and unbridled competition. This has resulted in governance within new networks and a repositioning from interventionist to regulatory state (Majone, 1996). Across the EU/OECD countries, new public management and programmes of modernisation were ubiquitous by the late 1990s. They have largely been driven by a desire for administrations to become more efficient, to have higher levels of transparency, to create a stronger customer orientation, to develop greater flexibility in operation and have much more of a focus on performance (OECD, 2005: 10). The means of achieving these aims have, however, been divergent since methods are often understood to be based upon pre-existing institutional and political agendas (Pollitt and Bouckaert, 2004), to which Ireland is no exception.

Although the Westminster model has continued to shape the structures of Irish government, there are departures from UK influence in the way public management reform has been approached. Ireland's reform experience has been different from other Westminster type systems in that ideologically driven, radical market reform has not been a central plank of its reform programme unlike practices in the UK or New Zealand. Prior to the late 1990s Ireland was reluctant to follow the global trend towards privatisation and the rolling back of direct state intervention in economic activity. The neo-liberal agenda that underpinned early privatisation activity in the UK was not embraced by Fianna Fáil and Fine Gael who dominated government in the 1980s. In addition, the trade union movement had effectively secured a veto on such initiatives as part of the Programme for National Recovery (1987).

In regard to reform of public administration, two reform attempts of note are the review by the Public Services Organisation Review Group culminating in the *Devlin Report* (1969) and the White Paper *Serving the Country Better* (1985) which emphasised the need to install management systems based on personal responsibility for results and value for money. Neither was destined for comprehensive implementation and by 1987 reform became synonymous with retrenchment to the detriment of structural and operational improvements. This had little to do with a paradigm shift to New Public Management (NPM) *per se*, but attention focused on reducing the size and operation of the civil service in a period of fiscal austerity. At local government level there were no attempts at reform in the period 1973–85 (Keogan, 2003: 83). The changes encountered by sustained participation in the EU and the initiation of the social partnership process precipitated reform and innovation, but this was not mirrored at all levels of government, departmental structures or in horizontal coordination. By the mid-1990s there was little evidence within the Irish system of the more pronounced aspects of managerialism implemented in other Westminster type systems under the banner of new public management (Connaughton, 2008). Many aspects of the human resource and financial management systems were regarded by officials as outdated and unsuited to current needs and developments. In spite of an increased focus on the interdependence of the economy and politico-administrative system, public and private sectors, the organisational and institutional mechanisms with the capacity to identify and mediate these changes were not in place.

In 1994 the Taoiseach Albert Reynolds launched a process to underpin an emphasis on management change called the Strategic Management Initiative (SMI). In general senior civil servants influenced by reforms in New Zealand and elsewhere, felt that more attention should be paid to corporate governance within Irish public administration and that changes needed to be realised within the legislative framework. In May 1996 *Delivering Better Government* was published and outlined an overall framework for change, specifically within the civil service but with the intention of broadening the process to the wider public service. The proposed reforms included new frameworks for authority and accountability, human resource management, financial management and for information technology. At local government level a series of Acts (1991, 1993 and 1994) gave effect to the recommendations of the Advisory Expert Committee on Local Government Reorganisation and Reform (*Barrington Report*). Of key importance was the devolution of functions and extension of general competence to enable local authorities to act in the interest of their areas. *Better Local Government: A Programme for Change* was launched in 1996 as the modernising reform programme for local government. This was followed by guidelines in *Modernising Government: The Challenge for Local Government* (2000). It is argued that although local authorities have achieved change, they have been overly concerned with operational rather than strategic issues (Keogan, 2003: 96). A more ambitious reform agenda was launched in 2007 by the Minister for Environment, Heritage and Local Government, John Gormley. This emphasises the renewal of local democratic leadership as an overarching theme for reforms that include the introduction of a democratically elected Regional Mayor for Dublin.

It is noteworthy that the new approach to Irish public administration was championed by the senior civil service. In other countries reform programmes have been predominantly the prerogative of the politicians whereas in Ireland politicians endorsed the work initiated by the administrative elite (Connaughton, 2008). The overall blueprint for reform also attempted to promote a shift from a secretive culture, underpinned by the Official Secrets Act 1911 and British influence, to a culture of openness. This was supported by the introduction of the Freedom of Information Act in 1997 (amended in

Table 4.1 Directions in administrative reform since 1990

Chief strategies and legislation	*Year*
The Comptroller and Auditor General (Amendment) Act	1993
Local Government Acts	1991, 1993, 1994
Launch of Strategic Management Initiative	1994
Ethics in Public Office Act	1995
Delivering Better Government	1996
Delivering Better Local Government	1996
The Public Services Management Act	1997
Freedom of Information Act	1997
Quality Customer Service Initiative	1997
Management Information Framework Initiative	1999
Modernising Government: The Challenge for Local Government	2000
Local Government Act	2001
European Union (Scrutiny) Act	2002
Freedom of Information (Amendment) Act	2003
Houses of the Oireachtas Commission Act	2003
Local Government Act	2003
Public Service Management (Recruitment and Appointments) Act	2004
Civil Service Regulations (Amendment) Act	2005
European Communities Act	2007

2002, 2003).[6] The scope of administrative reform is illustrated in Table 4.1 which outlines the chief strategies and legislative change since 1990.

The SMI remains the bedrock of what is now referred to as the Public Services Modernisation Programme and while findings indicate that the civil service has evolved into a more effective organisation, implementation remains incomplete (PA Consulting, 2002). An Organisation for Economic Cooperation and Development (OECD) review of the Irish public sector in 2008 highlighted more profound challenges and called for a renewal of public service reform. The report argued that a decade of public service reform had resulted in uncoordinated development and introducing strategic vision, greater performance review and an integrated senior executive service was necessary (OECD, 2008). The review also indicated that despite major increases in public sector employment (Table 4.2) and expenditure, public disbursements remained small as a percentage of total GDP in comparison to other OECD countries and generally reflected a typical 'catching up' process.

In terms of EU adaptational pressures, the emphasis on the economic element of European integration shifted in the 1980s to encompass a far wider mandate, incorporating significant implications of a political and social

Table 4.2 Public-sector employment, 1990–2007

	1990	1996	2001	2007
Civil service	27,472	31,282	34,068	37,200
Garda Síochána	10,900	11,391	12,228	14,115
Defence forces	14,387	14,137	12,211	11,369
Education	53,364	61,744	67,845	85,777
Non-commercial state sponsored bodies	7,132	8,501	10,444	12,013
Health services	58,438	65,169	81,513	107,500
Local authorities	26,468	26,479	29,090	34,567
Public service	**198,161**	**218,709**	**247,399**	**302,541**
Commercial bodies	**71,967**	**61,883**	**47,423**	**39,003**
Public sector	270,128	280,586	294,822	341,544

Source: Adapted from the *Administration Yearbook and Diary* (2000; 2008).

character. A series of treaty changes deepened the impact of the EU on the member states and attention has become more focused on the way the EU as a political system actually functions. The concept of multi-level governance has been offered as a means of acknowledging the multi-layered and complex nature of the EU system with its emphasis on the shared and interconnected roles of different states' policy arenas and actors in the EU policy process (Bache and Flinders, 2004). The Single European Act (SEA) (1986) engendered the first significant changes to the EU decision-making process and institutional structures with the shift from unanimity to the introduction of qualified majority voting in the Council of Ministers and an enhancement of the European Parliament's role. The Treaty on European Union (1991) built on these reforms, enshrined the principle of subsidiarity and introduced the timetable for EMU. Further treaty revision has followed with the Amsterdam Treaty (1996), Nice Treaty (2001), the ill-fated European Constitution, and most recently the Lisbon Treaty defeated in Ireland in a referendum on the 12 June 2008. All have ramifications for representation and interests in the EU institutions. The Union has expanded to twenty-seven member states encompassing much of Central and Eastern Europe, with enlargement remaining a recurrent feature of EU development. This presents considerable adaptational pressure for all member states since there are trade-offs between protecting existing political and economic advantages in order to accommodate new(er) member states and maintain some degree of efficiency and effectiveness in the EU policy-making process.

The constitutional consequences of EU membership have transferred decision-making authority from the parliamentary level, both to the European

Parliament and the member state executives through their participation in the intergovernmental institutions. Membership also qualifies the exclusive role of the national courts, since the body ultimately responsible for the interpretation of the EU treaties is the European Court of Justice. In Ireland a referendum, as opposed to ratification by majority Dáil vote, must be held if the introduction of EU treaties results in new competences transferred.[7] Over time provision has been made for a more inclusive role for national parliaments in EU affairs. In 1989 the Conference of European Affairs Committees (COSAC) was created and given formal status via the Treaty of Amsterdam. The Laeken Declaration in 2001 sought to provide political impetus to transform these rather weak provisions into scrutiny powers for national parliaments in respect to EU legislation.

This was demonstrated in provisions of the 2004 Constitutional Treaty which presented the potential for national parliaments to bypass national governments and interact directly with the Commission. These provisions are unlikely to be abandoned since they remain relevant to galvanise popular support and enhance the democratic legitimacy of the EU (Malone, 2007: 120). The European Council clearly seeks to underpin this since in 2006 it requested the Commission to consider input from national parliaments in new proposals with particular regard to the principles of subsidiarity and proportionality. This is reflected in the Lisbon Treaty which gives European and national parliaments a larger role in the decision-making.

In Ireland, Dáil and Seanad committees were few in number until the 1980s, and even some of those that did exist were mere housekeeping committees looking after the internal affairs of Leinster House. The Fine Gael–Labour coalitions in the 1980s substantively increased the number of Oireachtas committees though this was retrenched by Fianna Fáil who appears to have a less favourable attitude to committees relative to other parties (MacCarthaigh, 2005). The post-1997 committee system is more effective and its structure generally matches the structure of government departments (see Table 4.3). In addition, the establishment of the Houses of the Oireachtas Commission in 2004, underpinned by legislation in 2003, provides for a handover of the authority and responsibility for the running of the Houses of the Oireachtas and administration and management of the Office of the Houses of the Oireachtas from the Minister for Finance. This marks a positive development in bringing the Oireachtas more into line with the existing arrangements in a number of its EU counterparts which were significantly better resourced. However, enhancing the role of national parliaments within the EU policy process presents an adaptational pressure to a 'whipped parliament' like Dáil Éireann.

Table 4.3 Government departments and Oireachtas committees

Government departments	Oireachtas joint and select committees
Agriculture, Fisheries & Food	Agriculture, Fisheries & Food
Arts Sport & Tourism	Arts Sport & Tourism
Community Rural and Gaeltacht Affairs	Community Rural and Gaeltacht Affairs
Communications, Energy & Natural Resources	Communications, Energy and Natural Resources
Defence	
Education & Science	Education & Science
Enterprise, Trade & Employment	Enterprise, Trade & Employment
Environment, Heritage & Local Government	Environment, Heritage & Local Government
Finance	Finance and the Public Service
Foreign Affairs	Foreign Affairs
	Implementation of the Good Friday Agreement
Health and Children	Health and Children
Justice, Equality & Law Reform	Justice, Equality, Defence & Women's Rights
Social & Family Affairs	Social & Family Affairs
Taoiseach	
Transport	Transport
	Climate Change and Energy Security
	Constitutional Amendment on Children
	Economic Regulatory Affairs
	Constitution
	European Affairs
	European Scrutiny
	Members' interests Dáil Éireann

Source: Adapted from www.oireachtas.ie.

Impact of Europeanisation: institutional change and administrative adaptation

Early membership and incremental adjustment, 1973–86

The initial years of EU membership had a more profound impact on the institutional framework of central government as opposed to sub-national level. European affairs were also viewed as a predominantly executive function even though accession had significant consequences for the Houses of the Oireachtas and their legislative autonomy. The EEC was regarded as an area for the attention of the 'elite' and there was little by way of debate outside the government itself. Rather, successive governments and senior officials 'were largely free to chart Ireland's course' upon membership (Laffan, 2000: 129). There was no precedent for dealing with its magnitude and complexity. The Devlin Committee did not consider the implications of membership for the domestic policy process and neither did the white paper in 1972 (Lee, 1984). Before any firm guidelines on the management of dossiers were put in place, however, an interdepartmental wrangle between Departments of Finance and Foreign Affairs had to be resolved (Laffan, 2007). Finance had been the lead department in accession negotiations but by 1970 leadership had gravitated towards Foreign Affairs although Finance still supplied principal inputs and continued to chair the interdepartmental committee. With the foreign policy dimensions to membership becoming more apparent, the recognition of participating in political terms rather than solely economic consolidated Foreign Affairs' victory. It had assumed leadership and control of the mission to Brussels in 1966 and now gained the primary role in policy coordination. EC activity imposed a framework on Foreign Affairs which greatly affected both its structure and staffing and consequently boosted its position in the ranking of departments.

Coordination arrangements were laid down in the *Arrangements Circular* drawn up by the Department of Foreign Affairs in 1973. This reinforced its central position as the department with the greatest overview of European affairs, but not with the authority or expertise to assess developments in the sectoral areas. The circulation of documentation was the department's responsibility and it published accounts, at six-monthly intervals, of Community developments of concern to Ireland. In general it operated as a type of post-box in a triangle consisting of the Permanent Representation, Foreign Affairs and the technical departments in Dublin. Finance retained primacy in all matters pertaining to national budget and public expenditure and continued to occupy a dominant position in that it had to be consulted by all other Departments on Community proposals with expenditure implications. The Department of the Taoiseach initially lagged behind Foreign Affairs and Finance in terms of the centrality of its position but the thrice-yearly meetings of the European Council initiated in 1974 brought the Taoiseach into regular contact with his European counterparts and stimulated attempts for the department to make a greater input into the policy-making process. Ireland's first EU Presidency in 1975 marked a critical phase in the adjustment of the political-administrative system's engagement with Brussels and marked the end of its apprenticeship period (Laffan, 2000).

The general pattern of administrative adaptation was reflected by the standard institutional response to novelty: namely, to find a routine in the existing repertoire of routines that can be used to cope (March and Olsen, 1989). EU business was incrementally absorbed in existing structures and work methods. There was some expansion and partial reorganisation of the central government machinery but it was not transformed in either structure or practice. A high-level interdepartmental committee called the European Communities Committee replaced the Committee of Secretaries formed during negotiations. The EC Committee was designated the administration's strategic policy mechanism in addition to several policy groups. The key response to coordination at cabinet level was the creation of a cabinet sub-committee for EC affairs in 1973. These formal structures did not work effectively since the EC Committee met once a month at most, the policy groups disbanded and the cabinet sub-committee fell into abeyance by 1977 when Fianna Fáil entered government. Despite being above the interdepartmental system with regard to responsibility for decision-making, the cabinet sub-committee was not considered effective either as a source of policy initiatives or as a forum for broader discussion in EC affairs. Rather, existing structures incorporated the new responsibilities and the supplementary structures were only revived during complex negotiations pertaining to 'vital national interests', such as formulating Ireland's position on the milk super levy in 1983. The basic approach was piecemeal and portrayed an administration whereby culture and size facilitated an informal approach (Laffan, 2005: 174). By 1980 it became apparent that Foreign Affairs' role as principal coordinator had eroded. The technical departments maintained their traditional autonomy within the Irish administration and by 1983 many of them had succeeded in establishing direct contacts with members of the Permanent Representation, rather than using Foreign Affairs as the channel for coordination.

Although couched in established institutional repertoires, the executive branch of government experienced the ramifications of membership far more acutely than the Houses of the Oireachtas. The EC Act 1972 provided the Oireachtas with a limited role in European affairs though the government was required to submit a twice-yearly report to both houses. A further by-product of executive–legislature relations was that the Oireachtas had no tradition of dealing with foreign policy issues (which is how EC affairs were largely regarded by deputies during this period). In terms of scrutiny the main innovation was the establishment of a Joint Committee on Secondary Legislation under the EC Amendment Act 1973. This committee was endowed with a statutory function and could recommend the annulment of regulations passed by both houses within one year of adoption. Although novel in theory the committee was severely under-resourced and generally ineffective in practice (Conlan, 2007). It was reduced to a passive role through the relaying of information via its selected reports and as educator of politicians by the technocrats, experts and interest groups consulted. As a result its potential to improve accountability and control was not fully exploited. The Houses of the Oireachtas demonstrated a poor track record in debating EC affairs during the early years of membership and the government's reports on developments in the EC were neglected. In general incremental adjustment reflected the experience of central government and executive dominance coupled with apathy distinguished parliament's induction to Europe.

Refining the institutional framework to balance strategic concerns and day-to-day operations, 1987–2000

The informal approach and style in managing EU affairs did not fundamentally alter between the period 1987 and 2000 though there is evidence of efforts to upgrade the strategic mechanisms of coordination. This reflects both economic and political developments at EU level and the efforts to define and capitalise upon Ireland's interests within Europe. In the bureaucracy the pressures of coordination were keenly felt as the management of dossiers was driven by the immediate. Although EC/International sections remained in existence they performed a largely post-office type role in the line departments. The traditional compartmentalisation of Irish administration was compounded by the high level of autonomy in specialised sections for formulating and coordinating official briefing for the sectoral councils. The role of the Permanent Representation was also accentuated and they became the 'eyes and ears' of Dublin in Brussels (Laffan, 2000; 2007).

Departments that had been more marginally involved between 1973 and 1986, for example Environment and Justice, also gained substantial EU responsibilities or were brought more directly into EU decision-making fora. The availability of resources became a vital concern in terms of servicing the immediacy of the Brussels machine and the implementation of its outcomes. Officials opted for secondary legislation, rather than acts of the Oireachtas, as the main vehicle to expedite transposition. Administrative circulars were also used to notify departments and local authorities of changes in practice but were abandoned amid criticism from the Commission for their lack of transparency. The launch of major initiatives at European level commencing with the internal market programme placed further pressures on the civil and public service. A strict embargo on recruitment left departments, the Attorney General's office and parliamentary draftsman's office, acutely short of trained personnel to cope with drafting for complex legislative changes. Ireland's slippage in implementation league tables and the particular challenges with internal market legislation was one of the pressure points in motivating an upgraded approach to managing European affairs in Dublin.

By 1987 the influence of EU membership in modernising the Department of Foreign Affairs was discernible. As a result of its general EU coordination role and participation in negotiations, it was also more integrated into the fabric of the domestic system of administration. Finance also remained pivotal and preparation for the internal market impacted on the department in areas of taxation and banking. The designation of Finance as the national authority for the structural funds led to new mechanisms to manage the Community Support Framework (CSF) and a special unit was established to monitor its implementation and for preparation of the National Development Plan (NDP). The role of the Taoiseach's department was mainly in the realm of 'high politics' with the Taoiseach directly involved in the negotiations with Presidents Delors and Santer regarding vital national interests. The period 1987–2000, however, marked a greater input by the Taoiseach and the department in efforts to develop a more strategic perspective on Europe and reinvigorate the performance of existing institutional mechanisms.

In the mid-1980s the EC Committee met infrequently and even fell into abeyance for a two-year period. This was largely due to the Department of Foreign Affairs' day-to-day preoccupations with upcoming deadlines for meetings of the Council of Ministers. In 1987 Charles Haughey became Taoiseach and created a portfolio of Minister of State for the coordination of government policy and EC affairs. Foreign Affairs lost its chairship of the EC Committee which was transferred to the International Division of the Taoiseach's Department and chaired by the newly appointed Minister of State. It was viewed that Mr Haughey was not satisfied with the management of EU affairs and the absorption of the EC Committee into the Department of Taoiseach reflected his leadership style as more chief than chairman.

In 1988–90 Haughey also convened a Committee of Ministers and Secretaries with the dual function of presiding over the publicity campaign for the internal market and the negotiations on the Community Support Framework with the Commission. In November 1989 he initiated a small ministerial group to oversee final preparations for the Irish Presidency in 1990. The conclusion of the Presidency and the advent of Albert Reynolds as Taoiseach in 1991 resulted in a suspension of high-level committees which was surprising given the Intergovernmental Conferences on EPU and EMU were underway. This was a temporary lapse and from 1992 the EC Committee was reconvened. Up to 2002 the format of a coordination mechanism with membership of senior officials endured in the Department of Taoiseach. Although reincarnated under different titles, its remit has consistently been to provide an overall supervisory role in EU policy and track negotiation strategy. A further example of the upgrading of EU affairs was Taoiseach Bertie Ahern's decision to set up and chair a cabinet sub-committee on EU affairs in 1998. The performance of the committee system has accelerated depending on the issues at stake. For example, the negotiations for *Agenda 2000* received sustained attention at the highest political level, given that vital economic interests such as agriculture were at stake (see chapter 8).

The developments within the central government apparatus during this period illustrate that despite the primacy of a 'lead department' in the sectoral areas, the Department of Foreign Affairs, Finance and Taoiseach evolved into a cooperative partnership which has been dubbed the 'Holy Trinity' (Laffan, 2001). Foreign Affairs may have lost chairship of the top-level coordination committee but it was permanently represented and remained the department with the greatest overview and network in Brussels. Finance's trump card remained its veto on expenditure while the increased intervention of Taoiseach brought the weight of the Head of Government behind EU initiatives. All three departments remained highly networked in Brussels, working closely with the Permanent Representation and the cabinet of successive 'Irish' Commissioners, thereby being informed of all critical developments. As Laffan (2001: 52) notes, 'The three departments are complementary rather than competitive in their relationship because they must pool their limited resources to adequately manage the interface with Brussels.'

The impact of Europeanisation was far less overt in terms of institutional structures and official awareness within local authorities. Nonetheless, structural funding and EU policies in areas such as environment, health and safety and rural development had consequences for working practices. The territorial demarcations of the sub-national level were more profoundly affected, at least in theory even if not in practice (chapter 6). In order to comply with Commission guidelines on the structural funds the Irish government established seven regions in 1988. These territorial adjustments along with the emphasis of the principle of partnership, concentration, programming and additionality represented a perceived dilution of the highly centralised system of policy-making and drew attention to the need for inclusive decision-making. In the early 1990s, engagement with EU regional policy contributed to changing the basis upon which intergovernmental relations operated as well as institution building at the sub-national level (Rees, Quinn and Connaughton, 2006). Most visible was the creation of eight Regional Authorities in 1994 that continue to coordinate some of the county/city and sub-county activities and play a monitoring role in relation to the use of EU structural funds. Following a decision to split Ireland into two regions in 1999, two Regional Assemblies were also created under new structures for regionalisation (chapter 6). Initially a lack of routines to involve state actors implied a lack of change. Over time Commission encouragement and the strategic integration of a variety of non-state actors through initiatives within consecutive National Development Plans facilitated new codes and guidelines for governing (Adshead, 2005; Rees, Quinn and Connaughton, 2004).

The scale of institutional change in the Houses of the Oireachtas emulated the experience of the early years of membership. The Joint Committee on Secondary Legislation continued to operate intermittently and there was a palpable lack of interest in the committee or its reports. It may have managed to elevate the awareness of the politicians sitting on the committee during the particular parliamentary term but had little other impact. Its mandate restricted its role to secondary legislation and restricted its flexibility to consider wider dimensions of European integration. Rather, the dwindling significance of the dual mandate concentrated attention on how to maintain effective contact between the Oireachtas and the European Parliament. The Fianna Fáil/Labour coalition's programme for government in 1993 revived the idea of a more extensive committee system. Ironically, the Joint Committee on Secondary Legislation was not re-established but subsumed within a new Joint Committee on Foreign Affairs. It could be interpreted that this relegated EU affairs to a 'sub-category' of foreign affairs and the initiative was short-lived (Barrett, 2007). The Rainbow Coalition upgraded this situation and introduced a Joint Committee on European Affairs in 1995 which was given a wider remit than its predecessor. The committee was retained by the Fianna Fáil-Progressive Democrat government in 1997. The broader terms of reference did not signify a real shift in the effectiveness of monitoring legislation given the ingrained problems of the Irish parliamentary committee system. The solution suggested 'more pragmatism than critical parliamentary scrutiny' (Conlan, 2007: 183) and oversight of Ireland's relations with the EU continued to be dominated by the executive.

A punctuated equilibrium: the referendum outcome on the Nice Treaty
and its aftermath, 2001+

In spite of modernisation influences, some upgrading of coordination mechanisms and territorial re-alignment, it would appear that a fundamental shift in Ireland's conduct of EU affairs did not occur between 1987 and 2000 – even though this was a period of considerable change in the EU. The events surrounding the Nice Treaty referendums (chapter 3) altered the status quo and it has been argued that Nice 1 constituted a 'critical juncture' in Ireland's relationship with Europe (Laffan, 2007; 2005; Laffan and O'Mahony, 2007). The adaptation to new conditions has been reflected in a distinct formalisation of the management of EU dossiers and more effective oversight mechanisms in the Houses of the Oireachtas.

The 'no' result of the referendum on the Nice Treaty in June 2001 instigated a new departure for the policy-making elite since it questioned Ireland's traditional 'pro-Europe' credentials. During the campaign the EU's 'democratic deficit' had been highlighted and this was fed into the domestic debate through concern for the Oireachtas' lack of scrutiny of Ireland's EU policy and the growing legislative role of the Union. The low turn-out and result also signified a lack of public awareness surrounding the substance of the Nice Treaty. An immediate response to this impasse was to announce a second referendum and concerted action to address public concerns through a more informed debate. A National Forum on Europe was established in October 2001 in order to address the information deficit and general lack of visibility of EU affairs beyond the administrative and political elite. It held open sessions with participation from political parties and groups from civil society in an effort to engage a diffident public and address concerns regarding Ireland's future engagement in an enlarged Europe. As noted in chapter 3 the second referendum was passed in October 2002 following a more vigorous and more organised campaign.

The experience of the Nice referendums constituted an external shock to the Irish system and prompted lessons for the policy-making elite. It was recognised that a formal institutional response was required in order to present a more coherent and structured approach to EU affairs and that the Oireachtas system must be more effectively embedded within these procedures. An informal approach to EU affairs had long been perceived as the Irish norm and this contrasted with a more institutionalised approach in the majority of other member states. The small size and personal nature of the Irish administration had reinforced informality and a 'must do' culture that emanated from informal contacts and networks. These assets needed to become implanted within new processes and procedures given the contentiousness of Nice and in order to respond adequately to a more complex EU policy regime. The result was a deepened formalisation of the existing system and the establishment of new rules for managing the Brussels interface within the core executive (Laffan and O'Mahony, 2007; Laffan, 2005).

Renovation of the committee system was accompanied by personnel changes at the upper echelons of the Departments of Foreign Affairs and Taoiseach. The cabinet sub-committee chaired by the Taoiseach met more frequently and was assisted by an Interdepartmental Coordinating Committee on European Affairs attended by senior officials from every department. Following the general election in May 2002 the portfolio of Minister of State for European Affairs was re-created in the Department of Taoiseach as reinforcement of the significance of European integration issues on the agenda. The absence of such a ministerial post for Nice 1 had been perceived as a void in the administration (Laffan, 2005; Conlan, 2007). The greater formality has ensured that the committees do not fall into abeyance and more attention is paid to upcoming meetings and strategic goals. The new guidelines also embodied a reinforcement of Foreign Affairs' role as the general coordinator of EU affairs. The Economic Division was renamed the EU Division and Foreign Affairs is the liaison point for the new information system between the administration and the Houses of the Oireachtas. New guidelines were put in place for Irish embassies to upgrade coordination of dossiers and a new Permanent Representation was appointed.

Nice 1 also acted as a catalyst for addressing issues of executive–legislature dominance and the emphasis on protocol extended to relations with the

Houses of the Oireachtas. Laffan and O'Mahony (2007: 185) have commented that 'following the original circular on the management of EU business in 1973, the guidelines on Oireachtas scrutiny are the next most significant formalisation of the management of EU business in Ireland'. The new procedures for parliamentary oversight are underpinned in the enactment of the European Union (Scrutiny) Act 2002. Information notes outlining the purpose, significance and implications of proposed EU legislation are prepared by the relevant department and forwarded to the Department of Foreign Affairs. These are passed onto a sub-committee of the select committee on European Affairs. This sub-committee is unique in that it has been created by statute rather than by standing orders (MacCarthaigh, 2005: 144). The scrutiny sub-committee identifies proposals meriting further deliberation and refers them to the relevant sectoral committees in the Oireachtas. One exemption anticipated by the Act is if the relevant Minister believes that time does not permit prior parliamentary scrutiny, this will not delay the processing of the proposal. The practice of Ministers appearing in person before the committees is encouraged though not mandated. Although the above reflects change in practice it is recognised that the Oireachtas is restricted in EU matters since relevant Ministers are obliged to have regard for the committee's opinion but are not bound by a veto or scrutiny reserve for negotiations in the Council of Ministers (Barrett, 2007; Conlan, 2007; Laffan and O'Mahony, 2007). Thus while the Oireachtas now has potential for influencing government (Conlan, 2007: 184) it is apparent that pragmatism prevails. But a more active role for national parliaments is evolving and the Houses of the Oireachtas, in line with other parliaments in the EU, have established a permanent representative to the EU with an office in the EP building in Brussels. If brought into effect the Lisbon Treaty would substantively advance the role of national parliaments. They would acquire a direct input into the EU political process which would likely require reform of Dáil and Seanad procedures.

Assessment of change

In an examination of the UK experience, Bulmer and Burch (1998: 606) concluded that a pervasive Europeanisation of British central government has remained consistent with the developmental trajectory of the Whitehall system. To a large degree this commentary is resonant of the Irish case. The challenges of Europeanisation have largely been mediated through the existing institutional structures, values and historical legacy of the Irish political-administrative system. This system has remained remarkably centralised around a small group of individuals and institutions at the national level. EU membership provided new opportunities and stimulated modifications to the nature and practice of public administration – but it did not revolutionise its implementation habitat (Connaughton, 2008: 108). In understanding the nature of change in the Irish system it is also necessary to view other factors such as economic challenges, social partnership,[8] public management reform, growing interdependence between public and private sectors and the necessity to modernise structures and practices to meet contemporary governance requirements. The political settlement in Northern Ireland has also resulted in the development of an institutional framework for fostering cooperation and dialogue between Northern Ireland and the Republic of Ireland.[9] Thus while participation in the EU is a powerful factor in prompting the need for improved domestic coordination, it is not the only adaptational pressure for institutional reform. The Public Services Modernisation Programme, influenced by international reform trends, is ongoing and complements the adaptation induced by the EU. The EU, however, also employs many modes of governance that impact on domestic paradigms – regulation, intergovernmentalism, and a comprehensive *acquis communautaire* that envelops additional principles of governance such as partnership and additionality. The Lisbon Agenda also makes use of new modes of governance such as the Open Method of Coordination (OMC) that do not necessitate legislation but involve government departments through adherence to benchmarks and targets.

Laffan and O'Mahony (2007: 167) note that while adaptation to the multi-level system of governance has been path dependent it has also been sufficiently flexible to serve Ireland appropriately as the EU policy regime expanded and evolved. Ireland is unfamiliar with continental traditions of administrative law and formalisation of structures and processes. By 1983 many of the committees established at accession were no longer operational. The introduction of policy planning units was very limited – coloured by the anticipation that by and large existing structures would incorporate new responsibilities. The Irish experience therefore conformed to a general analysis that EU policy-making reinforces trends towards departmentalism and sectoralisation in national administrations (Page and Wouters, 1995: 213). Given the small number of officials involved in decision-making a position could be reached relatively quickly and assembled coherently. However, the Irish system of departmental autonomy may have led to individual departments guarding their specific policy domains to the neglect of linkages between issues and strategic action. The horizontal dimension of policy-making has long been diagnosed as a problem in Irish administration (e.g. the Devlin Report in 1969). Part of the challenge is the difficulty of working through the traditional civil service structures and the resultant silo mentality. Yet, horizontal policy coordination was not comprehensively addressed by the Public Services Management Act 1997 although there is provision for assignment of responsibility in respect of cross-departmental matters. In practice these have not been used (Whelan *et al.*, 2003) though efforts were made to reorganise and evaluate positions for EU business. This is evident from the experience of the Department of Enterprise, Trade and Employment which reviewed its conduct of EU business in 1999. The resulting *Whitney Report* recommended the designation of a section to lead in respect of cross-divisional EU issues and recognised the need to upgrade official training for participation in EU meetings.

Those members of government and senior civil service involved in EU negotiations are viewed as a *cadre* or as *boundary managers* who translate EU norms, policies and practices into the domestic arena and project domestic preferences back to the EU level (Laffan and O'Mahony, 2007; Bulmer and Burch, 1998). The discourse, interaction, networking and socialisation between these domestic policy-makers and their counterparts in other member states can itself be seen as an instrument of policy-making. In the Irish case domestic change has been mediated by such informal institutions and 'change agents' at central level. This aligns with Checkel's (2001) view that European values and policy paradigms are internalised at the domestic level, shaping discourses and identities. Due to the small and cohesive nature of the Irish civil service the same officials return to participate in EU meetings and the Permanent Representation is not wholly composed of diplomats from Foreign Affairs but also staffed from line departments. It may also be argued that the experience of being selected to work with Irish Commissioners in Brussels or in EU agencies shaped the personal career outlook of civil servants. To some extent insights from abroad facilitated the transfer and absorption of ideas and practices or provided an argument for introducing change within the Irish administration. For example, the continental idea of the Commissioner's personal cabinet was loosely experimented with in the early 1990s by the Fianna Fáil-Labour (1993–94) and Fine Gael (1995–97) coalitions through the introduction of the programme manager system and the subsequent growth in the number of special advisors.[10] In addition the learning involved in the practice of evaluation, monitoring and planning of EU projects and regional policy has been recognised as beneficial and emulated in domestic administrative practice.

Ireland has, however, been referred to as a 'selective centraliser' (Kassim, 2003: 95). In the absence of a defined ambition for the European project, coordination is focused on ensuring that national interests are effectively 'uploaded' in sensitive policy areas. The Department of Foreign Affairs has consistently occupied a central role in EU coordination but its dominance was eroded in the first ten years by the sectoral ministries who became more directly involved in EU policy-making. The increasing involvement of the Taoiseach in EU matters has also increased the input of the Department of Taoiseach which aims to undertake a more strategic perspective of Ireland's relationship with Europe. Prior to accession, the Department of the Taoiseach had long remained a small administrative unit with a coordination function for arranging government business and ensuring that government decisions were carried out. The influence of the department was seen as depending a great deal on the Taoiseach in office and his style of leadership. Greater internationalisation and more frequent meetings of the European Council have necessitated that the Taoiseach is supported by an International Division. The department's chairing of the top-level interdepartmental committee, cabinet sub-committee and a Minister of State for EU affairs is indicative of the prioritisation of EU matters. Table 4.4 illustrates the formal EU committees established in the Irish administration.

The impact of the EU regulatory framework has also contributed to institutional change and the creation of agencies. National agencies like the Environmental Protection Agency, Health and Safety Agency and the Equality Agency are part of a wider network of European regulatory agencies. These developments not only reflect the impact of EU legislation but necessary administrative reforms as the Irish economy and society modernised from the late 1980s. State-owned enterprises have since undergone considerable change with activities such as telecommunications, banking, insurance and food production privatised. The precise driver of privatisation has varied from case to case (Reeves and Palcic, 2004: 533) but European integration measures since the mid-1990s have impacted upon public enterprise policy. For example, the requirement of liberalisation of utility markets influenced decisions to privatise Telecom Eireann. The number of non-commercial public service bodies has expanded in response to new responsibilities and in some cases a response to

Table 4.4 EU committees in the Irish administration

Committee	Department chair	Dates
European Communities Committee	Finance	PreAccession
European Communities Committee	Foreign Affairs	1973–84
European Communities Committee	Taoiseach	1987–90
Ministers and Secretaries Group	Taoiseach	1988–90
Ministerial Group on the Presidency	Taoiseach	1989–90
European Communities Committee	Taoiseach	1992–94
European Communities Committee	Taoiseach	1994–97
Ministers and Secretaries Group	Taoiseach	1994–99
Senior Officials Group	Taoiseach	1994–98
Expert Technical Group	Taoiseach	1998–99
Cabinet Sub-Committee	Taoiseach	1998–
Senior Officials Group	Taoiseach	1998–2002
Interdepartmental Coordination Committee on EU Affairs	Taoiseach	2002–

Source: Adapted from Laffan (2005).

the exigencies of new public management. Instead of a whole-of-government approach, however, agencification has led to an increasingly fragmented (particularly at the sub-national level) and less accountable governance system. Given the interdependence of many of these bodies there is evidence of more networked based approaches to governance emerging, though largely operating in the 'shadow of hierarchy' (MacCarthaigh, 2007: 85–6). A rationalisation of these agencies is probable in light of the OECD review of the public services in 2008 and reduced government finance.

In terms of territorial administration and politics the EU has had an 'ambiguous' impact (Laffan, 2000). In the first decades of membership local authorities remained reactive and any relationships with Brussels were conditioned by central government dominance. Kassim (2005) notes that regional elites are strengthened by the process of European integration, though this appears to be conditional in Ireland. Developments such as the reform of the structural funds, emphasis on subsidiarity, creation of the Committee of the Regions and the Commission's promotion of the partnership principle have led to opportunities for local authorities but the prerogative has remained with central government. Despite this, territorial reform through the establishment of an albeit ineffectual regional tier of authorities is unlikely to have occurred without EU influence. But the reforms do not constitute the replacement of old structures with a comprehensive set of new ones. The change reflects adjustment by patching new administrative structures onto the existing system in order to accommodate the 'Europe-imposed' policies (Heritier, 2001). The weakness of the regional institutions has not alleviated local competition and this is reflected in policies such as the geographical dispersal of departments under the government decentralisation programme announced in December 2003.

Despite this, the absorption of EU structural funds and EU legislation has implied a number of changes to procedures and organisation within local authorities which denotes a particularly Irish *logic of consequentialism* (Rees, Quinn and Connaughton, 2004: 383). The contribution of *Better Local Government* and the partnership approach have complemented EU reforms and contributed to a widening of the range of actors in the policy process. This has influenced aspects of the reform of local government evidenced in structures such as City/County Development Boards and Strategic Policy Committees (SPCs) that formally involve non-state actors within the local government system. Local authorities have also become more active in establishing their own representation in and dealing directly with Brussels. A challenge for the central level is, however, to address the void in arrangements for ensuring that individual local authorities can raise issues of concern on draft EU legislation (Callanan, 2003). The relationships between all levels of government can be strained by allegations of poor enforcement on the behalf of local authorities when Ireland is perceived to have infringed its EU obligations. Europeanisation of the sub-national level has therefore been strongly mediated through the pre-existing balance of institutional structures and values. Adaptation has been 'politically pragmatic, administratively ambitious and institutionally limited' (Rees, Quinn and Connaughton, 2004: 402).

Despite the prominence of political parties, national parliaments have the historical legitimacy and potential to call the executive to account. In contrast, as member states have transferred sovereignty to the EU, power was relinquished not to the European Parliament but rather the Council of Ministers, Commission and European Council. The anticipation is that EU policy-making will trigger institutional adaptation and alter the domestic rules and institutional distribution of means for effective participation in the EU (Wessels *et al.*, 2003: 14). Historically the system of parliamentary scrutiny on EU business in Ireland has been one of the weakest in Europe but there is evidence post-Nice of more tangible change which would be greatly enhanced by the provisions of the Lisbon Treaty. The heretofore weak adaptation is partially explained by ingrained characteristics of the Irish political system, namely 'the danger of talking oneself out of the house' (Barrett, 2007; Malone, 2007). The lack of electoral incentives to be a good committee member, the limited resources of committees and the partisan behaviour of many committee members have impeded the effectiveness of the committee structure and make it questionable whether parliamentarians would be willing to engage in an expanded role within the EU policy-making process. Yet, the new document tracking system and more systematic procedures for scrutiny have strengthened the committee system in addition to bringing more transparency to EU affairs (Conlan, 2007: 194). The potential this brings needs to be consolidated but there is evidence that the committees are not meeting as regularly as they should in order to keep momentum going (Barrett, 2007; Conlan, 2007). Criticism has been levelled at the process because the sub-committee on scrutiny normally receives documents later in the policy process and therefore its ability to alter policy is limited (MacCarthaigh, 2005). It is not generally informed about what happens to policy after it has been passed on to the relevant sectoral committee and ministers are not bound by recommendations. While an improvement on the past, this does not suggest that the legislature has imposed real accountability on the executive. The operation of the system is summed up in Barrett's commentary, '[it] involves a somewhat peculiar institutional logic to compel a legislature seeking to hold account a government minister to depend on that Minister's department for virtually all of the information it needs to carry out this task' (2007: 210).

MacCarthaigh (2005: 298) has further commented that the media coverage in relation to the Joint Committee on EU Affairs and its subcommittee on scrutiny is negligible. He argues that the National Forum on Europe would not have been necessary (or retained) if there had been better media coverage of the work of the committee system. Although the National Forum on Europe contributed to the debate on Europe it is arguable whether it met the expectation of its advocates, who hoped for meaningful popular engagement (O'Brennan, 2005: 128) and whether it really raised public knowledge of EU affairs. The practice of inviting elites from other EU member states to address the forum and the Joint Committee's efforts to partake in dialogue with its counterparts in Europe do, however, indicate positive developments. Despite remaining in the shadow of the executive it is evident that there has been a learning process regarding the Oireachtas' experience in European affairs. Debates on Europe have improved. Further effort needs to be made to transfer this education upwards to other deputies not on the committee and downwards to the populace. In the main, the government retains the role of gatekeeper and the operation of scrutiny in the Oireachtas differs from the situation pertaining in Denmark and Austria since in practice executive flexibility endures.

In conclusion, this overview of the principal features of the political-administrative framework indicates that the pre-existing formal and informal institutional arrangements were resistant to major change and significantly shaped participation in the EU policy-making process. The 'No to Nice' in 2001 constituted an external shock resulting in adjustment and greater formalisation of procedures to manage Ireland's relationship with Europe. However, Europeanisation of the institutional architecture remains characterised by incremental and pragmatic adaptation. The essential characteristics of Irish government are largely unaltered and the pre-existing balance of domestic institutional structures such as central–local government relations and executive dominance over the legislature are predominantly intact. In this sense Ireland is no different from other member states in that structural diversity persists across Europe and core structures of domestic government have been retained. Europeanisation has precipitated learning and afforded opportunities for innovation. It is not the only reform and modernisation influence and has shaped but not fundamentally altered core features of the Irish polity and policy style.

Notes

1 For example Fabbrini and Dona's (2003) study suggest that Europeanisation strengthened the executive's power relative to that of the legislature in Italy.
2 The size of the government is fixed at not less than 7 and not more than 15 members. The legal office advising the government is the Attorney General who is not a member of the government.
3 The doctrine of *ultra vires* applied to local government up to 1991. If a local authority purported to do something in exercise of its powers but was acting beyond the powers, it was said to be acting *ultra vires* and could be restrained by

the High Court. In order to get over this restriction, a general competence provision was introduced.

4 Examples of commercial SSBs include the ESB (electricity supply) and Bord Gais (gas). Non-commerical SSBs include Teagasc (agricultural advice and research), Forfás (national policy and advisory board for enterprise, trade, science, technology and innovation), Fás (training), Bord Failte (tourism).

5 Vincent Wright (1994) referred to these pressures for reform as: internationalisation, communitsianisation, economic and financial pressures, general paradigm shift, changing policy agendas, rapidly changing political environment, technological change, democratic pressure, generalised disgruntlement at the performance of the public sector and so-called managerial revolution.

6 The amendments to the Freedom of Information Act diluted the intentions of the original act and militate against efforts to make the public policy-making process more transparent. Government papers will no longer be released after five years and there are new curbs on the publication of letters between ministers and senior civil servants, or between cabinet sub-committees and ministers. There are also new restrictions on the right of appeal to a court in cases of refusal of disclosure, where a policy matter is judged to be ongoing. Fees have also become significantly more expensive.

7 In 1987 the Crotty case challenged the constitutionality of the proposed ratification of the SEA and this was upheld by the Supreme Court. Crotty contended that the Single European Act surrendered sovereignty to Brussels, which only the people themselves, and not the Dáil, could do, as the people were the repositories of sovereignty.

8 Institutional adaptation is evident within the partnership mechanisms. In addition to the National Economic and Social Council (NESC) there is now a National Economic and Social Forum (NESF) established in 1993 to contribute to the formulation of policy and in particular unemployment, equality and social exclusion. A National Centre for Partnership and Performance (2001) promotes the partnership concept in the workplace. The three institutional structures are coordinated more closely following the establishment of the National Economic and Social Development Office (NESDO) underpinned by legislation in 2006.

9 Through the North South Ministerial Council the administration of Northern Ireland and the Irish government have agreed to hold collaborative discussions in twelve policy sectors: agriculture, education, environment, food safety and health, Foyle, Carlingford and Irish Lights Commission, health, inland waterways, language, tourism, trade development, transport and special EU programmes. Six of these issues have been formalised in north–south bodies. Chapter 6 outlines the institutional architecture with regards to EU funding initiatives.

10 The programme managers were perceived as a combination of advisors and managers operating along the lines of an underdeveloped ministerial cabinet system and within the blurred borders between politics and administration. Prior to the introduction of this system was a tendency to loosely refer to advisors as constituting a ministerial cabinet. Only the Tánaiste Dick Spring had what could conform to a cabinet since all his political staffs were outsiders. In the continental European style the programme manager system could not be interpreted as a cabinet and its emphasis was as a coordination mechanism for implementation.

5

The Irish economy and Europe

Nicholas Rees

Introduction

This chapter considers how Europeanisation has impacted on Ireland's economy and the implementation of economic policy. The case study examines economic developments by focusing on indicators of change, such as new policy directions and administrative adaptation, with a view to examining the purported reasons for change. The objective is to map the changes that have occurred by focusing particularly on the mediating structures and the discourse amongst the actors concerned, with view to understanding the stated reasons for change and whether they are attributed to Europeanisation, domestic factors or globalisation. The chapter begins by considering the pre-existing policies and polity that existed prior to EEC membership with a view to understanding the underlying domestic political and economic arrangements, which shaped Ireland's economy. It considers how European policy developments and adaptational pressures have influenced domestic economic and monetary policy. By exploring Ireland's adaptation to the strictures of the Single Market (Internal Market), Economic and Monetary Union (including the single currency), the Lisbon Strategy and increasing global economic pressures, it illustrates the degree to which Europe frames Ireland's economic policy choices and highlights the importance of domestic mediating forces. How domestic actors respond is likely to be shaped by actors' preferences and the degree of policy fit, as suggested in the literature that examined policy fits/misfits in Europeanisation. However, in the absence of strong European adaptational pressures, change may be driven at the domestic level and may reflect the type of developments in other European states. Europeanisation may, then, be a 'messy process' with adaptational pressures coming from many different directions (domestic, European and global). As Dyson notes, 'In explaining particular changes to domestic economic governance or policies it is difficult to disentangle Europeanisation from other processes – not just global but also domestic' (Dyson, 2007: 291).

It is argued that domestic economic and political considerations played a considerable part in shaping Ireland's economic development leading to a change in government economic policies and practices, including fiscal policy and the development of social partnership agreements. The success of the Irish economy depended on the ability of domestic decision-makers, especially key political leaders and officials in the Department of Finance, who took advantage of EU membership. It will be argued that Ireland's initial economic adaptation to Europe was conditioned by EC policies, which generally favoured the state and its economy in the 1970s, but by the 1980s the weaknesses of the Irish economy were evident and successive governments mismanaged the economy, failing to understand the dynamics of European integration and the impact of global forces on it. The situation was retrieved following the relaunch of Europe, with the Single European Act, and reinforced by the decision of the newly elected Irish government in 1987 to adopt a social partnership approach. The approach adopted was largely one devised at a domestic level, although the influence of the EU and other member states' economic ideas may have played a role in shaping Ireland's approach to social partnership. Ireland, while vulnerable to international economic change pro-actively managed its economic policies to ensure that the state was able to take advantage of its position in Europe and its economic relationship with the USA.

Historical context: institutions and policy

In order to understand the impact of Europeanisation on Irish economic policy, it is important to begin by considering the historical and economic context. Ireland's early economic development was shaped by the political decisions made by the new leaders of the Free State and the continuing economic dependence on British markets. At the outset the state had a strong infrastructure, civil service and education system, as well as a functional democratic system with many of the structures and institutions inherited from Britain. It was, therefore, in a relatively strong position at independence (Garvin, 2004: 2). It had strong ties to Britain and powerful allies in the USA (see chapter 1). The economy during this period was overwhelmingly an agricultural one with over half of the population of three million employed in agriculture as reported in the 1926 census, whereas as only 4.3 per cent were employed in manufacturing. As a result, the first government's priority was to encourage agricultural exports, which earned valuable income for the country. The government policies of the Cumann na nGaedheal party in the 1920s were focused on free trade, maintaining low taxes, and keeping the link with sterling (Haughton, 1998).

The election in 1932 of the Fianna Fáil government led by Eamon de Valera resulted in a significant change in economic policy direction. The new government pursued a policy of protectionism and import substitution, which was aimed at trying to ensure a better balance between agriculture production and industrial development. The policy generated new industrial development, with almost a 50 per cent increase in industrial production between 1931 and 1938 (Sweeney, 1999: 33), but such firms were small and found it difficult to expand into export markets and were largely dependent on importing their raw materials and equipment. This had the unfortunate effect of adversely affecting the state's balance of payments, leading to a significant deficit and economic stagnation in the economy. It also led to concentration of economic power in the hands of political, social and business elites with 'a large chunk of the economy being controlled by state monopolies, and market considerations were subordinate to political and 'national' considerations and priorities' (Garvin, 2004: 61). Throughout this period, the Department of Finance was presided over by Secretary J. J. McElligot (1927–53), who was opposed to state intervention in the economy and believed that taxes should be kept low (Lee, 2008: 36).

The economy between 1945 and 1949 did grow, stimulated by Marshall Aid and in response to the post-war environment. In 1948 Eamon de Valera's Fianna Fáil was defeated at the polls and an inter-party government was formed, led by John A. Costello, and made up of Fine Gael, the two Labour parties and Clann na Talmhan (western small holders), and Clann na Poblachta (People of the Republic). The government lasted for three years before being replaced by a Fianna Fáil government, led by Eamon de Valera. By 1955–56 Ireland was experiencing severe balance of payments problems, economic recession, high unemployment and mass emigration. The emphasis still remained on agriculture, which was considered to be a key economic driver. There was little interest in developments in Europe, with the focus mainly on America, and there was little confidence in Ireland's ability to develop as an economy. This was in marked contrast to the re-emergence of social capitalism across Europe, with Marshall Aid providing most states with a much needed boost leading to economic growth. Ireland was in marked contrast to its European counterparts, poor, underdeveloped and peripheral to these developments. The political elite seemed to lack the ideas and ability to change things, a tendency reinforced by the Catholic Church, the Gaelic League and underpinned by the clientelist political system (Garvin, 2004).

By the late 1950s Ireland began to become more outwardly focused, learning from experiences with the OEEC and joining the IMF and World Bank in 1957 and engaging in discussions with other states such as France about the future direction of the Irish economy. T. K. Whitaker notes that, 'One of our key priorities in the Department of Finance at this time was to get whatever help or advice we could from different quarters in developing new and effective economic policies' (Whitaker, 2007: 52). In 1959 Sean Lemass replaced Eamon de Valera as leader of Fianna Fáil and Taoiseach and initiated a policy of modernisation, which was to lead the state out of economic stagnation (Kennedy and Dowling, 1975). The government moved from a policy of protectionism and import substitution to one that adopted liberalisation and an outward looking policy of internationalisation. The objective was to modernise the Irish economy by refocusing indigenous industry and attracting inward investment to Ireland. T. K. Whitaker, as the new Secretary to the Department of Finance, appointed in 1956 (see chapter 1), led the development of the new *Programme for Economic Expansion*. The programme called for the dismantling of tariffs, the adoption of incentives to stimulate industrial investment, government spending to be used to support productive enterprises and more support for agriculture. The economy also grew by 4 per cent per annum from 1960 to 1967, reflecting a mix of factors including the government's new approach and favourable international economic conditions arising from the growth of the world economy, especially investment by MNCs in Ireland (Leddin and Walsh, 2003: 88). Much of the investment was in labour intensive industries in areas such as clothing, footwear, textiles, plastics and light engineering, shifting towards the end of the 1960s to electrical products, machinery, pharmaceuticals, medical devices and equipment (Laffan and O'Donnell, 1998: 159).

This was a critical turning point, leading to significant changes in Irish economy policy and foreign policy outlook. By the early 1960s Sean Lemass had become more confident that Ireland could economically compete with other European states in a larger European market place (Murphy, 2003). This led Ireland in July 1961, ahead of Britain, Denmark and Norway, to lodge its EEC membership application. Lemass was assured that Ireland could accept the political implications and that the economy was sufficiently strong to stand up to European competition – that the base for economic development was in place and Ireland would benefit from membership of a larger market. In the face of de Gaulle's veto, the government concluded a new Anglo-Irish Free Trade Agreement with Britain in 1965, which aimed to expose Irish industry to free competition within a decade, and joined the IMF and GATT (1967). At the same time the government sought to promote economic development at home through the adopting of successive economic programmes in 1964–70 and 1969–72, which established varying growth targets. The economy was buoyed-up during this period through the attraction of significant inward investment (using a mix of tax incentives and industrial grants) from other parts of Europe, especially the UK and Germany, and from the USA. The success of these economic programmes is debatable, with the economic planning approach being abandoned by the 1970s (Leddin and Walsh, 2003: 89).

Adaptational pressures: global, European and domestic

Global pressures

The developments described above meant that Ireland was likely to be affected by changes in the global economic system in a number of ways (O'Sullivan,

2006; Smith, 2005). First, changes in the rules, norms and policies developed by international organisations such as the World Trade Organisation (WTO), World Bank and IMF required domestic adaptation. Ireland has economically benefited from liberalisation, which has ensured greater access to international markets for Irish products, although this has exposed Ireland to outside competitors. For example, the WTO talks which were ongoing during 2008 and which included proposals on agriculture that would have adversely affected Irish farmers were opposed in Ireland. The threat of a revolt by Irish farmers in the lead-up to the Lisbon referendum, prompted European Commissioner Peter Mandelson to be conciliatory and offer reassurances to farmers that he would protect EU agricultural interests at the WTO talks.

Second, Ireland has been vulnerable to economic changes in the USA, given its dependence on US foreign direct investment in Ireland. Notably, a downturn in the US IT sector in 2000–1 quickly had economic consequences in Ireland, with US MNCs shedding workers. A further illustration of this vulnerability has been evident in the international financial crisis in 2008, stemming from the US mortgage market, which had a significant impact on Ireland and other EU states. These types of crisis quickly reverberate around the globe, affecting developed states with open economies that are integrated into the international economic system. In the Irish case, the state is highly globalised, at least in economic terms. For example, on one index that measures economic globalisation (2008), Ireland is now ranked fifteenth, reflecting a drop in its placing in recent years.[1] The evidence suggests that Ireland is dependent on a select number of economic markets in the USA and Europe, whereas the discourse around globalisation tends to emphasise Ireland as 'globalised'. The importance of global pressures can be overplayed and need to be placed in the context of Europeanisation and the domestic polity, politics and policy.

European pressures

In addition to global pressures, the growing role of the EU as an economic policy actor and the creation of a Single European Market have directly impacted on the manner in which national economic policy is formulated and implemented. The member states have come under increasing, if differentiated, adaptational pressures from the EU in this policy sphere. In its earliest form, arising out of the Treaty of Rome, the then EEC was focused on creating an economic community based on a common market providing for the free movement of capital, services, goods and labour across borders. The EEC aimed to create a common market (article 2) whereby the removal of barriers, such as customs duties and quantitative restrictions, would promote economic growth and prosperity. In the 1960s the community of six member states were committed to progressively removing the barriers to trade across the common market (e.g. tariffs and quantitative restrictions were removed by 1968) while engaged in developing a limited array of common policies around areas such as agriculture and commercial policy. In this period the member states economies experienced considerable economic growth, with increased US investment, and in the context of a positive international economic environment. In general, economic integration provided a positive impetus to growth while requiring limited adaptation by the member states.

By the mid-1970s the economic climate had significantly deteriorated, with the collapse of the Bretton Woods system and external events, such as the Yom Kippur war (1973), the first oil crisis (1973–74) and the second oil crisis (1979–80) negatively impacting on the Community. This led to increasing currency volatility, inflation and unemployment across Europe in the 1980s. There was also increasing internal dissension inside the EC, including failure to agree on proposed reforms[2] (institutional paralysis) and the prolonged discussion of Britain's budgetary contribution (which was not resolved until the Fontainebleau Summit in 1984). In addition the enlargement of the EC in 1981 (Greece) and 1986 (Spain and Portugal) to twelve member states considerably changed the political and economic nature of Europe. The enlarged Community now included states with weaker economies thereby increasing regional economic divergence. It also placed a considerable burden on the EC budget with more demands being made on it by these poorer states (e.g. Integrated Mediterranean Programmes). All of this highlighted the inability of the EC to address fundamental economic problems in the member states and the recourse to different policy approaches in Germany (monetarism), France and the UK (Keynesian).

By the 1980s, there was a growing focus in all the member states on monetarism reflecting a desire to address the issues of rising interest rates and growing public debt. This was reinforced at a European level, by the Franco-German proposals made at the Bremen European Council to create a European Monetary System (July 1979), including an Exchange Rate Mechanism, a European Currency Unit (ECU) and a European Monetary Cooperation Fund (for short-term borrowing). The UK opted not to join the Exchange Rate Mechanism (ERM), but did propose that sterling be included in the EMS currency basket. The objective was to reduce currency volatility and ensure greater stability, which was seen as key to economic growth. This latter initiative was successful at the outset, with the Germans maintaining a tight monetary policy, although there were frequent realignments of the French and Italian currencies. Spain, Britain and Portugal joined the ERM helping to stabilise the system. This lasted up until the currency crisis of 1992–93, when Britain and Italy dropped out of the ERM, with the Spanish government devaluing the peseta. There were similar attacks on the currencies of France, Portugal, Ireland and Denmark leading to devaluations in most of the currencies.

There was a new focus during the late 1980s on competitiveness, privatisation and deregulation in many of the EU member states, developments which were mirrored at the EU level. The key to future economic success lay in the combination of strong political support from German Chancellor Kohl and French President Mitterrand and strong leadership from the European Commission allied with growing concern among major industrialists that Europe needed to act. In 1985–86 the European Commission under the direction of its new President, Jacques Delors, and Commission Vice President Lord Cockfield embarked on a new drive to create a competitive Single European Market. This was followed in 1990–91 by new proposals for an Economic and Monetary Union, including a single European currency. These developments considerably changed the economic rules of the game on the European landscape. The move to create a Single European market (or internal market) reflected the concerns of the European Commission, the member states and industrialists that the EU was losing out to its US and Japanese competitors, who were able to produce high-quality goods at lower prices. The European response was to seek to complete the single European market by removing non-tariff barriers (e.g. physical, technical and fiscal barriers) that were considered as impeding economic growth and development in Europe (Lord Cockfield's white paper in 1985 contained 279 measures). However, this move was not accompanied by any attempt to provide the European Commission with a greater role in economic policy-making, which remained the prerogative of the member states; rather, it was placed in the position of score keeper (the 1992 Scorecard). The removal of these non-tariff barriers did have an immediate impact on member states, both in terms of what was required of their public administration systems and very directly on promoting growth.

The move to create a Single European Market by 31 December 1992 was quickly followed by a decision taken by the member states at the Hannover European Council (1988) to begin considering how the EC might create an Economic and Monetary Union (EMU). A committee was established under the chairmanship of President Delors to study and propose concrete steps to establish EMU. After intensive discussions of both EMU and Political Union during 1990–91, this culminated in the Treaty on European Union which was signed in Maastricht (February 1992) and committed the members amongst other things to forming an EMU (Title VI). In essence, the treaty and follow-on developments led to the creation of a single European currency in 1999 (thereby locking exchange rates together), a single European Central Bank (as the key decision-maker) and the stability and growth pact (governing excessive deficits and convergence criteria). In order for states to become members of EMU monetary union they were required to meet a strict set of economic criteria including: (1) a debt at less than 60 per cent of GDP (2) government deficit of under 3 per cent of GDP (3) a low inflation rate at 1.5 per cent of the three lowest rate inflation countries (4) long-term interest rates should not be higher than three lowest states, and (5) the currency should be part of the ERM for at least two years. The objective was to create a stable economic zone in which monetary policy would ultimately be set by the European Central Bank. However, the strictures of these criteria proved problematic and had to be lessened to ensure that eleven EU states were eligible to join (Greece was not considered ready), with Britain, Denmark and Sweden opting out.

Recently, the EU has sought to address concerns about economic performance of the member states (especially competitiveness and unemployment) through the Lisbon Strategy agreed at the European Council in March 2000. The objective of the strategy was to create a competitive and dynamic knowledge-based European economy able to sustain growth with more and better jobs and greater social cohesion. A particular emphasis was placed on better policies for the information society and research and development (R&D), as well as structural reform for competitiveness and innovation and by completion of the internal market. Other elements included modernising the European social model, investing in people and addressing social exclusion. This was to be supported by developing a healthy economic outlook and favourable growth prospects by applying an appropriate macro-economic policy mix (European Council, 2000). In order to achieve these objectives, targets were set in areas such as employment and R&D, although these proved to be problematic and were not achieved leading to the appointment of a new taskforce chaired by Wim Kok (former Dutch Prime Minister), to review progress and comment on what might be done to improve the situation.

In March 2005 the European Council endorsed a review by the Commission of the progress made towards the Lisbon Strategy and proposed a number of amendments.[3] This reflected the fact that progress in the member states had not achieved the goals of the Lisbon Strategy, perhaps reflecting the limits of Europeanisation! In fact the adapted strategy included a set of twenty three 'integrated guidelines' which covered a mix of macro-economic, micro-economic and employment guidelines (Gowland *et al.*, 2006: 382–3). The objective was to bring together a range of European policies aimed at addressing the objective of the Lisbon Strategy, namely to build a dynamic knowledge-based European economy and society. This required member states to draw up *National Reform Programmes* on the basis of the EU's *Integrated Guidelines for Jobs and Growth, 2005–08* (including broad economic policy guidelines and employment guidelines) and in consultation with regional and national stakeholders. This has been updated, with new Integrated Guidelines adopted by the member states for 2008–10 (March 2008). From the perspective of Europeanisation, the focus on member states coordination and the use of guidelines have minimised the European-level adaptational pressures. In effect this means that the achievement of the goals of the relaunched Lisbon Strategy will depend on the ability and willingness of domestic actors to integrate such guidelines into domestic policy.

In summing up, global and European adaptational pressures have played a role in shaping the domestic preferences of policy-makers and conduct of economic policy. In the economic arena, there is a complex interplay between domestic, European and global pressures that make generalisations difficult. In the next section, it is argued that Irish policy-makers have adeptly used European pressures to progressively frame and pursue their own economic policy preferences.

Impact of Europeanisation: institutional and policy adaptation

Early economic gains, 1973–80

Ireland joined the EC at an inauspicious time when there was both an energy crisis and a global recession. Global forces beyond Ireland and the EC's control impacted on the Irish economy and framed much of the discussion at national and European levels. The expectation was that Ireland would economically benefit from membership, although there was less certainty what that would mean in financial terms. The government's first white paper on European Community membership, published in April 1970, examined the economic, constitutional, legal and political aspects of EC membership. The economic attraction of EC membership was considered to be obvious, given the possibilities of Irish participation in a larger market where Irish food and manufacturing exports could be sold at much higher prices than at home and access to structural supports and agricultural subsidies. At an economic and political level, membership also offered the government a means of offsetting Ireland's dependence on the UK and the possibility of accessing these new markets. The EC offered what many believed was the only way forward for the state in the 1970s, as the alternative appeared to be a stark economic future.

The EC that Ireland joined had evolved during the 1960s from being a customs union and common market, but was something less than an economic union (Matthews, 1983: 112). By implication this meant that Ireland accepted the core tenets of these arrangements and thereby had to adapt to become part of the customs union. In the accession negotiations Irish representatives sought to protect Ireland's indigenous industries by looking for transitional arrangements to enable the industries to prepare for foreign competition. These included a five-year transition period, safeguard measures and a special anti-dumping regime. In addition, the government attached a Special Protocol on Ireland's industrial and economic development to the Treaty of Accession highlighting the state's economic situation. However, the 1972 white paper, *The Accession of Ireland to the European Communities*, concluded that at best these traditional industries would hold their own, whereas it was anticipated that growth in employment would occur from the attraction of multi-national corporations (MNCs) to Ireland. In practice, the economy performed reasonably well during the first period of membership from 1973–79, weathering the international economic slowdown and the oil crises of 1973–74 and 1979–80. At a domestic level, successive Irish governments while benefiting from Europe faced the challenge of addressing these new global pressures and coming up with sound domestic economic policies. Responding to the first oil crisis, the Fine Gael/Labour government (1973–77) led by Liam Cosgrave embarked on a spending programme without increasing taxation, thereby exacerbating inflationary pressures. There followed in 1976 a policy reversal, with the government raising taxes and curbing expenditures, which seemed to address the immediate economic problems (Leddin and Walsh, 2003: 94–5). In 1977, a new Fianna Fáil government took office under Jack Lynch and changed course again engaging in tax cuts and increased public expenditure leading to an increase in the budget deficit and fuelling inflation.

In this period EC membership did lead to a rapid growth in the export of manufacturing goods to European markets (McAleese, 2000: 82). In 1961 manufactured exports accounted for 20 per cent of total exports, which grew to 74 by 1995. Equally the dependence on UK markets declined from 75 per cent in 1961 to 44.5 per cent by 1978, just prior to membership (see Table 5.1). Imports into Ireland also rapidly grew during this period, sometimes adversely affecting domestic industry. This resulted in a decline in employment in the traditional manufacturing industries in Ireland, especially among indigenous companies, with the loss of 20,000 jobs during the 1970s (FitzGerald, 2000: 72). New employment was created by an influx of new largely US and some Japanese investors in areas such as pharmaceutical, metals and machinery. Such MNCs were attracted to Ireland as it offered a secure base inside the EU, a low corporate tax system (10 per cent) and IDA supports. US investment was particularly important, growing by over 38 per cent per annum in the 1970s,

Table 5.1 Irish exports and production, 1961–72, and 1972–81

	1961–72	*1973–81*
Industrial exports	13.4	11.6
Agricultural exports	4.6	2.8
Total exports	7.8	7.9
Industrial output	6.2	4.3
Agricultural output	1.7	0.6
GDP	4.1	3.4

Source: McAleese (1984: 152).

or over three times the EC average (Matthews, 1983: 119). The industrial growth rates of 8.5 per cent predicted in the 1972 White Paper were not achieved, with the annual rate being 4.3 per cent.

The economy was also supplemented through financial transfer from the Agricultural Fund (FEOGA), European Social Fund (ESF) and European Regional Development Fund (ERDF). In the case of the Social Fund, Ireland received a disproportionately large share of the fund relative to its population size. Similarly, while quotas were fixed the ERDF, the state was able to maximise its take from the fund, ensuring the funding of a number of large-scale infrastructure projects. The significant transfer of financial resources during this period required major adaptation and change in the manner in which government and public administrative system sought and managed these funds (see chapters 6 and 7). The transfer of resources indirectly contributed to economic growth, but provided much needed financial support to the exchequer which could be used to improve the state's physical and human infrastructure, thereby supporting economic development (FitzGerald, 2004: 74). These early experiences provided invaluable lessons for Irish officials, who became adept at working with their European counterparts and learning how to manage the system to Ireland's benefit. At the same time, however, Irish officials had to adopt key EU directives on health and safety, collective redundancies and acquired rights into Irish law. All of which ensured improved rights and protections for Irish workers bringing them into line with their European counterparts.

By the late 1970s Irish politicians and officials faced a new European policy challenge in the form of the European Monetary System (EMS). The EC had been committed since the late 1960s to creating some form of monetary system to address instability in the exchange rates which were considered damaging to trade and price stability. In Ireland this raised concerns about whether joining EMS would remove from government control a key national economic policy instrument, which could be used to preserve the price competitiveness of traded goods (Matthews, 1983: 128). It also raised the spectre of a break with sterling that had existed with Britain since 1826 and which had directly influenced Ireland's monetary policy. The merits of EMS membership were discussed in a government white paper (1978) and debated in the Dáil, where the general view was the advantages outweighed the risks. On the plus side, it was considered beneficial to trade, foreign investment, CAP and economic integration. It was also important from the perspective of the other EC member states that Ireland join, given that Britain had decided not to do so, and there was a concern about the emergence of a variable Europe (Scott, 1994: 21). On the negative side, there was a risk that any devaluation of sterling against the EMS basket of currencies might adversely affect Irish exports which remained dependent on UK markets. In the lead-up to the Bremen European Council

(July 1979), Ireland held a series of bilateral meetings with the other states, during which it was offered guarantees of financial assistance. EMS was agreed at the Bremen European Council and Ireland was granted a mix of grants and loans to ensure that the state was cushioned against any devaluation (O'Kennedy, 1999).

The decision to join EMS was significant on a number of levels. First, it demonstrated Ireland's commitment to supporting further European integration, and thereby its willingness to relinquish some economic sovereignty in this domain. Second, it provided an important learning experience for Irish officials, especially from the Department of Finance. The department had previously lost out to the Department of Foreign Affairs, who had the primary responsibility for coordinating EU affairs. This placed the Department of Finance in a strong position to lead on EC economic and financial matters, especially relative to other spending ministries at home. In practice, Ireland's experience within EMS was mixed, with inflation increasing between 1979 and 1981 and peaking at 19.4 per cent in 1984. Also, contrary to expectations, the British economy grew during this period, largely as a result of North Sea Oil with the value of sterling appreciating rather than depreciating as expected.

From economic stagnation to the Single European Market, 1980–88
Ireland in the early 1980s, like most other European states, experienced global recession, with the EC member states falling behind the USA and Japan. In this period European economic growth rates fell to less than 1 per cent (FitzGerald, 2004: 77). All of this fuelled political unrest and tensions between employers and trade unions, leading to three general elections between 1981 and 1982 (Kitchin and Bartley, 2007). Ireland's economic performance, however, was worse than its European counterparts (NESC, 1989: 144). The economy was characterised by high inflation, a growth in the national debt as a result of high public spending (over 10 per cent of GDP), huge unemployment (rising from 7.8 per cent in 1979 to 18.2 per cent by 1985) and emigration. There was also a contraction in the number of MNCs based in Ireland, with over £2 billion (7 per cent of GDP) leaving the country in 1986 (O'Hagan, 2005; Haughton, 1998: 45). The vulnerability of the economy to such foreign companies was highlighted in the report published by the Telesis Consultancy Group (Industrial Policy Review Group, 1982) and reiterated in the Culliton Report, *A Time for Change* (1992). The former report led to the publication of a government white paper on *Industrial Policy* (1984) and the significant reorganisation of the Industrial Development Authority (IDA) aimed at ensuring Ireland could attract in FDI. The latter directly impacted on the policy adopted in the second *National Development Programme, 1994–99*, highlighting the link between national decisions and the utilisation of EU supports.

In Ireland, the general inability amongst those in government during the 1980s to understand the relationship between developments in the Irish economy and the impact of external economic and political forces (internationalisation) contributed to Ireland's economic problems. Moreover, domestic electoral volatility, the continuing change of governments and the election of weak governments (see Table 5.2) ensured that economic policy did little to address fundamental underlying economic problems including reducing public spending. A variety of different economic plans were formulated during this period, although most rested on assumptions that included public expenditure would stimulate growth (e.g. *National Development 1977–80*; *Proposals for Plan, 1984–87*, and *Building on Reality, 1984*) (Leddin and Walsh, 2003). One commentator, O'Donnell suggests that the 'Organisational and institutional arrangements capable of identifying and mediating these mechanisms and pressures were not in place, and seemed beyond the capability of Ireland's political, administrative and interest-group system' (2000: 176).

By the late 1980s, European-level economic thinking and developments became an important source of change providing a significant boost to the Irish economy with the EC's commitment to economic liberalisation extended from the goods sector to services, the development of the single market programme with its emphasis on removing physical, fiscal and technical barriers, and further significant transfers through the structural funds (McAleese, 2000: 89). As McAleese notes, 'the liberalisation of the services sector was forced upon us by Brussels' (2000: 89). This focused attention in Ireland on the state run companies in transport, energy, telephones and steel and led ultimately to liberalisation in these and other sectors such as banking and insurance during the 1990s. This was not uncontested and there was considerable opposition amongst those groups with vested interest in these areas, such as existing management and trade unions. It did, however, lead to greater economic growth, especially during the 1990s. EC policy requirements also impacted

Table 5.2 Irish governments in the 1980s

Taoiseach	Parties	Years
Charles Haughey	Fianna Fáil	1979–81
Garret FitzGerald	Fine Gael/Labour	1981–82
Charles Haughey	Fianna Fáil	1982
Garret FitzGerald	Fine Gael/Labour	1982–87
Charles Haughey	Fianna Fáil	1987–89
Charles Haughey	Fianna Fáil/Other	1989–92

Source: Coakley and Gallagher (2005: 475).

on the domestic polity in a number of other ways. It led to an increasing alignment of Irish competition law with European law and a greater emphasis placed on the role of the Competition Authority. In addition, increasing European restraints were placed on state aids, which were viewed as anti-competitive and likely to have market-distorting effects. Finally, there was also an increasing focus on public procurement practices, which were seen as favouring domestic companies with new procedures and requirements introduced by Brussels. These developments coincided with the election in 1987 of a new Fianna Fáil government committed to economic change and neo-liberal market solutions (see next section).

It was, however, the European Commission's proposal to complete the single European market, which promised the possibility of significant economic gains for Irish citizens and businesses. The Cecchini Report (1988) estimated that that GDP across the EC would grow by 2.5 to 6 per cent arising out of cost reductions (cited in Mulreany *et al.*, 2007: 60). In Ireland, the government and the major parties welcomed the proposals to create a single market, although this was tempered by concerns about the effects of market integration on the Irish economy. It was likely to provide further opportunities for indigenous and MNCs operating from Ireland, with a further reductions in non-tariff barriers reducing the costs of doing business in Europe. There was, however, a concern that regional problems might be exacerbated by the creation of the single market with poorer peripheral regions unable to take advantage of the economies of scale. Ireland, in conjunction with other peripheral states, obtained a commitment to double the structural funds under the Delors I budgetary package (Brennan, 2008). This ensured that there would be sufficient financial transfer to Ireland to offset any potential negative consequences arising from further economic integration and enable them to develop their human capital and build up their physical infrastructures (see Table 5.3, also chapter 6). As a consequence, Ireland's structural funds receipts totalled 2.6 per cent of GNP per annum during the period 1989–99 – significantly higher

Table 5.3　EU transfers to Ireland, 1973–98 (IR£m)

Year	CAP price supports IR£m	Structural fund IT£m	Total IR£m	SFs % of total	SFs % of GNP
1973	37.1	0.0	37.1	0.0	0.00
1983	441.7	286.0	727.7	39.3	2.10
1989	963.4	331.9	1,295.3	25.6	1.50
1993	1,281.6	963.5	2,245.3	42.9	3.35
1998	19,415.4	10,576.1	29,991.5	35.3	1.73

Source: Adapted from McAleese (2000: 96).

than other member states when measured on a per capita basis (McAleese, 2000: 93; also Matilla, 2006). This significantly boosted the Irish economy during a period of European wide recession (1991–93).

In the end the move to complete the internal market has been judged to have been a key factor in Ireland's economic success during the 1990s (Sweeney, 2008; O'Donnell, 2000: 182–3; NESC, 1989). The internal market led to an increase of FDI in Ireland by US and Japanese MNCs, who were eager to be inside the EU and fearful of a fortress Europe. Equally, it provided an impetus to indigenous industry eager to do business in Europe, as well as making the service industries more aware of competition. It led to an alignment of Irish competition policy with that of Europe and led to a better monitoring of state aids. More generally, it copper-fastened the formation of Irish economic policy to developments taking place at EU level, further demonstrating the impact of Europeanisation on Ireland. This was clearly demonstrated in the development of the first Irish *National Development Plan, 1989–93*, which highlighted the impact of EU policy on the development and implementation of Irish economic policies (see chapter 6). At the same time that this was occurring, it should be noted that there was also an expansion of EU social policy which benefited many in Ireland. Notably the Charter of Fundamental Social Rights of Workers was adopted in December 1989, while the Maastricht Treaty provided for qualified majority voting on workers' rights and introduced a new consultative procedure between the Commission, employers and unions on social policy.

The origins and evolution of the 'celtic tiger', 1987–2008
The period from 1987 to 2008 was characterised by an increase in the role played by EU institutions in economic and monetary affairs, as well as in other related areas such as social policy. In 1994 the Commission published the white paper on growth, competitiveness and employment which moved the debate beyond monetary issues and deregulation to investing for the future, competitiveness and innovation (Cassells, 2000: 71). A range of major EU initiatives, including the completion of the Single European Market, EMU and the Lisbon Strategy significantly impacted on the formation and implementation of economic policy in states such as Ireland. In this context, Europeanisation has led to the formation of a complex system of economic governance that brings together key EU and member state representatives to discuss and coordinate economic policies. The development of such a discourse at European level has informed and influenced national-level economic policy thinking, as well as having progressively impacted on the autonomy of member states. In the Irish case, however, it is worth noting that the EU neo-liberal focus during this period was mirrored among a number of prominent Irish political leaders responsible for developing economic policy during the 1980s and 1990s

(e.g. Alan Dukes, 1982–87; Charlie McCreevy 1997–2004). The following discussion examines how these key developments have impacted on the Irish economic polity, politics and policy since the 1980s.

The first key EU development during this period was the move to create the Single European Market. In Ireland, these developments coincided with the election in 1987 of a new minority Fianna Fáil government led by Charles Haughey, which was able to take advantage of EU developments and the domestic desire for a radical change enabling it to address the problems of Ireland's economy. Its policies were focused on cutting public spending, a public-sector pay freeze, and a reduction in borrowing to bring the economy under control. The cuts introduced by Ray Mac Sharry, Minister for Finance, led to a fall in state spending from 50 per cent of GDP in 1986 to 37 per cent by 1988 (McSharry and White, 2000; Haughton, 1998: 45). It also sought to create a social consensus through a partnership approach.[4] In essence, the objective was to quell industrial unrest and gain support to implement a programme of spending cuts. It led to agreement between the government and the social partners on a *Programme for National Recovery, 1987–1990*, which provided the basis for an agreed strategy to manage public finances. This model brought Ireland's market-driven model closer to other European states, where the notions of partnership and consensus building were more the norm (see Table 3.3). Most importantly it recognised the need to develop Ireland as a competitive international economy in order to achieve all other economic and social goals. As a result government spending fell from 50 per cent of GDP in 1986 to 30 per cent by 1998 (Haughton, 1998: 45). There was an increase in foreign investment, inflation dropped and the Irish pound was secure within the European monetary system. All of this enabled the government and business to take advantage of the Single European Market.

Ireland had by the mid-1990s one of the fast growing economies in Europe, outperforming its European neighbours, with Irish per capita GDP having grown from 66 per cent of the EC average in 1972 to 115 per cent by 2000. The average growth of GNP, 1993–2000 was 8.3 per cent, with GNP at 4.4 per cent in 2007 (see Table 5.4). In a European context, Ireland had the second highest GDP per capita (138.9), second only to Luxembourg. Employment also grew by 45 per cent between 1993 and 2001 (Clinch *et al.*, 2002: 25). Unemployment had dropped from the highs of the 1980s to about 4 per cent in 2000–4 with over 1.920 million people in employment by 2004. Its population had grown to over 4 million, with a significant increase in returning migrants, immigrants from many central and east European states, and birth rates (ESRI, 2007).

Ireland's economic success in the 1990s was underpinned by a mix of EU, domestic and global developments. First, at EU level the introduction of the Single European Market (for exports of computers, pharmaceuticals and

Table 5.4 Ireland: GNP and GDP

Year	GNP	GDP
1980	2.6	2.9
1985	0.2	1.9
1990	6.5	7.7
1995	8.0	9.6
2000	12.3	11.8
2005	4.9	5.9
2007	4.4	4.7

Source: Sweeney (2008: 200–1).

chemicals), EMU, and EU structural fund transfers (see Table 5.5) supported Irish economic development. Ireland was by the far the largest net recipient of EU funds with each person annually receiving €550.00, 1995–2002 (Mattila, 2006: 42). Second, at a domestic level, the government's continued commitment to social partnership agreements, the maintenance of stable public finance and price stability, a low corporate tax and an associated presence of a large number of MNCs, and investment in training and education helped to secure economic growth. There was a regular supply of labour, with a large proportion of the population of working age, higher levels of participation by women in the work force, and immigration, including a high percentage of returning Irish and an influx of Central and East European labour. Competitiveness was accepted by all the social partners, trade unionist, business and government as a key economic driver. Finally, from outside of Europe foreign direct investment from the USA, a favourable trading environment, advantageous exchange rates against sterling and the US dollar, a growing US economy, low energy prices, and IT and communications improvements led to increased productivity (Clinch *et al.*, 2002; Sweeney, 1999).

O'Donnell suggests that:

> The boom of the 1990s can be seen as a process in which a range of domestic and international factors made it possible for Ireland's regional economy to greatly expand its export sector. The combination of a consistent policy approach, social partnership and improvement in indigenous business produced a virtuous circle. (2003: 2)

External global factors played a key part in Ireland's development with US direct investment provided an important stimulus to the economy. In Ireland, the Industrial Development Authority (IDA) played an important role in recognising the heterogeneity of MNCs looking to locate in Ireland and operated a high degree of flexibility around incentives tailored to meet those needs (Ruane, 2008: 44). Ireland offered a low-cost, English-speaking state

Table 5.5 Structural Fund programmes in Ireland (€m)

	1989–93	*1994–99*	*1989–99*	*2000–06*
National Development Plan (total)	12,275	16,800	29,075	57,111
Structural/Cohesion Funds as % of total NDP	29.91	41.20	36.43	6.55

within the EU, from which manufactured products could be exported. The companies were attracted by government subsidies and other supports, but the low corporate tax of 10 per cent for manufacturing was a significant inducement (dating from 1981 and extended to all corporate taxes at 12.5 per cent in mid-1990s). In the context of the late 1980s and early 1990s, the government also set about creating the infrastructure (with EU support under successive National Development Plans) to sustain this investment and to attract more highly skilled, high-end manufacturing, including research and development. Foreign Direct Investment (FDI) accounted for 50 per cent of Ireland's GDP by the late 1990s (Kitchin and Bartley, 2007: 7). The IDA's focus was on attracting industry in four sectors: financial services, chemicals, pharmaceuticals and medical devices. By the late 1990s the IDA's strategy had changed and it was eager to attract in the higher-end parts of the manufacturing and service companies, including their financial and business services, research and development, and marketing.[5]

The second key EU development that impacted on Ireland was Economic and Monetary Union (EMU) (Lynch, 2008). In Ireland, the proposed EMU was welcomed by all of the main political parties, IBEC and the trade unions. The government and particularly the Department of Finance believed it would prove to be important to Ireland's economic success, building on the benefits of the Single European Market. EMU appeared to offer the possibility of economic and financial stability, with low inflation and interest rates. This was seen as critical from the Department of Finance position, as the single currency offered a means of imposing and improving self-restraint on all levels of Irish debt and borrowing. It would ensure that Ireland's political leaders were kept in line and would avoid the worst excesses of public spending witnessed in the 1970s. It offered the benefits of making trade easier for exporters with other member states through use of the single currency and this was also likely to make it easier to compare prices across the Eurozone (McAleese, 2000). The elimination of exchange rate fluctuations was likely to lead to a reduction in interest rates. On the negative side, the UK opt-out and possibly sterling fluctuations might adversely affect Irish companies engaged in trade with the UK. There was also a concern that introducing the euro would be costly and would largely fall on business and the consumer. A further fear was that the loss of control over the setting of interest rates to the European Central Bank would limit Ireland's room for manoeuvre, although this was somewhat spurious given Irish interest rates were influenced either directly or indirectly by sterling. In the end the positive points outweighed the negative ones and the decision to participate in EMU and join the single currency on 1 January 2002 was endorsed by voters at the referendum on the Maastricht Treaty. The timing was also good for Ireland, given that it fitted well with the positive state of the economy.

In participating in EMU Ireland was signing up not only to a single currency, but was also agreeing to join in a fully integrated market and to coordination of national macroeconomic policies. The economic objectives of EMU included: growth, a high level of employment, price stability, convergence of economic performance, and economic and social cohesion. In order to achieve these objectives three instruments were to be used: (1) multi-national surveillance of economic developments in the Community (2) multi-annual economic policy guidelines to member states and secondary legislation, and (3) EC financial assistance to a member state threatened with difficulties (O'Donnell, 1991: 22). This represented a significant relinquishing of economic sovereignty and control thereby binding a member state to EU-level agreements. A noted Irish economist observed, 'EMU does [did] involve a further ceding of economic sovereignty from national government to Community institution and the supplanting of national policy-making powers by collective community decision-making' (Tansey, 1992: 6). In Ireland the government's economic policy approach was in accord with that being adopted at EU level, given its commitment to low inflation and low interest rates, tight controls on government borrowing and on the ratio of public debt to national income, and a stable exchange rate.

EMU brought with it new challenges for those who joined the Eurozone. Notably, the criteria imposed through the Growth and Stability Pact limited the actions that member states could undertake to manage their economies. Governments were meant to adopt relatively uniform economic policy to avoid inflationary pressures and maintain currency stability. Government borrowing was not allowed to exceed 3 per cent of GDP and they were to follow the Broad Economic Policy Guidelines agreed to at European level. In 2000 the Irish government ignored these requirements and adopted an inflationary budget, which EU leaders thought might lead to inflationary pressures and destabilise the Eurozone. As a result, Ireland was reprimanded by the European Commission and censured by the Economic and Finance Council of Ministers. These criticisms, however, were rejected by the Irish Minister for Finance, Charlie McCreevy, who disagreed with their economic assessment (McGowan and Murphy, 2005: 191–3; Rees, 2000). This highlights the role of the European

Central Bank, which decides on monetary policy, sets interest rates, controls the supply and production of new currency and manages inflation. Equally, fiscal policy is constrained by the Stability and Growth Pact, which limits each government's budgetary freedom.

Third, at EU level the growth of new structures, rules and practices around economic governance, including the Lisbon Strategy, have placed significant constraints on national economic policy-makers. In contrast to monetary policy, in areas of economic policy, such as employment and competitiveness, the EU depends far more on economic coordination among the member states and the EU's institutions given its more limited powers. The process is largely based on open coordination and annually peaks at the Spring European Council meetings, where economic matters are discussed by the heads of government and finance ministers. These annual meetings have also included assessment of the member states' success in achieving the objectives of the Lisbon Strategy and the implementation of agreed programmes. In the Irish case, this included the adoption of *Ireland's National Reform Programme, 2005–7* in line with the EU's *Integrated Guidelines for Jobs and Growth* arising out of the renewed commitment made at the March 2005 European Council to the Lisbon Strategy. In line with these commitments, the Commission publishes an annual progress report on each state's programme. In the Irish case, the state has been complimented by the Commission for its comprehensive and coherent national strategy.

In summary, the key EU developments discussed is this section – EMS (1978), the Single European Act (1987), the Maastricht Treaty (1993), the Euro area (1999) and the Lisbon Strategy (2000) – illustrate how Europeanisation has impacted on the formation of Irish economic policy.

Assessment of change: learning and adaptation

This chapter has demonstrated how the development of Irish economic policy, especially during the 1990s, became increasingly intertwined with EU policy and affected by global pressures. In the Irish case, past economic policy failure meant that the state was more than willing to take on the obligations of EU membership and adapt its existing economic policies and governance arrangements to meet European requirements as they evolved. There was strong domestic pressure for economic policy change, reflecting elite and public desire to participate in EU-level developments, ranging from EMS, the Single European Market, EMU to the Lisbon Strategy which were seen as bringing economic benefits and supporting economic growth. In the 1980s, as McAleese has observed, 'bad domestic policy went near to wrecking the Irish economy's capacity to utilise the advantages of market access. The fiscal situation was retrieved just in time' (McAleese, 2000: 104). In the late 1980s and early 1990s,

Ireland took advantage of its position in Europe and its access to these markets, to pursue national economic policies that proved successful in promoting economic growth and restoring confidence in the Irish economy for investors. The state was also buoyed-up by significant financial transfers from Europe at a time that coincided with a Europe-wide recession (1991–93) thereby ensuring that Ireland received a boost from EU funds at just the right time. Also, once Ireland joined the ERM and the EMU (1999), the state achieved much lower real interest rates supporting cheaper borrowing and housing investment boom.

The key to Ireland's economic success lay in the ability of its political leaders and their officials to adapt and learn from their experiences in Europe. Early experiences in the 1970s, including the first EU presidency held by Ireland, also boosted Irish confidence and the state's standing in Europe. They proved to be adept in European-level negotiations at winning financial support and other concessions for Ireland (see chapter 4). These officials were able to leverage Ireland's economic position in Europe to obtain valuable financial supports from Europe while usually trying to minimise what needed to change back home in Ireland. In particular, financial transfers such as from the ERDF and ESF grew after the Single European Act and constituted some 2.6 per cent of GNP per annum during 1989–99 (see Table 5.5). The growth of European economic and monetary requirements instilled new discipline among Irish officials, especially in the Department of Finance, who had to adopt new approaches to economic planning and public management. It also provided them with the authority, policy tools and means to manage the Irish economy – fending off the spending tendencies of other government departments and their ministers. For example, the adoption of various National Development Plans dating from 1988 required a carefully thought-out and planned approach to economic development. This included outlining economic policy objectives, broad spending priorities and plans for infrastructural investment. It also required a longer-term strategic view of investment including multi-annual programmes thereby ensuring a flow of funding to projects. Of course, this required agreement with other government departments and the European Commission, which was not always forthcoming and required considerable negotiation.

As the EU's role in economic and monetary policy has grown, it has significantly enhanced the role of the Department of Finance and led to administrative adaptation with EU matters permeating most divisions. In particular, the Finance and Budget and Economic Divisions have had the main responsibility for EU matters. The former has been responsible for monetary policy, the Irish contribution to the EU budget, financial regulation, and the Community Support Framework. The latter has responsibility for economic and social planning, including monitoring developments in the Irish economy and across the EU (Laffan, 2001: 46–7). Representatives of the department are now involved in the EcoFin Council, the Economic and Finance Committee, the Economic Policy Committee, the Eurogroup, ECB, and the Budget Council (Laffan and O'Mahony, 2003). The decision to join the single currency enhanced the position of the Department of Finance and the Central Bank relative to other spending ministries, as it was able to use the criteria for membership as a means of controlling spending and enforcing a fiscal policy aimed at keeping inflation low (Laffan and Tonra, 2005: 451). It also meant that the Irish Central Bank was represented on the ECB Governing Body, while the Department of Finance was involved with the Euro group of Finance Ministers. Aside from the Department of Finance, the Department of Enterprise, Trade and Employment has also been a key ministry responsible for EU business, especially in relation to the Lisbon Strategy. It has had to adapt its administrative structures to cope with the demands of EU work, including servicing the largest number of EU ministerial councils (Laffan, 2001: 54).

In assessing Ireland's changing economic policy in Europe, the state has become increasingly part of a system of European economic governance. This is a system in which policy competences are shared between Brussels and the member states and where much depends on the political commitment of the members to coordinate their economic policies. In this area, the introduction of Integrated Guidelines and a National Reform Programme in Ireland highlight how EU developments have led to national innovation and a change in planning practices. Ireland has been supportive of these developments, given that its own national economic policies have been in line with the EU's approach to economic growth and jobs. This is reflected in the state's policy commitment to maintain and build national economic competitiveness reflecting the belief that it is important to contain costs and increase productivity in order to remain internationally competitive and attractive to FDI. It has significantly invested in research and development in third level education, establishing a new Science Foundation Ireland (2003), as well as supporting research in industry through a range of Enterprise Ireland schemes. There has also been a significant focus in the *Towards 2016* partnership programmes on up-skilling workers and preparing them for the jobs of the future in the competitive knowledge-based economy. All of this resonates with the discourse being conducted at a European level, reflecting the degree to which EU developments have influenced Irish economic thinking and approaches to public policy problems. In summary, EC-level developments have significantly influenced the Irish economic process, fundamentally altering the relationship between the market, the state and society leading to the emergence of new patterns of governance. This is evident in policy areas as diverse as the environment, agriculture, regional and even foreign policy, as discussed in the following chapters.

Notes

1 Index of Globalisation, Swiss Federal Institute of Technology, Switzerland, http://globalization.kof.ethz.ch, accessed 13 February 2008).
2 These included the *Tindemans Report* (1975), *Report of the Three Wise Men* (1979) and draft Treaty on European Union (1984).
3 Commission Communication, *Working Together for Growth and Jobs: A New Start for the Lisbon Strategy* (2005).
4 NESC, *Strategy for Development* (Dublin: National Economic and Social Council, 1986).
5 Enterprise Strategy Group, *Staying Ahead of the Curve: Ireland's Place in the Global Economy* (Dublin: Enterprise Strategy Group, 2004), *Towards 2016: Ten-Year Framework Social Partnership Agreement, 2006–15* (Dublin: Department of the Taoiseach, 2007) , *Tomorrow's Skills: Towards a National Skills Strategy*, 5th Report (Dublin: Expert Group on Future Skills Needs, 2007).

6

Regional policy and politics

Bríd Quinn

Introduction

From its inception in the 1970s, the European Union's regional policy has effected significant change in member states, while itself evolving from a limited policy instrument to a fully fledged policy in response to expanding EU membership and changing priorities (Featherstone and Radaelli, 2003; Bache, 1998). Such change has been asymmetric between and within states. Ireland serves as an example of a member state wherein EU regional policy has induced perceptible adaptation while the state's experience also influenced the trajectory of EU regional policy. It is not surprising therefore, that a 2008 survey carried out by Gallup for Directorate General Regional Policy found that 64 per cent of Irish people were aware that the EU supported their region and 88.5 per cent believed that their region benefits from that support (Gallup, 2008). This chapter examines the impact of Europeanisation on regionalism and territorial politics in Ireland and reveals the pragmatic manner in which Ireland has adapted to European requirements. It explores Ireland's response to the various tenets and thrusts of EU regional policy, a response which involved exploiting the inherent opportunities and responding creatively to obligations and constraints. Having identified the underlying domestic socio-economic and political features which moderated and sometimes stymied adaptation, the chapter outlines the changes to policy, polity and politics, highlights the resultant institutional and processual modifications and charts changes to the structures and patterns of governance. It is contended that ostensibly the creation of regional structures and sub-national partnerships would suggest a transformation but in effect the changes have been cosmetic rather than systemic.

Historical context: institutions and policy

Ireland's adaptation to EU regional policy was affected by the existing domestic institutions and practices, the territorially undifferentiated approach to policies and the prevailing political culture. During the first thirty years after independence Irish economic policies were founded on protectionism and self-sufficiency. Such policies were designed to foster overall national development rather than encourage the growth of specific regions. The political structures put in place bolstered centralisation and sacrificed sub-national democracy in the interests of bureaucratisation and central control. Initially, efficiency, the elimination of corruption and the avoidance of anarchy in a post-civil-war society were listed as the reasons for the centralising thrust. Later, technical, administrative and financial complexity were cited as the justification for the continuing domination by central government and bureaucrats (Lee, 1989; Garvin, 1996). The centralised structures militated against any type of regionalism while the political culture precluded regional approaches which might threaten the authority and stability of the nascent state. The PR-STV voting system and the clientelist–localist political culture further diminished the possibility of a regional focus since politicians were more concerned with local votes than visionary regional strategies. From the 1930s onwards, the particular problems of Ireland's most peripheral regions, mainly along the west coast, were given sporadic attention by successive governments but this must be seen as attempting to address the chronic problems of the specific regions rather than as evidence of a regional policy, *per se* (Ó Tuathaigh, 1986). National problems such as the reduction in agricultural employment and rising emigration affected the west particularly and necessitated action in the early 1950s. Yet, despite the Underdeveloped Areas Act of 1952 and the 1956 Industrial Grants Act, the potential for a regionally focused development strategy was not realised. The Whitaker Report on *Economic Development*, issued in 1958, advocated an emphasis on national development but in 1959 a further attempt at regional development was made with the creation of the Shannon customs-free zone and the establishment of Shannon Free Airport Development Company Limited, a highly successful entity. Thus, the 1950s was a period of inconsistency in government attitudes to regional development and little impact was made on the regions.

Ireland of the 1960s witnessed waves of what could loosely be described as regional development activity although the emphasis was on the creation of economic growth poles. The Irish government's *Second Programme for Economic Expansion*, published in 1963, included a commitment to ensuring the coordination of economic and physical planning at regional and national level. To attain this goal nine planning regions were established in 1964 but they were not assigned either statutory powers or functions and merely served as administrative units. This failure to underpin the Local Government (Planning and Development) Act 1963 with a statutory regional mechanism meant that the opportunity for a clear hierarchy of development planning was once again missed (Bannon, 1989). However, the regional approach continued to be promoted in other aspects of public policy such as tourism. A further indication of the concern with regional issues during the 1960s was the creation of an inter-departmental committee to advise on regional policy. Later, Regional Development Organisations (RDOs) were established (in the mid-west in 1968 and in the other planning regions a year later). These bodies served a coordinating and dissemination role but again lacked financial and functional power. Despite these limitations the RDOs impacted in the regions, particularly in the east and Cork where an urban transport strategy was developed (Bannon and Lombard, 1996). There was, however, no coordination of the regional divisions for the various purposes and a multiplicity of regional boundaries resulted, a problem which still persists.

Several reports on regional issues were produced during this period, the most famous being the controversial Buchanan Report of 1968, which urged concentration on a small number of growth centres. The political will to implement these reports never materialised because the localist political culture prevailed and caused politicians to implement a localised, vote-getting industrial development strategy rather than a strategic regionalised approach. Accordingly, there was little institutional or administrative adaptation. However, government statements on regional policy were issued in 1965, 1969 and 1972. The latter 'advanced the concept of *regional balance* as the keystone of state regional policy' (Ó Tuathaigh, 1986: 123). The 1972 government statement had a strong industrial bias and listed the aims of regional policy as being: the reduction of regional disparities through industrial development, balanced regional development, minimisation of involuntary migration and restriction of Dublin's development. In retrospect, it is clear that the government's aims were not achieved but the proposed strategy was designed to ensure maximum benefit from imminent membership of the EEC.

Ó Tuathaigh concluded 'that the period between 1968 and 1973 was probably the most fruitful period in the past thirty years for the discussion of regional policy and for some moves towards structural and institutional reforms consistent with the development of a genuine regional policy' (1986: 122) but there is little evidence either of the embedding of such policy or of institutional reform to create regional structures. The regional dimension did feature in Ireland's negotiating stance on entry to the European Community. In July 1972, a memorandum was submitted outlining Ireland's regional development problems and seeking EEC commitment to supplementing national efforts at dealing with those problems and the development of a community regional policy which would take cognisance of Ireland's special problems. A protocol annexed to the Treaty of Accession referred to the Irish government's objective 'to eliminate under-employment while progressively evening out regional differences in levels of development' (cited in Maher, 1986: 315). As later sections of the chapter show, this objective was not actively pursued.

Thus, at the time of Ireland's accession to the EEC, although there was a demand for recognition of the country's regional development problems, there was scant evidence of any real attempts at addressing those issues. A number of factors contributed to this failure. These include the persistence of localism, failure to address the disproportionate growth of Dublin, the concentration of economic, administrative, political and academic expertise in the capital city and the unattainable focus on agriculture and manufacturing as the means to redress regional imbalances. The lack of coherent regional development policies and strategies was accompanied by underdeveloped administrative and political structures at regional and local levels. As Barrington asserts 'regional development in this country is usually held to mean something done *to* a region by a benign central authority, not done *by* a region for itself' (1982: 106). Local government structures, functions and finances were limited, so this level was not in a position to promote a regional dimension. There were no directly or indirectly elected regional political structures nor were there any public or elite demands for such bodies. Indeed, some civil servants held the view that local authorities were not to be trusted and were administratively inept. Although planning regions had been created they were only assigned a coordinating function. Similarly, the Regional Development Organisations lacked functional and financial impact. Neither was there evidence within the central administration of any coordinated approach to regional issues or a consistency with regards to regional policy. Yet, there was considerable interest in the EEC's moves towards a regional policy which it was hoped would bring Irish standards of living closer to those in prosperous parts of the Community (Barrington and Cooney, 1984).

Adaptational pressures: European, global and domestic

Opportunities and challenges, 1973–87

The regional policy of the European Community has continually evolved to reflect changing economic, social and political contexts. When introduced in 1975, the EEC's regional policy was based on a national quota system which meant that the European Regional Development Fund (ERDF) was perceived as a *juste retour* for countries contributing an above-average amount to the EC's budget. The system also meant that the funds were widely dispersed, covering 60 per cent of the Community's geographical area and 40 per cent of its population (Bache, 1998). The European Regional Development Fund was intended to complement the regional development efforts of the member states and the monies were expected to be additional to domestic regional policy expenditure. No specific role was assigned to subnational authorities in the process. During this period a number of amendments to the ERDF regulations and processes were adopted. These included the introduction of strategies to devise a systematic approach to analysing regional problems and the allocation of a 'non-quota' section of the ERDF to be used for integrated programmes of investment projects. In 1984 the rigid quota system was replaced by a more flexible system of allocative ranges. These were incremental steps towards a Community regional policy but the member states continued to dominate the sphere and in its early years and the Community's regional policy had little impact on member state institutions and practices.

This was a period of change both domestically and within the EEC. Notwithstanding the explicit concern for balance and economic dispersal in Irish government pronouncements, the dynamic of regional development altered during the 1970s, with regional development being identified only with the regional section of industrial policy. This change in focus reflected the Irish government's articulation of a policy which would make industrial development incentives available throughout the country rather than only in underdeveloped regions (Bannon, 1989; Ó Tuathaigh, 1986). The white paper on *National Development 1977–80*, which formed the basis of the regional development programme which Ireland submitted to Brussels did not refer to regional policy as a means of reducing internal disparities. However, the regional dimension continued to gain prominence in other areas of Irish life. Two distinctive regional development organisations continued to operate, Údarás na Gaeltachta[1] in the Irish-speaking districts and Shannon Development in the mid-west. Regionalised structures, such as regional health boards, regional fishery boards and regional technical institutes were put in place and training and industrial development organisations operated on a regional basis. The failure to coordinate the regional designations for the differing purposes resulted in an administrative farrago. Throughout the 1980s, attention again swung towards national issues and the improvement of national economic performance. Rather than striving to attain inter-regional equity, the IDA sought to attract industries with a high-added value which would improve the country's general circumstances. Thus, it became clear that the commitment to any form of regional development policy had waned (Bannon and Lombard, 1996). During the late 1970s and early 1980s Ireland made only a limited and half-hearted commitment to regional policy and local development, reflecting the realities of Irish economic development and the impact of external factors. The most significant external factors included the worldwide economic recession, which severely affected Ireland; exchange rate fluctuations and membership of the, then, European Economic Community.

The European Regional Development Fund emphasised the need for Ireland to attain convergence with more developed parts of the EEC and so fostered national development rather than regional development or the reduction of disparities within Ireland. Between 1975 and 1983 Ireland received IR £276.39 million in ERDF payments. This varied from IR £5 million in 1975 to IR £64 million in 1982 (Hart, 1985: 226). The geographical imbalance of the infra-structural proposals submitted by the Irish government for funding under the ERDF did little to redress inter-regional disparities during this period (Bannon and Lombard, 1996; Drudy, 1984). Holmes and Rees (1995) and Drudy (1984) also draw attention to the perceived unequal distribution and impact of the funds, with the eastern part of the country appearing to receive a greater share. However, it is difficult to isolate the specific impact of the ERDF funds from that of domestic policies and payments because of the lack of regionally disaggregated data. It was only from this period onwards that regional statistics and data became more available, providing objective evidence of Ireland's regional imbalances.

The lack of progress in the area of true regional development during the 1970s and early 1980s may be partly explained by the decision to designate Ireland as a single region for EEC funding purposes. As O'Donnell and Walsh assert 'this postponed the development of political, representative and adminis-trative structures for regional development in Ireland' (1995: 225). In relation to other Nomenclature of Territorial Units for Statistics (NUTS) II regions, Ireland was somewhat unusual as it was double the size of the average NUTS II region, both in terms of population (average size was 1.8 million in population), as well as in physical territory. There was also a prevailing view that as Ireland was a small state, regionalised structures were not necessary and that local government was not particularly strong or capable of acting on behalf of local communities. Administration of the ERDF in Ireland was highly centralised with funds being allocated sectorally within the national Public Capital Programme rather than on a regional basis and with no specific role for local authorities. The Department of Finance thus retained its tight control on spending. There were doubts among civil servants about the capacity and expertise of local government to take on additional responsibilities (Holmes and Rees, 1995). Thus the implementation of EEC regional policy in its early years, while inducing some administrative change, served to reinforce Ireland's centralising mode of governance. The greatest achievement of the period was the translation of the rhetoric of regional development into the reality of targeted interventions.

A period of change, 1988–99

From the mid-1980s there had been an upsurge of concern for regional development in Ireland, brought about partly by internal forces and impelled by developments in Europe. Among the internal forces propelling the regional development movement were a shift in industrial policy to the fostering of indigenous firms (in accordance with the tenets of the Telesis review of industrial policy in 1982); a shift in economic thinking; a change in the relationship between the various policy-makers as evidenced in national agreements which have become the norm since the 1970s; a growing acceptance that social problems can be better dealt with on a regional or local basis; a groundswell of local initiatives aimed at socio-economic improvement and an awareness of the 'democratic deficit' between the politico-administrative elite and the citizens, a deficit which might be counteracted by regional political structures. Although such forces were at play and pro-regional rhetoric was widespread, their impact was minimal until the external catalyst of the structural fund reforms of 1988.

Operational changes were brought about by the 1984 reform of the ERDF and were designed to bring about an emphasis on programming rather than projects. However, the Irish government continued its project approach, submitting 160 projects for support in 1985 (Holmes and Rees, 1995: 244). Iberian enlargement, moves towards a single market and EMS added impetus for reform of the EEC's regional policy. A European Parliament committee, chaired by John Hume MEP, prepared a *Report on the Regional Problems in Ireland* in 1987. The Hume report was critical of the Irish government's approach and strategies and such external criticism stung. The general lack of functional integration, the problem of territorial inconsistency and the absence of coordination among regional structures meant that the Irish government was not prepared for the implications of the changes in European regional development policy initiated by the 1988 reform of the structural funding process.

The reformed EU regional policy was based on the principles of partnership, programming, concentration and additionality. The resultant adaptational pressure led to administrative and policy change in Ireland. The Delors I package obliged the Irish government to submit a development plan. Because the country was regarded as a single region for Structural Fund purposes this implied preparation of a national development plan. Consequently, since the late 1980s successive Irish governments worked with the EU in developing the National Development Plans/Community Support Frameworks and specific operational programmes, thereby moving from a project and annual focus to a multi-annual and programming approach. The National Development Plans (NDPs) (1989–93) and (1994–99) articulated the government's priorities for investment, the targets for development and the strategies to achieve them. The 1989–93 Community Support Framework (CSF) consisted of twelve Operational Programmes with CSF related expenditure amounting to IR£8.64 billion of which IR£3.2 billion was drawn from the EC. Over 45 per cent of this funding came from the ERDF, 37 per cent from the European Social Fund (ESF) and 17 per cent from the European Agricultural Guidance Guarantee Fund (EAGGF) (*ibid.*: 244) leading to EC involvement in many aspects of Ireland's public administration. The Treaty on European Union added a new dimension to the EU's regional policy strategy – the

Cohesion Fund whose goal was to assist the convergence of national economies in preparation for monetary union (Brennan, 2008). For Ireland this meant a significant allocation to be expended on transport networks and environmental projects. The 1994–99 CSF involved a budget of more than €2,105 million from the Cohesion Fund, of which €1,496 million was provided by the EU (NDP, 2000–6: 285). Again, there was little emphasis on the regional dimension with the whole country continuing to be regarded as one region for EU regional policy purposes. There was, however, growing domestic opposition to the manner in which the government formulated and implemented the plan, issues which also concerned the European Commission. The Cohesion funding processes reinforced a national as opposed to regional emphasis. The funding emanating from EU regional policy interventions complemented and supplemented public and private expenditure and national polices adapted to comply with EU priorities and strictures. Such adaptation was particularly evident in the agricultural and environmental spheres as chapters 7 and 8 illustrate.

Change did come about in the processes used for planning, implementing, monitoring and evaluating EU regional policy interventions with sub-national actors being involved, particularly at the implementation stage. Institution building at regional level also resulted, albeit on an incremental and piecemeal basis. In response to Brussels' insistence on consultation/partnership with sub-national actors, seven regional committees were put in place during preparation of Ireland's submissions for the 1989–93 funding period. These were transformed into monitoring committees for the CSF 1989–93 (Laffan, 1996). The European Commission provided administrative and technical assistance to the regions to help with preparation for the 1994–99 round of funding. The regional submissions fed into the National Development Plan which was the basis for the second CSF. The regional committees were perceived by Brussels as a cosmetic response and in 1994 eight Regional Authorities were created (Holmes and Rees, 1995). Their mandate was to promote the coordination of public services at regional level and to monitor and advise on the implementation of EU funding in the regions. Regional Authority members are appointed by the constituent local authorities who also fund them. Although created to mollify Brussels and maximise Ireland's gains from EU regional policy, the Regional Authorities have become implanted in Ireland's institutional architecture despite their continuing functional and financial limitations.

During the 1989–93 funding period the Irish economy expanded at an average rate of 5 per cent per annum with real and nominal convergence being achieved in addition to significant growth in investment (NDP 1994–99). This economic growth was in part stimulated by the financial transfers from Brussels which exceeded what Ireland should have received based on its *per capita* GDP.

These significant transfers occurred at a time when the rest of Europe was experiencing economic recession. During the 1994–99 funding period GNP growth averaged about 7.5 per cent in real terms (NDP 2000–6). Despite the general economic improvement, the impact on Ireland's regions was uneven. The mid-term review in 1997 indicated that the regions, which had started out on a relatively more developed basis, were prospering to a much greater extent than those in the west, north-west and midlands. The creation of Regional Authorities, although externally impelled, did lead to a regional focus in development planning[2] and provided an institutional framework at regional level, albeit an insubstantial one. Yet, regional inequalities persisted and inter-regional differences become more pronounced. Table 6.1 illustrates the inter-regional gross value added (GVA) variations and also sets the Irish regions against the EU average.

These changes occurred in an Ireland in which global forces had induced significant economic and social change. The high rates of growth achieved by Ireland's economy affected all facets of the polity. Globalisation had both 'enabling and constraining impacts' (Smith, 2005). As in other countries, globalisation exacerbated the differentiated regional capacity for development in Ireland and contributed to inter-regional economic polarisation (Pike *et al.*, 2006). This period also brought further international pressures for social change with a strong flow of migrants arriving in Ireland from the mid-1990s. Between 1995 and 2000 about a quarter of a million people moved to Ireland (Tovey and Share, 2005). This led to a more multi-cultural society within Ireland but also raised a number of social, political and economic issues with regard to managing migration and achieving integration. Some of these integration issues changed the focus and nature of local interventions supported under the EU's regional policy instruments such as the Local

Table 6.1 Per capita GVA relative to EU average, 1994–96

Region	Average 1994–6, EU = 100
Dublin	122.4
South-west	102.1
Mid-west	88.2
South-east	86.8
Mid-east	78.9
Border	76.5
West	71.3
Midlands	66.4
State	**95.0**

Source: CSO, November, 1998.

Development Social Inclusion Programme. Furthermore, the Single Market and the TEU consolidated Ireland's placing within the EU which thenceforth delimited the economic and social policy instruments which Ireland could select. Thus, global and European pressures combined to induce further adaptation, adaptation which was mediated by the Irish government and public service. This period may have resulted in the creation of regional structures but the structures created were strangled by their limited remit and were loosely overlaid on the institutional architecture, rendering them impotent to effect any real change.

Increased obligations, reduced opportunities, 1999–2007

As the previous sections showed, the first two rounds of EU Structural Funding brought significant financial gains to Ireland and induced administrative and policy change. The third round had less financial impact but continued to induce political and administrative adaptation. As preparations for the 2000–6 programming period got under way Eurostat data made it clear that the whole of the country was no longer eligible for Structural Funding. Initially, the Irish government sought a politically pragmatic division of the country in order to maximise funding but Brussels insisted on a division based on the NUTS III (Regional Authority) areas. Irish negotiators were also concerned to ensure Irish agricultural interests were protected in the Commission's *Agenda 2000* package. Arguably, there was a stronger farming lobby than a regional one. Ireland was divided into two regions for Structural Fund purposes and in 1999 two Regional Assemblies – the Border, Midland and West Regional Assembly and the Southern and Eastern Regional Assembly – were created. These NUTS II regions promote coordination of the provision of public services in their areas and monitor the general impact of all EU programmes of assistance under the CSF. They were given responsibility for managing Regional Operational Programmes under the Community Support Framework 2000–6. Although active in EU regional policy, the Regional Assemblies seem loosely overlaid on the Irish political landscape. The power that has been given to the Regional Assemblies is restricted, their resource base is quite limited and their designation is not based on any evidence of regional identity so there is little public or political affiliation with these regional entities.

Notwithstanding the superficial regional structures, the NDP and CSF 2000–6 articulated a commitment to balanced regional development, listing it as one of the four overarching objectives of the NDP. The allocation of management responsibility for the two regional operational programmes to the Regional Assemblies had some political and administrative implications, marking as it does a modicum of decentralisation and creating regions with differing eligibility criteria for support. The 2000–6 CSF amounted to €6.42 billion, within an NDP expending €58.36 billion (Fitzpatrick, 2005). Elements of all seven Operational Programmes were co-financed with 26 of the Priorities and 112 of the measures delivered under the Operational Programmes receiving EU support. The CSF made up about 11 per cent of the overall NDP, a smaller proportion than had been the case in previous NDPs. The need to comply with EU requirements for the CSF elements affected the planning, implementation and evaluation of the NDP. These effects were noticeable in the multi-annual programming and the expansion of the partnership approach at both local and national levels. The monitoring process was strongly influenced by the EU approach with the NDP 2000–6 stating that reports on all non co-financed expenditure and measures 'be submitted to the Monitoring Committees and the CSF Monitoring Committee. It will be open to the Monitoring Committees to consider the progress and impact of such expenditure and to make recommendations in such regard' (1999: 211). There is also evidence of EU influence on investment patterns. Fitzpatrick points out that a 'more consistent level of investment has continued to be achieved in co-financed than in non co-financed parts of the NDP' (2005: 8). The evaluation does go on to speculate about whether the programming approach might continue when the 'glue of the Structural Funds largely disappears' but is buoyed by the fact that both Department of Finance capital guidelines and the initial plans for the NDP 2007–13 were based on a programming approach. Thus, it is clear that EU regional policy requirements have led to conceptual and administrative adaptation, some of which seems likely to persist.

For the latest funding period 2007–13, the EU's approach embodies the Lisbon and Gothenburg strategies and focuses on achieving sustainable economic growth by fostering convergence, competitiveness, employment and territorial cohesion in an expanded Union. It also takes account of the impact of enlargement to twenty-seven members. The link between regional policy and the Community's priorities has been made more explicit. The new approach emphasises alignment with other EU policies, prioritises sustainable development, highlights the importance of good governance and the prevention of discrimination, allows greater discretion to member states (albeit within an indicative framework) and reiterates the importance of the territorial dimension. Subsequently, member states were obliged to draft national strategic reference frameworks (NSRF) which outline the national policy orientations that underpin operational programmes. These innovations fostered differing reactions. Germany opposed the whole approach while in Italy significant adaptation has taken place, resulting in alignment of EU cohesion policy, domestic regional policy and various sectoral policies for the first time (Bachtler and Wishlade, 2005). Thus, EU regional policy continues to induce adaptation but adaptation which is everywhere moderated by domestic institutional and political considerations.

For Ireland the amount of EU funding for the period 2007–13 has dropped to €750.7 million over seven years. Yet, the priorities, processes and procedures of EU regional policy strongly influence the organisation and implementation of Ireland's development strategy. The thematic and territorial priorities outlined in Ireland's NSRF reflect the opportunities inherent in the Community's strategy and aim to objectify the horizontal principles of sustainable development and equality. Three operational programmes have been agreed. Two are territorial and will lead to investment of €146,603,534 in the Southern and Eastern Region and €228,758,838 in the Border, Midland and Western (BMW) region with both allocations emanating from the ERDF. The Human Capital OP will lead to an investment of €375,362,370 from the ESF (NSRF, 2007). The revised EU arrangements also require member states to ensure coordination and clear demarcation of interventions under the various funding instruments. A Committee for the Coordination of EU Funding was established in 2007 and includes departmental representatives as well as representatives of the implementing bodies including the Regional Assemblies. Thus, institutional adaptation in response to EU regional policy continues.

Despite the interventions under previous CSFs and NDPs regional inequities persist in Ireland. The inequities are both economic and infrastructural and have social and political as well as economic consequences. Nowadays, the inequalities are better understood and documented than was the case when Ireland joined the EEC in 1973. In addition to national and European interventions, bodies such as the Western Development Commission provide policy analysis and promote economic and social development. Nevertheless, the NSRF sees as one of the national weaknesses the 'continuing imbalances in regional development even though all regions have achieved significant economic and population growth in recent years' (2007: 35). The ESRI mid-term review of the 2000–6 NDP forecasts congestion problems and costs in the Southern and Eastern region and the continuation of infrastructure-related problems in the BMW. Analysis carried out in preparation for the NSRF showed that the BMW region (with 26.7 per cent of the population) accounted for 18.6 per cent of national gross value added (GVA) in 2003, while the Southern and Eastern region (with 73.3 per cent of the population) generated 81.4 per cent of total GVA. The regional imbalance is further illustrated by GDP per capita growth patterns as shown in Table 6.2.

Therefore, it is clear that Ireland's regional development issues have not been solved. However, more attention is being paid to the regional dimension in national strategies. Attempts are being made to coordinate efforts at regional development and to link European, national and sub-national approaches. The NSRF has been linked to the NDP 2007–13, the National Spatial Strategy, the social partnership agreement *Towards 2016* and the National Action plan for

Table 6.2 GDP per capita in purchasing power standards (PPS), (EU-27 = 100)

	2000	*2004*
Ireland	132.3	141.4
BMW region	91.5	100.1
S&E region	147.0	156.5
EU-15	115.2	113.2

Source: Adapted from NSRF (2007).

Social Inclusion. Furthermore, regional actors are involved in the preparation and delivery of all these strategies with the Regional Assemblies being represented, for example, on the high-level committee charged with preparing Ireland's NSRF. Thus, steps are being taken to continually involve regional actors as advocated in the Lisbon strategy, the Community Strategic Guidelines and other EU documents pertaining to the implementation of regional policy. Nevertheless, the Regional Assemblies themselves (Press Release, 7 March, 2008) have criticised central government for lack of consultation of regional and local bodies regarding policy issues so it cannot be asserted that the regional bodies are automatically regarded as vital players in the policy process.

A noteworthy impact of EU regional policy has been its positive influence on relations between Northern Ireland and the Republic. Hayward (2007) refers to the compulsory, enabling, connective and constructive influences of the EU on cross-border relations. There has been an emphasis on cross-border collaboration as the most effective means of addressing the concentrated problems of peripherality in Ireland's north-west region which straddles the border. EU initiatives such as INTERREG and the PEACE programmes strongly influenced regional development strategies on both sides of the border as well as facilitating cross-border collaboration. Over the years, particularly, since the Good Friday Agreement, EU regional policy has acted as a catalyst for collaboration. The establishment of bodies such as the North South Ministerial Council, the British–Irish Council and the Special EU Programme Body (SEUPB) led to administrative and processual change. These entities created a formalised structure for cross-border activity within the governance architecture while also institutionalising mechanisms for the implementation of EU regional policy.

Having reviewed the adaptation induced by EU regional policy, Ireland's introverted and instrumental response becomes evident. What emerges is a situation wherein structural change has been superficial and tentative while processual adaptation has been more apparent but centralisation persists and Ireland's regional policy continues to lack substance and political status.

Assessing change: polity, policy and politics

EU regional policy has instigated a combination of structural, superficial and at times symbolic changes within Ireland's polity, policy and politics. Regional policy is a domain in which there is evidence of institutionalisation of the formal and informal rules, procedures, policy paradigms, styles, 'ways of doing things' and shared beliefs and norms referred to in Radaelli's definition of Europeanisation. Despite this evidence, it cannot be asserted that Ireland's governing elites have been converted to regionalism or that a regional approach has become the norm in general policy-making or implementation. Attention to the regions is still sporadic and short-term and government commitment to the regions is more rhetorical than real. Institution building has been manifested in the form of the eight Regional Authorities (1994) and the two Regional Assemblies (1999) as well as the Structural Funds Units and the Committee for the Coordination of EU Funding. The Irish Regions' Office, a government initiative established in 2000, provides a nexus for Irish regional interests in Brussels and issues reports and updates on regional policy issues as well as assisting regional interests in their lobbying endeavours. The Association of Irish Regions serves as a national forum for the regional bodies, disseminates information and advice and represents them in national negotiations. The cross-border institutions which have developed over the years to deal with the specifics of EU regional policy are further illustration of institutional adaptation in response to Europeanisation. However, one must question the degree to which the various EU-induced bodies are embedded in the polity and whether they will continue as funding ends. There is little political attachment to or public identification with such structures which are largely perceived as administrative entities. Politically, the adaptation has been pragmatic and opportunistic. Administratively, learning and adaptation has yielded increased efficiency and effectiveness. The implementation of measures emanating from EU regional policy has, because of their regional/local nature, increased the salience of the EU for regional and local actors and the general public. But the effects of Europeanisation on regional policy have been circumscribed by the retention at the centre of political and financial control and by enduring reluctance to delegate real power.

The Irish polity's administrative structures have undergone continuous adaptation influenced by EU regional policy as evidenced, for example, by the monitoring and implementation structures which have evolved. However, many of these are programme-specific and have been overlaid on rather than subsumed into the politico-administrative system. Administrative structures have been adapted to take cognisance of the EU's requirements at the planning, implementation and evaluation phases of regional policy implementation. Multi-annual budgeting was imposed by Brussels for the 1994–99 round of funding but has now become the norm and has been welcomed by national and local bodies. The EU's regional policy instruments have financed technical assistance which led to improvements in the administrative capacity of member states and Ireland has been no exception. Bachtler and Wren cite Ireland, Denmark and the UK as countries which have 'used evaluation more actively for improving the management of the Funds' (2006: 149). A culture of evaluation is now embedded within Ireland's administration and its genesis can be traced to a combination of the exigencies of Europeanisation and the influence of international public management reform trends. Through its involvement of sub-national actors in the various processes, the EU's regional policy has affected intergovernmental relations in Ireland as well as changing the processes and mechanisms for regional policy. In conforming to EC regional policy reforms, the Irish government has been obliged to give greater voice to regional policy interests (Adshead, 2002). The consultative processes employed in preparation of strategies, although imperfect, have become more comprehensive over time. This is evident in the involvement of regional actors in the preparation and implementation of the NSRF, for example. Thus, there is evidence of Europeanisation of the administrative and policy-making processes induced by the EU's regional policy requirements.

These developments in the polity have accompanied ongoing political developments. Dimensions of EU regional policy have received attention in parliamentary debates and within the deliberations of the various EU-related Oireachtas committees which existed at different times since Ireland's accession in 1973 (see chapter 4). The EU's championing of the regional dimension has contributed to the greater aspirational attention to regional development in government strategies published since the 1990s such as the NDP 2000–06, NDP 2007–13, the *National Spatial Strategy* and the Regional Planning guidelines. Thus, the rhetoric of regional recognition has become ingrained but significant lacunae remain with regard to implementation.

Since the creation of the ERDF, Europe's regional policy has generally been perceived as one of the positive outcomes of membership. The financial benefits to Ireland have featured in many electoral campaigns and have elicited positive public opinion. This complex policy area has also affected interest intermediation and contestation. The EU's promotion of partnership accorded with a national focus on partnership as an effective means of policy-making. Even though the model of concertation used in the Irish case is effectively imposed from the top, new sets of relationships between the state, business, trade unions and community groups have developed horizontally at the local level and vertically between the local and national level (Walsh, 2007). Laffan asserts that 'the insistence of the Commission on partnership in the deployment of EU structural fund monies loosened the grip of central administration on territorial politics in Ireland' (2004: 123). However, it is widely believed that without Brussels' insistence on sub-national partnerships, partnership as a *modus operandi* would not have been implemented at sub-national level. The support for partnership approaches in the EU regional policy processes has reinforced the use of partnership within Ireland's political system and has led to its widespread usage at subnational level. Thus, new patterns of governance have emerged, albeit within centralised practices.

The various development programmes funded under EU Structural Funding provided legitimacy and focus for local and regional actors and bodies. Interventions such as LEADER and social inclusion programmes facilitated animation, capacity building and skills training as well supporting local economic development. Such interventions also provided tangible evidence of the EU in local communities and reinforced partnership as *a modus operandi.* Although strengthening the position of sub-national actors within the regional policy processes, some local partnerships have operated as independent entities outside of the control of local government. This raises questions about accountability and representativeness while the forging of formal linkages with the system raises questions about the 'colonisation' of the voluntary sector. EU regional policy also mobilised occasional protests. When differentiated designation of the country for structural funds purposes was mooted in 1999, the fifteen-county committee organised a concerted campaign for retention of Objective One status. In October 2007, one LEADER group made a formal complaint to Brussels about ministerial plans to subsume the organisation into a new county structure. Thus the EU's regional policy has led to differing forms of political adaptation as it became embedded in the Irish system.

The regional policy agenda in Ireland has been framed by the EU and reflects the obligations and opportunities inherent in the EU's evolving regional policy. Although the initial impact of EU regional policy reinforced centralisation, the reform of 1988 set in train attempts at a more regionalised approach. Furthermore as O'Donnell points out 'the doubling of Structural Funds and the significant reform in their principles and procedures had an important effect in re-introducing developmental thinking and procedures to the Irish public service' (2000: 186). The norms and goals of Ireland's regional policy have been influenced by the EU's focus on social and territorial cohesion and balanced regional development. Thus, the NDP 2007–13 includes a strategic framework for regional development which is integrated with the plan's economic and social goals. The policy instruments and style of EU regional policy have led to emulation and innovation in Ireland. Community initiatives such as LEADER have led to the mainstreaming of such an approach to rural development in Ireland and the introduction of a national LEADER programme. The embedding of a partnership approach to policy-making and implementation at sub-national level and the resultant actor networks have broadened the range of development interests involved, enhanced the communication channels, improved the focus of regional policy interventions and maximised their impact. Yet, as Hayward assesses the EU has served 'to complicate rather than coordinate the workings of sub-national government in Ireland' (2006: 20).

EU regional policy processes have created opportunities for subnational actors from Ireland to interact with EU bodies and with their counterparts in other member states. This has resulted in learning and some policy transfer as well as raising the profile of these actors at home and abroad. Irish local authorities have become involved in specific programmes and transnational collaborations under the aegis of EU regional policy and have contributed significantly to initiatives such as INTERREG or projects under the different framework programmes. The BMW Regional Assembly's Operational Programme 2007–13 includes plans to participate in the Atlantic Area Programme, the Northern Periphery Programme and the North West Europe Programme under the EU's Territorial Cooperation Objective. These linkages have opened new horizons for those involved, yet there is little public interest in such processes. Again, in this sphere, the Europeanisation effect has been specific rather than general.

Conclusions

EU regional policy is one policy sphere which has significant impact on Ireland, leading to institutional and policy change. Because of the indeterminacy of regional policy prior to membership, the impact of EU regional policy is discernible. The paucity of regional development strategies in place in Ireland prior to accession has begun to be addressed and policy development has occurred, spurred by the obligations and opportunities of the EU's evolving regional policy. Yet, it would be an exaggeration to assert that Ireland's government has been convert to regionalism. The resources available through EU regional policy interventions impacted on Ireland's regions, particularly from the mid-1980s to the end of the 1990s. Although regional disparities persist, the money made available through structural funds did make a difference to the economic development of Ireland's regions while the processes surrounding EU regional policy increased their salience in the national polity. Within Ireland's regions there is evidence of improved infrastructure, innovation, mobilisation and experimentation, as well as increased competence, capacity and confidence. Policy-making and implementation in the regional sphere have changed and become more complex, involving multiple actors and multiple arenas. There is evidence of new integrated approaches to spatial planning and the tackling of social problems which have been influenced by the processes and outcomes of EU regional policy but were mediated by domestic considerations and seem likely to embed themselves in the new governance processes. However, much of the adaptation, as and when it has occurred, has been in response to demands made by Brussels.

The process of Europeanisation has resulted in learning and adaptation, particularly during the second and third rounds of funding. It is, nevertheless, important to note that other factors contributed to learning. Such factors included radically changing economic situations, public management reform, changing social norms and changing patterns of political activity. The consonance between the changing emphases in EU regional policy and the prominent issues in Ireland (unemployment in the 1980s, social inclusion in the 1990s and, more recently, integration) ensured a 'goodness of fit'. Because of this correspondence of issues and the appropriateness of the EU regional policy approach to dealing with these issues, the influence of Europeanisation is more readily visible in the sphere of regional policy than in other policy areas. Furthermore, the absence of pre-existing structures for regional development necessitated institutional innovation rather than adaptation.

Europeanisation in the regional policy sphere has resulted in some new patterns of governance in Ireland such as the adoption of a multi-level governance approach involving local, regional, national and European actors, the embedding of partnership as a mode of governance in this policy sphere and the successful creation of cross-border bodies. New structures have emerged in the regions and some limited decentralisation has occurred. New local and regional actors and networks have become involved in governance. However, although there has been some procedural change, the role and powers of local authorities have not changed significantly and the regional structures that have been put in place lack authority and resources. Neither has the balance between pre-existing structures been altered so the centre still rules. Nationally, there is evidence of recognition of the diversity of regional problems and the need for these to be addressed. This awareness seems to be enduring despite the rapidly dwindling funding from the EU regional policy pot but there is little evidence of commitment to implementation of a regionally focused strategy. The green paper on Local Government Reform published in 2008 does not convey government support for stronger regional structures so centralisation seems likely to prevail.

Ireland's judicious use of the funds available, the deliberate emphasis on interventions which would increase human capital, the complementarity of other domestic policies (education and industry, for example), the pragmatism and creativity in the responses of politicians and administrators to EU regional policy developments and their ability to learn and adapt combined to make Ireland a success story in this policy domain. In the regional policy sphere Europeanisation has undoubtedly led to domestic adaptation. However, rather than radical institutional innovation and transformation, what has occurred is an ongoing realignment to cope with new demands, a realignment tempered by domestic and global as well as European considerations.

Notes

1　A partially elected regional authority which continues to facilitate preservation of the Irish language by developing the economy of the Gaeltachtaí (Irish-speaking districts).
2　In 2004, the Regional Authorities were charged with developing regional planning guidelines which aim to link national, regional and local planning strategies.

7

The politics of environmental policy

Bernadette Connaughton

Introduction

Ireland's environmental policy is largely shaped by a generally low level of environmental awareness and the dominance of economic priorities on the national policy agenda. Yet Ireland's environmental performance is regarded as relatively strong (EPA, 2005) and illustrates evidence of progress in terms of policy and institutional framework (OECD, 2000). In contrast to this are the increasing pressures to which Ireland's physical environment is subjected. These include factors such as a weak decoupling of economic growth, population increase, urban sprawl and changing patterns in individual consumption and behaviour. These challenges are reflected in environmental problems such as climate change, waste management and nature conservation. Ireland's progress in environmental policy development must also be measured in terms of its effective compliance with EU legislation, since it is argued that most contemporary national environmental legislation in Europe is driven by, or closely correlated with EU legislation (Jordan, 2005). Ireland is not an 'uploader' of environmental policy initiatives (Borzel, 2002) and it is claimed that while Europeanisation has stimulated the increase and modernisation of the content of Irish environmental policy, the policy style and institutional structures have been less 'Europeanised' (Flynn, 2004: 118). In terms of effective implementation, the Irish record has come in for strong criticism with references to a 'general and structural failure' (European Court of Justice (ECJ), 2004). What factors account for this lack of instiutional response to various international and domestic 'pressures' and to what extent is this likely to condition effective compliance?

This chapter discusses the impact of domestic pressures and the Europeanisation of environmental policy on the domestic institutional framework. It investigates factors that illustrate the responsiveness (or lack of) in relation to environmental policy implementation in Ireland. The chapter argues that Europeanisation has led to adaptational pressures resulting in legal harmonisation and some institutional innovation. However, the necessary change for effective compliance remains bounded by pre-existing features of the Irish polity, politics and policies. The government's approach to policy-making and public attitudes over time are also significant; since many environmental problems reflect social and economic dilemmas which necessitate more than environmental policy initiatives for their solution. It will be ascertained whether the progressive change that has occurred in environmental policy, and the way in which public and private actors seek solutions to environmental problems, are reflected in new patterns of governance.

Historical context: institutions and policy

Prior to EU membership, the environment did not feature on the Irish policy agenda and the environmental regulatory regime was weak and under-developed. This has been described by Flynn (2004: 118) as a 'minimalist and British-influenced corpus of environmental regulation.' This picture was not out of step with other European states prior to 1973 since it was not until the late 1960s that environmental policy emerged as a central area of governmental activity (Knill, 2006: 249). The major policy priorities of the independent Irish state largely reflected aspirations to increase population and energy generation, intensify agricultural production and boost industrial activity (O'Donnell, 1991: 121). Ireland was predominantly a rural society with agriculture as the principal economic activity (see chapter 8) and was correspondingly far less developed in comparison to many of its European counterparts. Environmental awareness was low and remained low since the perceived lack of threat to the physical environment did not provoke a reaction of concern amongst policy elites or the public. Late industrialisation and urbanisation implied that the environmental degradation encountered in the UK and mainland Europe was only marginally experienced in Ireland. Policy proceeded with more emphasis on continuity rather than change during the period 1922–55, with a decidedly 'laissez faire' approach to heritage and the physical environment. One explanation for this was the inward approach to finding policy solutions pursued by the state. Ireland's regime of environmental regulation, however, needs to be observed in conjunction with an examination of the historical interaction between the Irish and UK regulatory systems (Taylor, 2001: 371), which prior to 1922 were considerably interlinked.

One consequence of political independence was that the ideas and policy initiatives that would generally originate in Westminster and trickle down to Ireland only did so after a significant time-lag (Mawhinney, 1989: 90). In some cases such lesson learning was absorbed in a subdued form or was unlikely to occur at all. Given the low priority of environmental affairs on the agenda, domestically and internationally at this time, in tandem with the weak economic situation in Ireland, it is not surprising that there was little motivation to initiate a process of conservation. The launch of the programmes for economic expansion by T. K. Whitaker in 1958 marked the beginning of a new era of economic and social change. It led to an influx of multi-national companies encouraged by grant aid to locate in Ireland, the modernisation of Irish agriculture and so began the long delayed processes of industrialisation. In addition, from 1958 onwards the geographic pattern of population began to shift from rural to urban and the 1960s heralded several initiatives such as the Buchanan Report in 1968 which promoted balanced regional development. Despite this sea-change, policy proceeded on an essentially ad hoc basis, with little consideration given to longer-term considerations such as what to do when the new industries matured or whether there would be environmental repercussions (Yearley, 1995: 659).

The apparent invisibility of environmental affairs as a policy precedent is also reflected in the institutional arrangements for its formation and implementation. A central government department for the environment did not exist and the principal institutional innovation in the 1960s appears to be the establishment in 1964 of An Foras Forbartha, the National Institute for Physical Planning and Construction Research. This institute undertook work in the areas of conservation and amenity planning (heritage, tourism). It would appear that environmental problems were perceived as issues connected to planning and heritage/conservation and little regard was given to pollution control. The vacuum at the national level in terms of institutional framework and policy implied that local authorities were left to deal with environmental dilemmas without adequate guidelines or concrete policy initiatives. Environmental administration followed that regulators be allowed discretion with a preference towards the establishment of voluntary codes of practice and pragmatism prevailed (see Flynn, 2004; Taylor, 2001). Local authorities operationalised environmental regulation with reference to outdated legislation and largely through the incorporation of environmental conditions in planning permission with no detailed emission standards in operation until the late 1970s (Scannell, 1982).

The 1963 Planning Act, largely drawn from the British Town and Country Planning Act 1959, is of significance (Taylor and Horan, 2001: 385) since it formed the legal basis of the Irish environmental planning system. Agriculture and forestry, however, were both omitted from local planning controls. The 1963 Act gave strong emphasis to conservation and provided planning authorities with an array of special conservation powers (Mawhinney, 1989: 99). In addition, the act introduced public participation in the planning process which was of significance for environmental matters. It accommodated a third party right of appeal on development proposals and has been described as 'a landmark in the development of environmentalism in Ireland, in that it routinised public participation and created an institutional channel that has been central to the action repertoires of environmental groups in the 1980s' (Mullally, 1994: 140 cited in Yearley, 1995). One group long in existence is An Taisce, also known as the National Trust for Ireland, which was established in 1948. An Taisce promotes sustainable development through advocacy, education and heritage ownership. It is noteworthy that local authorities were compelled to consult An Taisce on a number of development proposals and inform them of planning applications in areas of scenic beauty and heritage significance.

Public interest in environmental affairs was awakened by the rapid industrialisation and modernisation of Ireland during the 1960s/1970s and environmental controversies such as Wood Quay in Dublin. The latter was a site of Viking settlement which was identified as the location for the offices of Dublin City Corporation. A high-profile, but unsuccessful, public campaign was launched in order to halt the development but failed. However, these instances became accompanied by new social movements, including ecology groups (Mullally, 2006) and a shift in emphasis from land use and planning toward environmental issues. Despite this, environmental matters were not evident as part of the dialogue of the principal political parties prior to EU membership, with the discourse focused on issues such as agriculture or neutrality. Environmental protection remained residual in the trade-off with economic growth, and was largely exercised on an ad hoc basis through the existing institutional framework. In general, the Irish approach to environmental policy-making prior to EU membership 'can be safely described as consensual and reactive, as environmental issues were underdeveloped and not a priority' (Flynn, 2004: 130).

Adaptational pressures: global, European and domestic

International and EU developments in environmental policy-making and implementation

Despite the apparent lack of development in Ireland regarding environmental policy-making, the late 1960s and early 1970s marked a surge of multilateral activity. The publication of scientific evidence of environmental deterioration, greater public awareness and incidences of environmental damage (such as the Seveso case in 1976) acted as a catalyst for the politicisation of the environment. In the early 1970s, green parties began to contest and win parliamentary seats and the mobilisation of several high profile international NGOs such as Greenpeace and Friends of the Earth gathered pace amidst mounting public concern. The political pressure placed on elected governments, the transboundary dimension of environmental problems and the emergence of global economic pressures led to formalised efforts to confront environmental degradation. This is most apparent through international cooperation involving the EU, OECD and the United Nations (UN). From this period onwards the environment has developed into a highly differentiated policy sector which is characterised by a range of subfields and policy approaches (Knill, 2006: 249). Although Ireland remained aloof from this emerging international concern for environmental protection, its fledgeling membership of the EU implied that any binding decisions in this area would provide significant adaptational pressures for domestic change.

A landmark initiative was the Stockholm conference on the human environment which was convened by the UN in 1972. Following on from this was the establishment of the United Nations Environment Programme (UNEP) which continues to pursue environmental protection on a global platform with many initiatives in developing countries. In the context of the EU it is argued that prior to 1973 there was no environmental policy in principle (Hildebrand, 1993). However, early policy action dates back to the 1960s even though the environment was not formally included in the Treaty of Rome 1957. The precursor to the first environmental action programme (1973) and the formal entry of environment to the EU agenda was a meeting of the European Council in Paris in 1972 (Jordan, 2005). To this end, the member states agreed upon a series of goals which still largely underpin EU environmental policy and acknowledged the necessity for a transfer of policy arrangements. The international dimension to environmental questions precipitated awareness that pollution needed to be tackled at source, cross-border cooperation was imperative and that European citizens needed to be informed in order to act responsibly with regard to environmental problems. Although many of the early environmental action programmes were largely aspirational, sufficient progress was made so that by 1980 some fifteen EEC directives relating to water, waste and air had been issued, as well as regulations dealing with waste and air (Hildebrand, 1993). This was during a period of international economic turmoil due to the oil crises and the subsequent period of 'Eurosclerosis'. The necessity to support green measures at the European level seemed of little relevance to Ireland yet impinged upon the Irish system in terms of implementation responsibilities.

The formal inclusion of environmental policy in the Single European Act (1987) facilitated a further harmonisation of national environmental policies and the completion of the internal market. Economic imperatives were clearly influential since a principal objective in these developments was to reduce intra-European trade distortions. The prior achievements of environmental policy were consolidated, however, since the demand for higher standards ensured the increased output of environmental rules. Further revisions in the Treaty on European Union (1992) and Treaty of Amsterdam (1997) strengthened the treaty basis through the inclusion of measures such as the precautionary principle and sustainable development as an overarching objective of all EU policies. Sustainable development was catapulted to prominence by the report of the World Commission on Environment and Development (WCED) in 1987 ('Brundtland Report') and formally endorsed by political leaders at the Rio Earth Summit in 1992. The term is now deeply embedded in the international discourse on environment and development issues (Bomberg, 2004; Lafferty and Meadowcroft, 2000). The formal commitment to put environmental goals on the same level as economic and social is illustrated in the goal of environmental policy integration (EPI) in the definition and implementation of all sectoral policies. This has gained momentum through initiatives such as the European Council 'Cardiff Process' in 1998 and its stocktaking completed in 2006. The principles of sustainable development for the Union were set out at the Gothenburg Summit in 2001 with the launch of the Sixth Environmental Action Programme *Environment 2010: Our Future, Our Choice.* This was further boosted by the adoption of a Renewed EU Sustainable Development Strategy by EU heads of state in June 2006.

In terms of an Irish position on these developments it is apparent that Ireland, unlike Germany or Scandinavian member states, has never been an 'uploader' of EU environmental initiatives. Scarce administrative resources were generally directed towards negotiations involving vital national interests such as EU supports around agriculture and regional policy. A greater realisation of the potential financial costs associated with legislative compliance has led to a more coordinated national position on EU environmental proposals, as opposed to passive acceptance. An example of a more proactive Irish stance is the wider international negotiations on climate change that originated in the late 1980s. A combination of official and political activity, through alliances with other cohesion countries, ensured that Ireland retained flexibility within the parameters of the EU burden sharing agreements to pursue economic growth. What this example illustrates is the primacy of economic considerations within national politics and government agendas as opposed to championing better air quality. In addition, it demonstrates that the Department of Environment, Heritage and Local Government is guided by the advancement of environmental policy through EU fora and has been unable to encourage effective ownership for environmental issues across the other departments. The department focuses on developments in Brussels, is motivated to preserve the national position within the EU and for this to be reflected within the common EU position in global environmental negotiations.

The role of the Commission has been instrumental in steering many of these developments and the European Court of Justice significant in its endorsements. A current modus operandi is the introduction of thematic strategies in key areas such as air pollution and the marine environment. These represent a new approach to making policy through working with integrated themes rather than single pollutants or specific economic activities. Other current measures include the transposition of the Århus Convention on public access to environmental information (2003/04/EC), facilitation of public participation in environmental procedures (2003/35/EC) and a guarantee of public access to justice in environmental matters into Community law. For Ireland and other members of the EU the developments in environmental policy over time mean that the pre-existing environmental policies (be they substantive or phantom) are now politically and legally intertwined with EU environmental policy. As a result of participation in the multi-levelled system of policy-making that characterises the EU, member states have 'created an institutional entity to perform certain tasks which has, in turn, deeply affected the way they perceive and act towards environmental problems' (Jordan, 2005: 2). This Europeanisation process in turn creates new governance opportunities, challenges and constraints for the range of public and private actors involved at national and sub-national levels of government.

Of paramount concern to EU environmental policy development is its effective implementation which involves a multitude of actors and sharing of competences within a system of multi-level governance. Member states may accept the legal obligations of European policy convergence but one of the ramifications of this cross-national policy transfer may be significant costs entailed by economic and institutional adaptation. Responsibility for overseeing implementation lies with the European Commission although it must work through the bureaucracies of member states to ensure that governments translate EU policies into appropriate action at the 'street level'. The challenges associated with implementation are evidenced in Ireland's difficulties with effective compliance for directives to combat water pollution, biodiversity loss and waste management. Ireland was referred to the ECJ in 2007 for failing to adopt and provide correct information on measures to give effect to the EU's Public Participation Directive. Not once to date has an Irish higher court referred an environmental case to the ECJ.

At the wider EU level, the environmental policy sector exemplifies the difficulties of the 'implementation deficit'. This has profound economic considerations whereby non-compliance creates advantages for some and disadvantages for others (Sverdrup, 2003: 9). It increases the transaction costs and imposes problems for citizens and businesses when relating to several sets of rules. Clearly a dilution of standards through weak or non-implementation provides firms based in non-complying member states with a competitive advantage. At societal level resistance can arise surrounding issues such as costs involved or impact on local employment and the ability of non-governmental actors to mobilise opposition to European legislation. The weakness of environmental groups and the apparent willingness to compromise the environment in favour of economic development or powerful interest groups has been a feature of the Irish case. This is illustrated by the debacle with the farmers' associations over the implementation of the nitrates directive (1991). Although it was supposed to have been implemented by a deadline in 1995, the appropriate measures were not agreed upon until late 2005. Unlike business and farming interests, it may be argued that environmentalists perceive the Commission and the ECJ as their first and only true court of appeal.

In the late 1990s EU strategies sought to address this through slackening the pace of formulating new policy in an attempt towards consolidation through framework directives and efforts to address the problems associated with the implementation deficit. This evolved into a departure from a 'command and control' system to interventionist approaches increasingly linked with new forms of regulation and the introduction of New Environmental Policy Instruments (NEPIs), such as voluntary agreements or economic incentives (Knill, 2006: 249). This diversification of policy instruments is embedded in a re-orientation in modes of governance towards participatory and network-style forms of policy formulation and implementation. Despite this the perceived shift from government to governance is variable and contingent on differentiated national policy styles and instruments. It is argued that very few of these approaches are devoid of state involvement (Jordan *et al.*, 2005). This would imply that the new approaches can be effective but can also become encumbered by the methods and practices of traditional government and administrative tradition. An element of hierarchical steering from governments is implied since NEPIs have not supplanted regulation, though shifts towards governance will further adjust relationships between actors. Environmental policy and its implementation is perceived as the output of a process that involves interaction between non-hierarchically organised actors and inter-organisational collaboration (Knill, 2006; Knill and Lenschow, 2000) which reflects a plurality of state and non-state actors in a multi level setting. The cooperation and embedding of actors across different levels of government can also be illustrated through the development of initiatives such as IMPEL (Implementation and Enforcement of Environmental Law), a transnational expert network within which national bureaucrats can observe and learn from development in other countries. In all, it is clear that environment has developed into a major policy area with significant trans-border implications. The European Commission has illustrated leadership in attempting to promote the environment on a global agenda but the success of this policy area is reliant on effective compliance within the member states.

Domestic pressures: 'push' and 'pull' factors to develop an environmental policy regime

The earlier discussion illustrated that environmental policy was not a priority issue in the first several decades following Irish independence. Therefore EEC membership in 1973 did not catapult Ireland into a group of states which actively sought to promote environmental proposals congruent with high domestic environmental standards. Rather, the process of cross-national policy transfer, stimulated by the exigencies of EU requirements, has significantly shaped environmental legislation in Ireland. Nevertheless, the Irish record for the effective implementation of EU environmental legislation has been described as 'woeful' (Flynn, 2007) and the domestic monitoring of compliance remains problematic. One explanation for this has been the necessity to 'catch up' in terms of economic development which has resulted in an uneven balance in commitment to environmental affairs relative to economic factors. In common with the change in emphases at EU level, more recent attention focuses on sustainable development whereas prior to the mid-1990s policy-makers do not appear to have regarded the processes of economic growth and environmental protection as integrated. Irish public attitudes also appear to be changing whereby there is positive support for the development of state environmental regulations, and an increased sense of personal efficacy in terms of paying higher prices, or greater engagement in practices such as recycling (Motherway *et al.*, 2003; Doelg, 2003).

The years since 1970 saw Ireland increasingly open to, and influenced by, ideas and developments from outside the country. The modernisation process initiated at the end of the 1950s continued with the prominence of industry and urbanisation in Irish economic life. Economic development remained challenged by Ireland's peripheral position and further complicated by the uneven development within the country, concentrating on the east coast. In an assessment of the Irish economy prior to the 1990s, O'Hearn comments that Ireland's indigenous industrial sector declined rapidly following EEC accession and by that time the state was already heavily reliant on investment from multi-national corporations (2003: 35). The global economic down-turn stimulated by the oil crises of the 1970s inevitably had negative repercussions for Ireland. This was compounded by the poor economic management of successive governments from 1977 to 1987 which accentuated the crisis and deep recession. During this period indigenous industrial decline continued and was complemented by multi-national disinvestments and a failure to secure new jobs in sufficient numbers. The inadequacy of an industrial strategy based on foreign investments was emphasised in reports such as the Telesis Report (1982). The reality of persistently high levels of unemployment and emigration thus ensured that job creation remained at the top of the political agenda. The environmental threats which resulted from the pursuit of rapid industrial-isation since the late 1950s remained unchecked and were reflected in the rather lax environmental standards attracting operations such as the asbestos industry (Yearley, 1995: 659). Indeed Taylor (2005: 153) notes that the regulatory environment in which industry operated during the 1970s and 1980s was influenced crucially by the role undertaken by the IDA. The implication is that while environment was developing into a distinct policy sector internationally and establishing specific environmental standards, the domestic approach focused on minimal pollution control standards and the propensity to 'turn a blind eye'. The influence of the farming lobby on the policy-making process also made it difficult to enforce stricter environmental standards in order to offset the environmental damage resulting from the intensification of agriculture following accession.

A period of fiscal austerity launched in 1987 by the minority Fianna Fáil government and facilitated by opposition support in the wake of the 'Tallaght Strategy', marked the beginning of a reversal of fortunes in the Irish economy. The transition from economic failure to success is attributed to a variety of factors including EU membership and the wider experience of globalisation. In the context of environmental policy this did not translate into an automatic rise of conservation priorities on the national political agenda. O'Hearn (2003) comments that Irish governments 'bought economic tigerhood' through low corporation tax, subsequently putting up with lax standards. The advent of the structural funds, while imperative for economic growth in terms of building infrastructural capacities, has also had implications for conservation. Positive developments are apparent, however, through initiatives from the business community such as REPAK[1] and the introduction of BATNEEC (best available technique not entailing excessive cost) and IPPC (integrated pollution prevention control) stimulating ecologically friendly production processes and manufacturing systems. The modernising influence of the EU has therefore been beneficial in that it has provided 'ready made policy solutions off the shelf' (Flynn, 2004: 121).

Current discourse on the state of the Irish economy tends to stress the necessity to maintain national competitiveness, implying that the situation has evolved from securing jobs to also retaining these jobs in a highly competitive global economy. It has been asserted that this has led to a prioritisation of market forces rather than social issues (Kirby, 2002) or indeed environmental matters. Policy-makers and the business community can interpret environmental shortcomings as a symptom of infrastructural deficit and have become more conscious that poor environmental performance may undermine economic competitiveness. A former Minister for Enterprise, Trade and Employment, Mary Harney (PD), highlighted this in the foreword to a major report assessing infrastructural shortfalls in the waste management sector (Forfás, 2001). Her principal message implied that putting the infrastructural facilities in place would significantly address this complex challenge for sustainable development and maintain competitiveness in the state's industrial policy.

The emphasis on economy and the historical neglect of the environment and its integration within other public policies are reflected in several of

Ireland's current environmental challenges. Agricultural, regional and energy policies all have significant effects on environment. The challenge of horizontal policy integration is particularly evident in climate change whereby greenhouse gas emissions were at 125.5 per cent of 1990 levels in 2006. This was 12.5 percentage points higher than the Kyoto 2008–12 target for Ireland of 113 per cent of 1990 levels (CSO, 2008; EPA, 2007). Ireland has one of the highest per capita greenhouse emission levels in the EU (Flynn, 2007; EPA, 2005). In 2006 agriculture remained the single largest contributor to overall emissions by international comparisons but economic pressures on the environment remain the most dominant. The Minister of Finance, Charlie McCreevy's decision in 2004 to abandon the introduction of a carbon tax as a means of expediting and encouraging the attainment of climate change targets appears symptomatic of a tendency to give sway to the business lobbies. Its abandonment and replacement policy solution of buying carbon credits has been referred to as 'akin to "borrowing on the never never"; it simply puts off the day when the real bill must be paid' (*Irish Times*, 16 February 2007). The reviews of Ireland's Kyoto target in the period 2008–12 to limit emissions to 13 per cent indicate the rise of transport emissions as by far the largest source of increase, reflecting a 160 per cent increase on 1990 figures (EPA, 2007). This is largely the result of increasing investment in the transport sector, vehicle numbers with a trend towards purchasing larger vehicles, an increased reliance on private cars and increasing road freight transport (*ibid.*). The highlighting of some of the factors in the climate change problem illustrate the challenges Irish governments have in confronting the environmental pressures stemming from economic growth and the increased consumerism that has accompanied it.

In terms of the Irish public and the non-governmental sector exerting a positive influence on environmental policy, a rather mixed picture may be presented. The role of environmentalists and the public in general is crucial for effective compliance and the domestic monitoring of that compliance. Since the 1990s considerable emphasis has been placed on the improvement of consultation mechanisms in order to address information deficits and enhance public participation in policy formulation. The rationale behind this implies that positive domestic mobilisation through, for example, informal institutions such as advocacy groups and citizen associations will contribute to effective implementation (Börzel, 2000). What degree of influence does the environmental movement hold in Ireland? Do they have any leverage in the policy-making process to counteract the dilution in environmental standards that has been tolerated in agriculture, industry and planning? Mullally (2006: 150) argues that commentators may be forgiven for perceiving that 'Irish environmentalism is somehow a failed entity' when weighing up the movement's influence in terms of unity of purpose, mobilisation and national impact. On the one hand, there are the conservation groups such as An Taisce which has been allocated some formal access to the policy-making process. On the other hand, there are the 'populist environmentalism' issue based groups such as CHASE (Cork Harbour Alliance for a Safe Environment) or BAG (Burren Action Group) who direct(ed) their attention to environmental hazards in specific local communities and vocalise their demands through protest measures that can bring them into conflict with state agencies and influential interest groups. The diversified nature of the environmental movement may also account for its lack of empowerment in the formal policy-making process. There is also little support from the public for actions which may be perceived to potentially diminish living standards or result in higher taxation. Despite this, the parochial focus of many of these environmental protests has conspired favourably with the clientelistic nature of Irish politics, thus striking a more equitable balance between actors (Leonard, 2006; Yearley, 1995), producing local environmental clientelism and constituting an informal adaptation pressure. The environmental movement can also play an active role in policing compliance and acting as a conduit for the European Commission regarding information on the full implementation of EU law.

In conclusion, the development of a coherent body of European environmental law considerably shapes the environmental policy in Ireland. The efficacy of solutions and their management have been determined by a range of economic and social pressures. Ireland's size, geographical position, economy and a historical lack of environmental policy initiatives or public awareness have determined the contours of the domestic response. The following section presents an overview of the impact of Europeanisation on the institutional framework and policy change.

Impact of Europeanisation: institutional and policy change

From systemic to institutional agenda, 1973–87

It is asserted that environment remained a residual item on the Irish policy agenda in the period from accession to the Single European Act. This is reflected in the insignificant impact of environmental issues on the Irish polity and a regulatory framework described as aligned more to 'continuity than change' in the first two decades of EU membership (Taylor, 2001: 117). It may be argued that for the development of environmental governance in Ireland there were also clear institutional limits to change. The possibilities for building support for an effective policy regime were conditioned by existing institutional arrangements in agricultural and industrial policy, financial constraints and the system of central–local relations. This would imply that the formal adjustments required to moderate incompatibility between EU regulatory requirements and domestic arrangements were dealt with in a minimalist way.

An example of where adaptation to EU environmental policy change appeared to be more symbolic than effective was the renaming of the Department of Local Government to the Department of Environment in 1977. This was deemed to reflect the growing importance of environmental issues and that local authorities, the principal agents to whom implementation fell, were aligned to this department. In reality the direction of the department remained largely unchanged and fragmented. The formulation and coordination of environmental policy was not a dominant concern. The appropriate commitment or resources were not channelled to the section expected to cover all aspects of environmental policy and oversee international commitments (Taylor and Horan, 2001: 378). The mid-ranking position of the Department of Environment in the administrative hierarchy and the position of the minister in cabinet were not reflective of its remit as the 'green ministry'. Rather, it is on account of the department's large public works profile and high spending portfolio on infrastructure. This multitude of responsibilities is also reflected in the Houses of the Oireachtas whereby environmental issues are generally dealt with within the Joint Committee on Environment and Local Government. The Oireachtas joint committee has never undertaken an effective scrutiny role with respect to EU environmental proposals although scrutiny of EU proposals has become a regular agenda item in recent years. Officials and experts are invited to attend and provide information briefings as opposed to members actively debating or challenging the substantive content.

Of more significance during the first phase of membership was the progression of An Foras Forbatha in engaging in an expanding programme of environmental research and its operation of a conservation advice service for local authorities. In 1985 it produced a major report entitled *The State of the Environment* which illustrated an overview of indigenous resources and the rural and urban environmental challenges that were beginning to be acknowledged. The report was not acted upon and when public finance cutbacks gathered pace in 1987 An Foras Forbatha was disbanded and transformed into an Environmental Research Unit of the Department of Environment. Although this may have signified a shift in emphasis from land use and planning towards environmental issues (Bannon, 1989), it is also probable that public bodies in the environmental sphere were a less controversial target for administrative rationalisation. The down-grading of this institution has been regarded in hindsight as diminishing an agency with the potential to have become a fully fledged national environmental protection agency (Flynn, 2007: 90).

Perhaps the institutions most conspicuous in terms of their environmental remit were local authorities who ironically played a dual role of 'gatekeeper and poacher' (Coyle, 1994: 73). Their roles in development and in control of environmental functions created a conflict of interest whereby stringent environmental legislation and enforcement could jeopardise jobs and have a severe negative economic impact on dependent local communities. By the late 1970s the practice of adopting environmental conditions in planning permission as a method of pollution control had become widespread (Taylor, 2001: 19). Local authorities as polluters themselves remained exempt from many of the pollution controls they were attempting to enforce on others. The necessity to reform the regulatory framework and the role of local authorities therefore constituted a significant adaptational pressure. However, the practice of 'adding on' to the remit of local authorities, without substantively taking stock of the demands arising from new legislative requirements or providing the requisite expertise, appeared to be the norm (Taylor, 2001; Scannell, 1982).

The European influence started to become evident in the legislation introduced in the late 1970s, namely the Local Government (Water Pollution) Act 1977. This revised the Fisheries Act 1959 and reflected the focus on water quality issues at EU level. Coyle (1994) has reflected that the translation of such European directives into Irish law often 'lacked precision and clarity' whereby the relevant authorities were informed of new administrative procedures via circulars and memos on an ad hoc basis. An explanation for this is the differences in administrative tradition between Ireland and the continental states with their emphasis on administrative law. Public notices and departmental circulars were often used to implement a change in administrative practice. Such methods were criticised by the Commission and this method of transposition was abandoned in the late 1980s. It has been replaced by a tendency to transpose the European directives almost word for word into Irish legislation. Enforcement was weakly attended to by local authorities and in spite of this the central policy-makers did not transfer functions away from these bodies. The overall system appears to have been marked by a lack of dedicated professionalism and resources with little systematic control or monitoring emanating from the relevant regulatory bodies.

The 'business as usual' and ambiguous approach generally to dealing with environmental affairs in Ireland was also reflected in EU policy developments at the end of the 1970s. Given the impact of the oil crisis on national economies, political leaders were ambivalent and allowed environmental policies develop under their own impetus until the Single European Act. In Ireland while environmental issues were slowly nudged onto the institutional agenda by the obligation to incorporate European legislation, adaptation was conditioned by embedded characteristics of the politico-administrative framework (see chapters 3 and 4).

Political representation and institutional innovation, 1988–96
Up until the mid-1990s it was apparent that progressing the environmental policy agenda vis à vis other problems and policy fields was extremely difficult given the limited economic, societal and political resources available. From the

mid-1980s the discourse on environmental issues broadened as a result of disasters such as Chernobyl and the break-up of the oil tanker, *Kowloon Bridge*, off the coast of Cork in 1986. The politicisation of environmental issues beyond popular local concern about ecological threat was also heightened by growing concerns regarding risks of radioactive contamination in the Irish Sea from Sellafield. Over time this has resulted in the Irish government using international diplomacy and litigation to oppose plans by British Nuclear Fuels (BNF) to expand operations of the Sellafield nuclear power plant in Cumbria. EU influence has been discernible as environmental groups became concerned with the inadequate implementation of EU legislation and as networks developed they became more sophisticated in their lobbying and use of media promotion to highlight this. The global endorsement of sustainable development through the Earth Summit agreements also legitimised their campaigns and provided instruments through which to interpret Irish issues in terms of local reactions to economic globalisation (Mullally, 2006: 157).

In terms of formal political representation, the promotion of environmental issues was given a boost with the formation of the Green Party/Comhaontas Glas (formerly the Ecology Party) in 1982. The party won its first seat in 1989 when Roger Garland, representing a South Dublin constituency, was elected to Dáil Éireann. In the 2002 general election the Green Party secured six seats and have emerged as a 'non traditional' alternative to the big parties (Mair and Weeks, 2005). Many of the founding members of Comhaontas Glas formerly protested at the Carnsore Point controversy in 1979 when the government was forced to abandon its plans for a nuclear power station and/or have been involved in local and community activism. A bottom-up approach promoting decentralisation and sustainable development is a pillar of the Greens' policy and philosophy though they have maintained a critical voice on European affairs.

Irish governments also began to assert their green credentials and in 1989 the first Junior Minister for the Environment, Mary Harney, was appointed. In 1990 the government introduced legislation that banned use of bituminous coal in Dublin, established ENFO – an environmental awareness service, and published an Environmental Action Programme to provide a framework for environmental protection in Ireland. It may be argued that these developments are linked to EU influence. Ireland's experience of implementing the legislation passed in the 1970s had not been impressive and the responsibilities of the actors involved remained disputed, fragmented and uncoordinated over a decade later. This is illustrated by Ireland's experiences with the Habitats (1991) and Birds (1979) Directives (Laffan and O'Mahony, 2004) whereby the implementation process has been mired in conflict and contestation at the domestic and European level. The fragmentation of the environment portfolio is also reflected in the management of biodiversity policy which was initially divided between the Departments of Agriculture and Arts, Culture and Gaeltacht. Such conflicts were not exclusive to the Irish case and, as the 1990s commenced, it became increasingly apparent at EU level that there was a lack of systematic control and penalties emanating from the monitoring and judicial systems of the member states.

The decision to establish a European Environmental Agency (EEA), which commenced work in 1994, was an additional reinforcement and institutional-isation of environmental policy (Knill and Liefferink, 2007). The prospective EEA together with Ireland's hosting of the 'Green' Presidency in 1990 are perceived to have been catalysts for the proposal to establish an Environmental Protection Agency (EPA) in the government's action programme for the environment (McCarthy and Yearley, 1995: 258). It was formally established by the Environmental Protection Agency Act 1992 and section 62 specifically confers further powers on the agency in relation to the failure by local authorities to perform their statutory functions. Environmental regulation changed as a result of the introduction of Integrated Pollution Control (IPC) licensing streamlined through the EPA. On the one hand, the introduction of the EPA can be perceived as an upgrading of an ineffective institutional framework to manage environmental policy emanating from Brussels. Environmental initiatives were reflected in the environmental chapter of the NDP 1994–99 but adaptational pressure would have emerged mainly from the necessity to introduce better environmental standards due to the burgeoning corpus of EU directives to be complied with. On the other hand, commentators have recommended prudence in attributing too many domestic initiatives to EU influence, since the creation of the agency and shift to integrated permitting can also be ascribed to lesson learning from policy developments in the UK (Flynn, 2004; Taylor and Horan, 2001). It is apparent that while EU developments may have been a catalyst, a domestic solution was required to deal with the inefficiencies of the system experienced by developers and industry in obtaining permits and clear instructions regarding national environmental standards. The local authorities' simultaneous 'gamekeeper–poacher' role was therefore impinged upon but they retained their prominent role in the planning process generally (with appeals to An Bord Pleannála). This would imply caveats in the independent regulatory agency status of the EPA which has prompted comments that its role focused more on managing rather than conserving the environment (Taylor, 2001). Hence, while the decade marked some adaptation to environmental requirements, institutional innovation was characterised by the establishment of a new agency as opposed to significant reform of the existing institutions and economic growth and environmental protection were still regarded as mutually exclusive.

*Government to governance? Policy development and implementation
challenges, 1997–2008*

The period since the 1990s has witnessed more activity in environmental policy initiatives than in the previous two decades or so of EU membership. The improved economic situation has provided an unprecedented opportunity to funnel the much needed funds into improving and developing environmental infrastructure. In spite of this the emphasis of economy over society and quality of life persists. It is evident in the reluctance of both policy-makers and the public to face up to the environmental dimension of a wide tranche of public policies at national and local levels and their problematic legacy for the future (Flynn, 2007; Connaughton, 2005b; Taylor, 2005).

Regardless of 'reduced dynamics' in environmental policy activities at the European level (Knill and Liefferink, 2007), the EU has remained the principal engine of domestic policy change in terms of both strategy and legal framework (Connaughton, Quinn and Rees, 2007). The exigencies of EU membership and trajectory of increased environmental pressure on natural resources have resulted in the roll-out of several policy strategies such as Changing our Ways, 1998, and the National Climate Change Strategy 2007–2012. The substantive and procedural obligations defined in EU legislation have resulted in the modernisation of the domestic legal framework with the introduction of legislation such as the Waste Management Act 1996 and its amendment in 2001 which led to the advancement of waste legislation. This also prompted changes in the institutional framework since the act transferred authority for waste licensing and inspection to the EPA away from the county councils and insisted upon the development of regional plans to stimulate cooperation between local authorities to maximise economies of scale. It is unlikely that without EU steering such initiatives would have been introduced given their inconsistency with domestic institutional arrangements.

The reorientation of environmental regulation at the European level during the 1990s also prompted some limited experimentation with NEPIs in Ireland. The waste area is the principal example of where NEPIs have been applied through voluntary agreements (the establishment of REPAK in 1997 to manage packaging waste), the introduction of the landfill levy, plastic bag tax and more recently in emissions trading (climate change). EU stimulation is also apparent in the introduction of a charge in 2005 to cover the recycling of electrical appliances in order to comply with the directive on Waste Electrical and Electronic Equipment (WEEE). Despite the relative success of such initiatives it is unlikely that the Irish government would have been prompted to innovate without EU inducement (Flynn, 2007). Taxation and charging for environmental services remains a thorny issue on the political agenda, even when Ireland enjoyed an era of unprecedented wealth. This is evidenced by the abolition of domestic water rates in 1997 and the considerable public opposition to refuse collection charges.

This development of policy content and diversification of instruments since the 1990s is not matched to the same degree by significant institutional redesign or marked changes to repertoires and routines. Nonetheless, the conditions within which the politico-institutional framework operates for environmental policy are changing through, for example, moves to a neo-liberal agenda and a broadening of the array of actors in pursuit of solutions to the sustainable development agenda. At the sub-national level the role of regional authorities, the establishment of city and county development boards and strategic policy committees are regarded as institutional fora to facilitate the strategic coordination of environmental policy. The shift from government to governance is also apparent through greater onus on local authorities to incorporate local environmental/community groups into partnership arrangements in the promotion of Local Agenda 21 activities. However, despite the increased emphasis on participation and partnership it has been noted that community activists are increasingly wary of consultation measures that may be superficial and not allow for meaningful input (Fagan *et al.*, 2001). If anything, the public appear more alienated from the institutional mechanisms designed to represent them, given the rise in NIMBYism (Not In My Back Yard) and public protest directed towards environmental issues, ranging from water quality to incineration and planning.

At the national level a new institutional opportunity to nurture partnership emerged through the introduction of *Sustainable Development: A Strategy for Ireland* 1997 and the establishment of COMHAR, the National Sustainable Development Partnership in 1999. COMHAR brings together public and private actors (including expert and NGO representation) in a forum to debate and extend public consultation and participation in the sustainable development agenda. As part of its remit COMHAR gives recommendations on government policy but its activities are often frustrated by the failure of government to utilise and give genuine effect to its structures (Connaughton, Quinn and Rees, 2008). This would imply that the principle of partnership heralded in approaches to economic and social policy and heavily promoted by the EU in regional policy is not applied equally to environmental affairs. The demands of implementation and the costs associated with non-compliance of EU criteria have resulted in quite opposite solutions. For example, the reluctance of local councillors to approve of regional waste management plans in 2001 led to the introduction of the Waste Management (Amendment) Act 2001 which allowed city/county managers to make local waste plans. This was further enforced by measures in the Protection of the Environment Act 2003. On the one hand, the clientelist strategies employed by local councillors to object to politically unpopular initiatives such as incineration in local constituencies could be viewed as frustrating the development of much needed environmental infrastructure. On the other hand, the confiscation of the right of elected public representatives to take decisions on environmental issues is viewed as an attack on democracy.

The removal of public control over the management of environmental policy is further accentuated by the increasing trend towards the privatisation and contracting-out of the delivery of environmental services. This is particularly the case within the waste management sector where by 2002 the private sector had become the dominant actor in waste collection and recycling. Public Private Partnerships (PPPs) are also actively fostered by the government to provide the solutions for large-scale infrastructural projects. Whilst the impetus towards such approaches illustrate changing patterns in governance it also apparent that the added input of the private sector reflects the inability of the local authority level to address sound environmental management due to lack of expertise and resources. The worsening Irish record in complying with EU legislation and proliferation of illegal dumping resulted in the establishment of the Office of Environmental Enforcement (OEE) within the EPA in October 2003. A central role of the OEE is to audit the performance of local authorities and prosecute them if necessary for enforcement failures. Although some prosecutions have occurred, it is apparent that it is a last resort and the office is largely subsumed within the culture of the EPA itself as opposed to having an independent oversight role. Although the OEE may not be a policing office 'with teeth' it promotes increasing collaboration with and between actors such as the Gardaí and Department of Communications, Energy and Natural Resources and works with local authorities to find solutions to implementation dilemmas through capacity building. What is apparent is that the policy and institutional change emanating from the 'celtic tiger' era is conditioned by the ongoing challenge of implementation per se, tensions between economic interests and environment and the extent to which the adjustments in relations between actors constitute meaningful change.

Assessment of change: Limits of adaptation and domestic constraints

This chapter has illustrated that while Ireland has made considerable progress in developing an environmental policy, its adaptation to the EU policy agenda is constrained by pre-existing features of the polity, politics and policies. The new patterns of governance remain conditioned by the traditional trajectory of Irish government despite exogenous and endogenous pressures to alter it. The establishment of the EPA and reform of local government, interest group politics and domestic policy legacies emphasise the propensity of past practices, values and modes of operation to constrain policy actors in 'path dependent' ways. The domestic structure of the political system also militates against regional and local levels of government, playing a more concrete role in the promotion of sustainable development.

It is argued that the implementation of EU policy is but one example of the broader phenomenon of Europeanisation (Falkner *et al.*, 2005). In the Irish case the pressure to comply satisfactorily with EU directives has driven the development of an environmental policy. Börzel (2000) asserts that implementation problems and the variance in compliance among the different EU member states is the result of the interplay between both domestic and European factors and she develops a model to illustrate this. The 'push-and-pull model' is based on two major propositions. First, compliance problems only arise if the implementation of European policies imposes considerable costs on the public administrations of the member states. Hence, the less a policy 'fits' the legal and administrative structure of a member state, the higher the adaptational pressure in the implementation process. It may be argued that this has been the case in Ireland given the underdeveloped environmental policy framework, societal and political culture and unreformed institutional arrangements. Despite a mirroring of the international discourse shift to sustainable development, the consensus for comprehensive change to social and political institutions is extremely difficult to achieve.

Second, pressure from 'below' – where domestic actors may mobilise against ineffective implementation (pull) and from 'above' – where the Commission may introduce infringement proceedings (push) – may increase the chances of the effective implementation of costly EU policies (Börzel, 2000: 147–8). In relation to the former, Irish environmental groups have been active in bringing infringements to the attention of the European Commission since they are largely ignored at home. For the latter, the state's record for compliance with EU environmental legislation is characterised by drawn-out implementation processes, with reprimands emanating from the European level before any concrete action is taken (Connaughton, Quinn and Rees, 2007: 90). The government has tended to point towards a good record in terms of transposing legislation (*Irish Times*, 23 March 2007) but this deflects from 'bad application' and the deficiencies in enforcement. At the beginning of 2008 Ireland remained the only EU state not to have ratified the Århus Convention. Irish officials cannot claim that EU environmental legislation is a new departure. Paraskevopoulos (1998) argues that the learning process and elite socialisation to European models of governance are critical factors in explaining the relative success of structural fund programmes. So too, as elites gain familiarity with the EU, they acquire knowledge that influences the implementation of EU policy. Not only do national institutions need to mesh with European aims, but national elites too must learn how to cooperate. Therefore, as time passes, fewer infringement procedures should occur (Mbaye, 2001: 264). Irish officials participate in EU level working groups, initiatives such as the IMPEL, the environmental policy dimension of the department has been considerably extended with specialist sections and the EPA is networked with its other agency counterparts in Europe. But the 'street level' actors at local authority level remain largely divorced from the EU policy-making process and struggle in terms of capacity and expertise to comply effectively with the legislation.

In assessing change to the polity, politics and policies it is therefore apparent that a general paradigm shift resulting from the development of environmental policy has not occurred. This is evidenced by the aforementioned commentary of the ECJ in its reference to the 'general and structural failure' on behalf of the state to deal effectively with the application of EU legislation. The EU largely frames environmental policy parameters and there is no adequate strategic perspective employed at the domestic level in terms of controlling the negative repercussions of economic growth. It may be argued that Europeanisation has only weakly promoted the paradigm of ecological modernisation in Ireland (Flynn, 2004: 121) and that environmental discourse is shaped by a belief in the ability to provide technocratic solutions to environmental dilemmas (Taylor, 2005: 158). Environmental policy integration (EPI) at the national and local level in Ireland remains poorly integrated with cognate policy sectors such as transport, energy and agriculture. It is acknowledged that the strategy for sustainable development launched in 1997 (reviewed in 2002) is outdated and fundamentally more rhetorical than real. The government is committed to a renewed national sustainable development strategy under the terms of the social partnership agreement 'Towards 2016'. The revised climate change strategy published in 2007 was long overdue but has been presented as part of a package of policies in tandem with a white paper on Energy and a Bio-Energy Action Plan. Implementation of these new strategic departures will be problematic since the political culture, dominated by the Fianna Fáil party, does not prioritise the environment. Resistance to proposed solutions tends to be marshalled through classic lobbying tactics by local constituents and the business community within the clientelist party political system.

While central government may be condemned for a lack of consistent political leadership, it is apparent that environmental policy has moved up the agenda given increasing public concern with sustainable development and quality of life issues. A sea-change in the way environmental policy has been advocated is evident with the entrance of the Green Party into a coalition government with Fianna Fáil and the Progressive Democrats in June 2007. From an environmental perspective the Green Party secured two strategic ministries – Environment, Heritage and Local Government and Communications, Energy and Natural Resources. In exchange for participation in government, however, the Green Party appeared to compromise on the progression of some of their own environmental policies which have been excluded from the programme for government, and they also failed to change government transport policy on the controversial M3 route through Tara. Despite this, the Green Party managed to ensure that a carbon tax was once again back on the government agenda, a new landscape strategy and review of the EPA and its role and introducing changes to increase deterrents against environmental crimes. In the delivery of his first carbon budget in 2007, the Minister for the Environment, Heritage and Local Government, John Gormley, announced a move to a motor tax system based on CO2 emissions.

Whether or not a paradigm shift is likely to occur does not detract from the fact that changes in the mode of governance are evident as a result of the reforms introduced since the 1990s. As Flynn (2007: 177) asserts, however, there remains a mismatch between the institutional 'hardware' and 'software' which inevitably impacts upon effective implementation. The 'hardware' refers to Ireland's policy style and entrenched institutional framework, whereas 'software' reflects policy content which is more readily changed and 'Europeanised'. The introduction of new legislation, the proliferation of policy strategies and an injection of positive political will does not substitute for meaningful institutional reform, or the ability of agricultural and business interests to circumvent unpalatable environmental proposals. For example, the IFA have strongly lobbied to force any policies on land conservation to be tied to fiscal transfers and payments. This is demonstrated by the habitats and birds directives, the implementation of which also illustrates the cultural beliefs and sensitivities of Irish farmers regarding the interference of environmental law upon sacrosanct land rights. Business interests represented by the Irish Business and Employers Confederation (IBEC) have been regarded as more constructive and pro-active in pushing for technical environmental approaches driven by EU development. Unsurprisingly business representation is more likely to champion EU driven proposals that are more compatible with their interests and modernisation agendas e.g. waste management. This also indicates a more strategic approach to environmental policy interests since there is more attention paid to how environmental legislation will impact upon economic advances.

In all, it would appear that there have been misguided assumptions about the actual impact of environmental policies on domestic arrangements and a misinterpretation of the national and sub-national-level consequences of EU legislation, assuming that compliance is possible without changing domestic institutional structures (Connaughton, 2005: 46). Local authorities are weak actors in comparison to their counterparts in the majority of western European states and remain conditioned by local politics. The experience of waste management policy in particular is instructive of how dependent these authorities have become on the private sector to take the initiative to find solutions and deliver services to the consumer in line with the required standards. The privatisation of waste collections and the input of the private sector to develop large-scale infrastructure through public private partnerships (PPPs) are now part of environmental governance.

The principal example of institutional innovation is the establishment of the EPA. It has been referred to as part of an emerging ecological modernisation within the Irish polity (Taylor, 1998: 54) but it is also criticised for not having the desired level of regulatory independence. In accordance with the EPA Act 1992 the Minister for the Environment remains a highly significant actor with the authority to direct the EPA on various functions. It is the government that appoints the Director General, board of directors and advisory committee members of the EPA which tends to exclude rather than develop a distinctive role for the Oireachtas committee system. As noted, the role of the organisation and the legislation underpinning it will be reviewed in the period 2007–12. The policing component of the EPA's role has already been strengthened by the establishment of the OEE, largely prompted by pressure from the European Commission due to Ireland's numerous infringements. But it is not really a separate entity since it is an additional office within the EPA and, within its current remit, it is arguable that its policing role does not go far enough. What is apparent from the development of such new institutional fora and the enhanced role for the private sector, however, is that implementation while top-down in terms of policy direction, requires the interaction between non-hierarchically organised actors and greater inter-organisational collaboration. This has been largely driven by Europeanisation and public management reform. The membership of COMHAR or any designated environmental group has not to date been sanctioned to participate in the mainstream partnership bodies that have an input into determining national policy. This is changing since the Programme for Government 2007–12 includes a commitment to COMHAR's representation in social partnership institutions.

In conclusion, environmental pressures will proceed to increase rather than diminish in Ireland as a result of strong population growth, consumer preferences and ongoing economic development. Despite increased attention to environmental matters at the domestic level since the Green Party is now formally a government partner, the European dimension will continue as the driver of policy development. The challenge is to find a 'goodness of fit' between such policy content and the formal and informal institutional structures necessary to reinforce it.

Notes

1   REPAK is a voluntary initiative between industry and the Department of the Environment, Heritage and Local Government that seeks to meet industry's producer responsibility obligations under waste management legislation.

8

Does the CAP fit? Agriculture policy in Ireland and the EU

Bríd Quinn

Introduction

Agriculture was the main economic imperative for Ireland's application for EEC membership. It was expected that membership would help advance Irish agriculture and improve farm incomes. The dominance of agriculture in the debate on EEC membership is not surprising. Historically, agriculture framed Ireland's development, dictating decisions from the settlement choices of the earliest tribes to the country's late move towards industrialisation and the independent state's policy priorities. Consequently, issues of ownership, apportionment and utilisation of land have had huge political, social and economic influence. These issues have been affected by Europeanisation, particularly the Common Agricultural Policy (CAP). Therefore, agricultural issues have continued to dominate Ireland's involvement within the EU. Agriculture is a sphere in which domestic policy structures, the policy content and the policy discourse have adapted substantially as a result of Europeanisation. This chapter maps the changing position of agriculture within Ireland's economy and society and the adaptational pressures which have affected the sphere. It examines how Ireland's agricultural policy developed and analyses the changes that have affected policy, politics and polity. It is argued that while Europeanisation impelled significant adaptation in the agricultural sphere it is the complex interplay of domestic, European and global factors which determines this overarching dimension of Ireland's development.

Historical context: institutions and policy

Ireland's agricultural policy has evolved in a path-dependent manner and developments in the century prior to EC membership shaped the subsequent development of agriculture and agricultural policy. Successful attempts to improve the commercialisation and marketing of agricultural produce had been put in place throughout the nineteenth century. The emergence of the Co-operative Movement during the 1890s and the creation of the Irish

Department of Agriculture and Technical Instruction in 1899 were evidence of the continuing importance attached to agriculture. Farming during the 1920s focused on exploiting comparative advantage, raising standards and improving the quality of both inputs and outputs (Ó Gráda, 1997). The Free State's first Minister for Agriculture, Patrick Hogan, asserted that 'national development, for our generation, at least, is practically synonymous with agricultural development' (memo cited in Lee, 1989: 112). Thus, the fledgeling state prioritised agriculture as a social and economic bedrock.

Agriculture remained rather stagnant throughout the 1920s and although 51 per cent of those gainfully employed in 1926 worked in agriculture, the sector contributed only 32 per cent of GDP at current factor prices (Kennedy cited in Lee, 1989). Nevertheless, government policy towards agriculture encouraged profitability and productionism. The 1930s, however, brought a change of policy spurred by widespread economic recession, a move towards protectionism in the UK and various domestic developments which combined to lead to deterioration in quality of life for those engaged in agriculture. The post-1932 minority Fianna Fáil government emphasised self-sufficiency and supported a move from pasture to tillage. The unsuccessful tillage policy contributed to an increase in the number of emigrants from rural areas. The focus on domestic expansion coupled with the economic war of 1934–38 (brought about by Ireland's refusal to continue to pay land annuities and the UK's imposition of tariffs on imports from Ireland) meant that Ireland's farmers had less access to British markets and necessitated government bounties and subsidies on export. The 1940s was another bleak decade for Irish agriculture. World War II led to a policy of compulsory tillage with the acreage under grain almost doubling during the war. Even after tillage was no longer compulsory, agricultural output continued to fall, with a drop of 10 per cent in net output between 1944–45 and 1949–50. An Anglo-Irish Trade Agreement was negotiated in 1948 and a meat processing industry began to be developed at the end of the decade. Thus, the structure and significance of agriculture continued to change. Government commitment to agricultural development continued to be articulated strongly throughout the 1930s and 1940s. The Constitution of 1937 reinforced this commitment by including Article 45.2 which states: 'The State shall, in particular direct its policy towards securing that there may be established on the land in economic security as many families as in the circumstances shall be practicable.' However, commentators such as Girvin (2002), Lee (1989) and O Gráda (1997) are critical of the policies of successive governments during the 1930s and 1940s because of the inconsistent approach to sectoral issues, the focus on the social rather than economic dimensions of agriculture and the efforts to insulate Irish agriculture from competition.

The 1950s witnessed further deterioration in the agricultural sphere. Difficult climatic conditions, international economic recession, domestic balance of payments deficits and cautious fiscal policies all impacted on agriculture. The decade saw a decline of 17 per cent in the agricultural labour force with subsequent negative social impact on rural areas. Meanwhile government policy focused on supporting agricultural prices but An Bord Gráin was established in 1959 to deal with the purchase and marketing of Irish wheat. The decade witnessed several changes of government with consequent alterations in agricultural policy emphasis. The *First Programme for Economic Expansion* promoted expansion of the beef sector as the line of development most likely to yield positive results and advocated a reduction in price supports. However, neither aim was achieved during the Programme's lifetime with both prices and outcome remaining stagnant and the agricultural labour force continuing to decline. A *Second Programme for Economic Expansion* was published in 1963 and, unlike its predecessor, set targets for specific agricultural sectors; articulated a realisation of the need to promote output growth on small farms; introduced schemes such as the Small Farm (Incentive Bonus) Scheme and included direct supports for farmers owning less than thirty acres.

Interestingly, the problems facing Irish agriculture in the 1960s presaged those faced by the EEC in the 1980s, i.e. realisation that price and commodity supports were untenable and a growing awareness that the problems in rural Ireland were not just agriculture-related but that wider rural development issues existed (McDonagh, 2001; Commins and O'Hara, 1991). To address these issues an inter-departmental committee recommended action on structural policy; production and marketing; educational and social policy and industrialisation, tourism and fisheries (Daly, 2002). This led to the introduction of pilot area development programmes to support agricultural development in the western counties. In 1965 an Anglo-Irish Free Trade Agreement was signed which gave a guaranteed market for store cattle and lamb and increased Ireland's butter quota on the British market. This helped offset the constraints which Britain's cheap food policy had placed on Ireland's agricultural exports.

A young farmers' organisation, Macra na Feirme, had been established in 1944. The Irish Creamery Milk Suppliers' Association (ICMSA) was established in 1951 and the National Farmers' Association (NFA, later the IFA) in 1955. These farming organisations increased their profile from the mid-1960s, despite tension over whether the NFA or the ICMSA ought to represent farmers. Widespread protests were organised over declining agricultural incomes and what farming organisations saw as the lack of structures for involving them in negotiations on policy. The government took a strong stance and refused to yield to farming demands. A National Agricultural Council (NAC) was established as a forum for discussion between government and the various farming representatives but the main farming organisations refused to participate and the NAC was disbanded in 1969. Since that period the role of farming organisations has changed and they have played an important role in negotiations on agriculture and related issues (Greer, 2005b; Adshead, 1996).

The *Third Programme: Economic and Social Development 1969–1972* framed economic and agriculture policies immediately prior to accession to the European Economic Community. Its stated objectives for agricultural policy were 'increasing efficiency in production, processing and marketing, improving structures and securing better conditions of access to external markets' (Dooney cited in Crowley, 2006: 25). Changes in the nature and processes of agricultural production were evident during this period. Diversification in the dairy sector, an emphasis on improved quality in the meat sector, increasing mechanisation and a growing horticultural sector were among the indicators of change (Daly, 2002). Nevertheless, the decline in farming numbers and the mis-fit between production and market were causes for concern and the Department of Agriculture commissioned a number of policy reviews in order to address these problems. Thus, agriculture was both a priority and a problem as Ireland moved towards accession. As Sheehy points out 'in the years immediately preceding EEC accession the Irish exchequer was spending 3.4 per cent of GDP on the kinds of price subsidies on which today 0.6 per cent of the EU GDP is spent under the CAP' (1997: 285).

From independence, the Ministry for Agriculture was regarded as an important one, and the Department of Agriculture had shown itself to be responsive to changing problems. Little attention was paid to the needs of consumers and it was difficult to achieve consensus among the various organisations purporting to speak on behalf of farmers. The Department's administrative approach was traditional and bureaucratic so it was not well equipped to adapt to a more consultative form of policy-making. Differences in outlook emerged between the department and An Foras Taluntais (AFT), the progressive agricultural research body established in 1958. During this period there is little evidence of institutional innovation, apart from the creation of commodity specific agencies such as An Bord Bainne, CBF, An Bord Gráin and the Pigs and Bacon Commission. Neither had there been institution-building at sub-national level. The county committees of agriculture never evolved into influential bodies and the vocational education committees failed in their attempts to take responsibility for farmer education (Daly, 2002).

This overview of Ireland's agriculture prior to EEC membership highlights the productivist ideology of successive governments and their respective political parties which resulted in a regional imbalance in the impact of subsidies; inconsistency as to whether the home or export market ought to be developed; ill-judged decisions about which sectors to support; a tendency to ignore developments in other parts of Europe; the persistence of problems with land redistribution and a paucity of attempts to achieve any balance between the prospects of big and small farmers. These differences between the earning potential and level of political influence of farmers with different sized holdings had economic, political and social consequences which successive governments failed to address. Similarly, dualism about the economic and social dimensions of agriculture prevailed with modernisation and efficiency being advocated at the same time as retention of non-viable farms because of their preservation of the rural lifestyle. The review also shows that during the 1960s many of the elements of what is currently regarded as innovative rural development policy were being advocated in Ireland. Among those elements were regional and local responsiveness, off-farm employment initiatives, the promotion of agri-tourism and the support of local collective action.

Adaptational pressures: European, global and domestic

In the years immediately preceding accession to the EC, much hope was pinned on the CAP to solve the problems of Ireland's agriculture policy and dispel the prevailing pessimism. It was expected to provide stable prices for Irish produce, reduce Ireland's dependence on UK markets, provide access to a market of three hundred million people, lessen the proportion of government expenditure on farm price supports, lead to a rise in farm income and increased land prices as well as providing attractive retirement packages (Crowley, 2006; Sheehy, 1997; Commins, 1995). The Common Agricultural Policy had itself evolved in response to differing adaptational pressures, both internal and external.

Although the specific objectives of the original Common Agricultural Policy were outlined in articles 38–42 of the Treaty establishing the European Economic Community it was only in 1962 that the CAP was introduced. From its inception it operated along two strands market/price supports (administered under the Guarantee section of the EAGGF) and structural interventions (administered under the Guidance section of the EAGGF). Thereby, CAP has governed the production and marketing of produce within the Community as well as trade with non-member states. At the time the CAP was introduced, the EEC produced only 80 per cent of its food needs (Commission of the European Communities (CEC) 1996: 2). Consequently, the focus of the new agricultural policy was on promoting food security, encouraging farm modernisation and protecting the community's market. Intensification and expansion were encouraged, prices were kept artificially high and protectionist tariff barriers were put in place. In 1973 the CAP accounted for two-thirds of the total EC budget. Daly judges that at that time 'the Community's policy towards agriculture was much more developed than policies towards industry, the environment, education and social welfare' (2002: 505).

While the policy was successful in its aim of increased production within the Community, the knock-on effects were negative. Large, more efficient farms benefited more from the CAP measures thereby exacerbating regional and sectoral differences such as existed in Ireland. As Mac Sharry points out 'eighty per cent of the direct payments go to the top twenty per cent of farmers' (2000: 174). These gaps in income are a persistent problem. The intensification of farming methods sowed the seeds of environmental degradation and led to product surpluses. Product prices were agreed on a yearly basis and the annual agricultural negotiations led to conflict and compromise between the various member states. Further complexity was added by the financial mechanisms used such as Monetary Compensatory Amounts (MCAs).

The CAP has been repeatedly reformed with the catalysts for adaptation varying for each phase of reform and each set of reforms causing different adaptational pressure within member states. The reforms of the 1970s and 1980s represented incremental attempts at managing production levels but were hampered by the prioritisation of national rather than Community issues during every set of negotiations. The Mansholt Plan of the late 1960s sought to reduce the numbers employed in agriculture and urged the creation of larger units of production. Structural reforms in 1972 sought to achieve better balance between supply and demand. In 1975 a Disadvantaged Area scheme was introduced to ensure that farmers did not add to the rising levels of unemployment within the Community. A co-responsibility levy was introduced in 1977 and a 'prudent price policy' was put in place which broke any link between support prices and inflation. Growing awareness of the problems stemming from over-production and the high cost of intervention led to the introduction of milk quotas in 1984. Although the 1984 milk quota provisions were originally intended to be in place for five years, they have been repeatedly extended and are currently underpinned until 2014–15. Intimations of the significance of the environmental dimension of agriculture were evident in Article 19 of EU Reg. 797/85, a voluntary scheme for the designation and protection of Environmentally Sensitive Areas. The Mac Sharry reforms of 1992 sought to separate the Community's market policies from its farm income policies by introducing a system of direct payments to farmers, supporting measures to reduce the intensity of farming (e.g. set-aside and REPS), encouraging afforestation and providing for an enhanced early-retirement scheme.

Agenda 2000 was published in 1997 and negotiations on reform lasted until 1999 with a strong emphasis placed on the multifunctionality of agriculture. The reform package was multi-faceted, underpinning the 'European model of agriculture' which focuses on the environmental and rural development dimensions as well as the economic aspects of agriculture. Integrated rural development was designated as the second pillar of the CAP, thereby underlining its increasing salience within the EU's policy process. Although the changes in *Agenda 2000* were regarded as radical, a mid-term review (MTR) of the strategy in 2003 led to other substantial reforms such as the full decoupling of support payments and production for some important products (e.g. livestock, milk and arable crops). The resultant Single Payment Scheme (SPS) is linked to food safety, environmental and animal welfare requirements. The EU has come under adaptational pressure during successive negotiations with the WTO with the European Commission finding itself in a difficult situation trying to achieve agreement while respecting the mandate of the member states. In recent years, the EU has increased its focus on bio-technology and bio-fuels and this has led to linkages between EU research endeavours and the agricultural sphere.

The successive reforms of the CAP reflected changing conditions and priorities within the EU and led to significant adaptational pressure in Ireland which affected the composition and methods of Irish agricultural production, the design and implementation of its agricultural policy and the nature of the associated administrative and budgetary processes. As the various reform packages were negotiated Ireland played an active role in shaping the ultimate outcomes and forged strategic alliances with countries such as France. Ireland successfully sought support for sheep farmers in the 1970s (even taking a court case against France), fought for concessions such as increased milk quotas in the 1980s (even threatening to use the veto), achieved an increase in beef premia and avoided a reduction in milk quotas in the 1990s. Ireland was one of the seven countries which insisted that no explicit link be made between the CAP reform and wider trade reforms in 2002 (Greer, 2005a). Ireland was also instrumental in preventing renationalisation and achieving adjustments to the modulation processes in the Luxembourg package of 2003. Thus, Agriculture Commissioner Franz Fischler commented that 'Ireland fought its corner of the reform process well'.[1]

Adaptational pressure on Irish agriculture did not only originate in the EU. Globalisation with the attendant mobilisation, personal modernisation and mass communication has sparked social, political and economic change in Ireland which impacted on matters agricultural and combined with domestic factors to cause adaptation. Ireland's increased global interdependence has affected the food and agricultural spheres, specifically via GATT/WTO impacts as well as generally via technological and social developments. Economic change such as altered trade flows, capital mobility, new production and distribution methods as well as market liberalisation and increased competition have impacted on Ireland's governance practices and affected the agriculture and food sectors. The social changes outlined in chapter 3 have affected the purpose and focus of agricultural policy. Political change in Ireland, most recently, the move towards a developmental welfare state (NESC, 2005), has affected the context within which Ireland's agriculture policy is implemented.

As within the EU, there is tension between the government's conflicting desires for a more neo-liberal approach and its upholding of the public good functions of agricultural policy (Potter and Tilzey, 2005) and between consumer and farmer attitudes towards production. These varied adaptational pressures have combined with the evolution of the CAP to change the mode of farming and its role in Irish society since Ireland joined the EEC in 1973. As the next sections will show, the adaptation has been incremental but fundamental.

Adaptation to the CAP: opportunities and constraints

Great expectations and hard times, 1973–88

Not surprisingly, agriculturalists were among the most enthusiastic advocates of Ireland's campaign to join the then Common Market. Membership was expected to bring better prices, expanded markets and increased opportunities. The budgetary and trade transfers would expand opportunities and relieve the Irish exchequer of the burden of supporting farm incomes. The first years of membership fulfilled those great expectations with the 1970s regarded as the most prosperous decade ever for Irish farmers. Prices for Irish products increased by a multiplier of 4.5 between 1972 and 1978 and income from the CAP 'was a major contributor to the twenty-three per cent increase in the volume of the country's gross national product between 1972 and 1978' (Barrington and Cooney, 1984: 94). Initially, real farm family income increased significantly as Table 8.1 shows but farm income levels also varied according to national and supranational market and fiscal vicissitudes.

The structure of Irish agriculture changed more slowly. Land prices increased in the short-term but take-up of the farm modernisation/early retirement scheme was lower than anticipated. Between 1975 and 1983 only 614 persons opted for the retirement package (Commins, 1995: 186). Yet, between 1971 and 1986 the number of farmers in Ireland decreased by 34 per cent while the number of landholdings remained fairly static (*ibid.*: 187). The guaranteed incomes and price supports created an illusion of security and sustainability of income so from the mid-1970s Irish farmers began to borrow for land and machinery. Inflation, increased interest rates and exchange rate

Table 8.1 Farm family income (FFI) per family worker

1970s		1980s		1990s	
1970	100	1980	108.1	1990	118.6
1978	209.6	1988	217.3	1998	247.9

Source: Adapted from Sheehy, 1999.

fluctuations after accession to EMS in 1979 led to a serious debt problem among farmers in 1979 and 1980.

The euphoria of the 1970s was replaced by tempered enthusiasm for the CAP in the 1980s. By 1989 land prices in Ireland had fallen to half their 1978 level. The EEC faced pressure to adjust its policies and discourage over-production. Consequently, production quotas were introduced in 1984 with the dairy sector, a vital sector in Irish agriculture, a primary target. Ireland opposed the idea of quotas and threatened to use its veto power, causing political tension both at home and in the Brussels arena. Despite Irish farmers being given a 10 per cent bonus in their quota, milk production which had grown by 5 per cent during the 1970s was brought to a standstill by the 1984 quotas (McAleese, 2000: 87). Furthermore, the exodus from farming continued and the rate of reduction in the agricultural work force rose from 2.5 per cent to 7 per cent in 1984–85 when 12,000 left the land (Mac Sharry, 1987: 46). As chapter 5 illustrates, the general economic situation in Ireland deteriorated seriously during the 1980s and the agricultural domain did not provide grounds for optimism. However, the European Community offered a lifeline in the form of structural funding. A major reform of the ERDF in 1987 and the commitment to double the structural funds budget by 1992 was opportune for Ireland (see chapter 6) and promoted local development initiatives which impacted positively on agriculture and rural development policies.

Changing fortunes, 1988–97

The Commission's reform of the structural funding policy framework in 1988 sought to encourage governments to engage in more long-term planning through the adoption of multi-annual programmes. Consequently, Ireland's Structural Funding allocation was linked to production of an NDP and negotiation of a Community Support Framework with Brussels. Because of its significance to the Irish economy, agriculture was an important element of the NDP 1989–93 with 26.7 per cent of the total CSF allocated to agriculture, fisheries and rural development. Measures supported were aimed at forestry, rural development, environmentally friendly farming, tourism, sanitary services and the western package which provided support for the poorer western region (Walsh, 1995). The mobilisation effects of the CSF expenditure as well as the economic effects are highlighted by Laffan who comments on the *engagement* of agricultural, industrial, environmental and social actors in implementation of this tranche of Structural Funding and their eagerness to gain 'access to the funds and influence over their distribution' (1996a: 333). The NDP/CSF 1994–99 emerged, following major reforms of the CAP with Agriculture, Rural Development and Forestry being one of the nine Operational Programmes. One-sixth of Ireland's allocation from this second round of structural funding went to the (then) Department of Agriculture,

Forestry and Rural Development – with 47.6 per cent of this going on headage payments, 20 per cent on subsidies for animal welfare and pollution control and only 3.5 per cent on diversification measures (Daly, 2002). Although an additional 4.5 per cent was directed at the food industry, the distribution of supports reflects the Irish government's continuing prioritisation of farm incomes. At this time, the rhetoric of rural development was also beginning to gain credence and support, with the countryside beginning to be perceived not just as the workplace of farmers but as a leisure resource for urban dwellers and as an ecological entity warranting careful management. The alteration in EU agriculture discourse to an emphasis on rural development coincided with a reiteration in Ireland of the need for planned rural development and diversification in agriculture. Commins and O'Hara (1991) assert that rural development had been eclipsed in Irish politics from 1973 to the mid-1980s because of the expectations pinned on the CAP, the national focus on industrial development and the deteriorating national fiscal situation. The 1990s, however, witnessed an increased emphasis on rural development issues in Ireland, reflecting domestic and European pressures for adaptation and leading to new patterns of local governance.

The decision to include domestic agricultural supports as well as export subsidies and agricultural tariffs on the agenda for the GATT Uruguay Round placed considerable reform pressure on the Community and its member states. The 1990s also saw a growing emphasis on food safety in the EU following consumer pressure arising from the BSE and foot and mouth crises. Consequently, legislative and institutional reform regarding food quality took place and impacted on the CAP processes in Ireland and elsewhere. Thus, developments in Ireland during the late 1980s and early 1990s reflected European developments. In addition to the price support changes which affected Ireland's agriculture profoundly, the other measures such as set-aside also had a significant impact. The Rural Environment Protection Scheme (REPS) served to bring about agricultural restructuring, raise environmental awareness and provide alternative sources of income. REPS I ran from 1994 until 1999 and by 1999 more than 50,000 farmers were participating with total expenditure reaching €450 million (Mac Sharry, 2000). The number of farmers continued to drop during the 1990s with the number of sole occupation farmers declining at national level, by 24 per cent. Yet, despite these negative developments, EUROSTAT figures show that between 1990 and 1998 average agricultural incomes[2] in Ireland increased by 21.4 per cent in real terms. This was the fourth-best performance in the EU but statistics from the Central Bank of Ireland show that income from agriculture, forestry and fishing grew by only 24.4 per cent between 1990 and 2002 compared with a 200 per cent increase in non-agricultural wages, salaries and pensions. Thus, the income gap between farmers and non-farmers persisted.

A decade of change, 1997–2007

From the mid-1990s, impending enlargement, the ongoing inefficiencies inherent in the CAP, increased competition on the world market and the prospect of a new round of WTO negotiations combined to induce a new wave of reform within the EU. This trajectory had serious implications for Ireland. Irish negotiators disagreed with some of the initial proposals. They strongly opposed renationalisation of agricultural policy and fought for incremental adjustment and sectoral support. The final package of the CAP reform was in line with Ireland's priorities and the then Minister for Agriculture, Joe Walsh, described the outcome as 'the best possible deal that could have been achieved' (cited in Daly, 2002). Threatened reductions in milk prices were deferred, a higher milk quota was negotiated and an intervention process for beef reinstated. However, some aspects of the reform package were problematic. *Agenda 2000* provided for the decentralised application of the CAP, thereby placing adaptational pressure on the national administration system and increasing the bureaucaratic burden on the Department of Agriculture. The subsequent reduction of direct payments above €5,000 a year (compulsory modulation) totalled over €18 million for Ireland in 2006 (Greer, 2009). This was used for one-off payments but future modulation monies will be redirected for rural development purposes. Thus, multi-functionality is being institutionalised.

The Irish government published a white paper on Rural Development in 1999 which outlined an overarching strategy for rural development but which commentators such as McDonagh (2001) criticised for its aspirational approach. This move chimed with EU developments as rural development was being underlined as an intrinsic element of the drive for economic and social cohesion. For the 2000–6 funding period all member states were required to submit Rural Development Plans which conformed to a standard framework while facilitating appropriate responses to differing contexts and problems. Thus, Ireland prioritised environmental protection (allocating 40 per cent of payments to REPS), compensatory allowances (30 per cent), early retirement (15 per cent) and forestry (14 per cent) (Greer, 2005a). The EU's increased focus on food issues combined with domestic demands for greater emphasis on food safety and quality influenced developments such as the expert report *Agrifood 2010*, on the future of agriculture and food production in Ireland. In 2004 an Agri Vision 2015 committee of experts was established by the minister to undertake a broad-ranging policy review. The committee brings together farm leaders, academics, the food industry and relevant state agencies. It has produced a number of reports and an action plan for maximising the potential of the sector but Greer (2009) is critical of its challenge to the dominant policy focus on competitiveness.

The mid-term review (MTR) of the CAP in 2003 resulted in further adaptational pressure for Ireland. The MTR led to substantial reforms such as the decoupling of support payments and production for some important products (e.g. livestock, milk and arable crops). The resultant SPS is linked to food safety, environmental and animal welfare requirements. Although Ireland voluntarily opted for full decoupling of payment from production, the decoupling of direct payments is expected to lead to loss of employment, a further reduction in the number of farmers and changes in income and production patterns. One of the conditions attached to the SPS was compliance with the Nitrates Directive. For Ireland, resolution of this issue involved thirteen years of domestic and international conflict before agreement was reached on fertiliser levels in 2006. The nitrates issue is an illustration of strong adaptational pressure but also highlights the role of both the farming and environmental lobbies and their influence on governance processes.

The EU reform package also amplified the focus on rural development with agreement that specified percentages of direct/first pillar payments each year were to be 'modulated' to the second pillar. Meanwhile, REPS 2 and REPS 3 continued to influence Ireland's agricultural policies and practices by supporting 'bio-diversity' options and a revised Farm Waste Management Scheme. Ireland's Rural Development National Strategy Plan (2007–13) takes cognisance of national priorities as identified in the National Spatial Strategy and the NDP as well as EU priorities outlined in the Lisbon and Gotheborg strategies and subsequent documents. The *ex ante* evaluation of the plan asserts that 'the problems which need to be addressed can be summed up in terms of the three axes in the RDP: there is a threat to the competitiveness of Irish agriculture from a number of sources, there need to be incentives to preserve and enhance the rural environment and countryside, and supports are needed to create employment and generate economic and social activities and infrastructure in rural areas' (AFCON, 2006: 8). EU negotiations with the WTO in 2007 and 2008 have generated negative reaction in Ireland, with the farming organisations suggesting that up to 50,000 farmers could go out of business if the Mandelson proposals for trade reform are implemented. In May 2008 proposals for a the CAP Health Check were published. These suggest changes to the system of direct payments, an increase in transfers to the Rural Development budget by 8 per cent and a reduction in the number of market support instruments. Thus, the challenges confronting Irish agriculture reflect the complementary and conflictual pressures for change which emanate from domestic, global and European developments.

Assessing change: polity, policy and politics

The profound economic and social transformation occurring in Ireland since the 1970s would, of itself, have altered outlooks and outcomes so it is difficult to isolate the impact of Europeanisation. Furthermore, Ireland's championing of agriculture as a key driver of economic and social sustainability, prior to and during membership of the EU has meant that unlike other policy areas, there has generally been a 'goodness of fit' between Ireland's agricultural policy and that of the Union. Despite this accord, domestic forces mediated the impact of the CAP. Government actions, attitudes and processes, the demands of farming organisations, the postulations of civil society and the needs of consumers shaped the implementation of the CAP in Ireland and affected policy formulation and the choice of policy instruments in the agriculture sphere. Changes resulting from the Good Friday Agreement also affected the politics of agriculture. These domestic policy preferences were ardently promoted in the Brussels arena, in turn nuancing the CAP. Global influences have added complexity and intensified economic, social and cultural pressures for change. Specific global-level developments such as the WTO negotiations have impacted on Ireland's agriculture policy. Nevertheless, it is possible to identify adaptation induced by Europeanisation within the polity, policy and politics of agriculture in Ireland.

The adaptational pressure on the product composition of Ireland's agriculture has been dramatic. When Ireland joined the EEC in 1973 dairying was the cornerstone of the agriculture industry, beef was important, the sugar-beet sector was significant and the food-processing sector was embryonic. Today, many Irish farmers are 'envelope' farmers (in receipt of direct payments decoupled from production); the sugar industry has disappeared as a direct result of the CAP reform; there were only 22,386 active milk producers in 2005 compared with 86,300 in 1984 (prior to the introduction of quotas) while beef exports in 2005 represented only 18 per cent of total Irish agri-food exports (Department of Agriculture and Food (DAF), 2006: 23). The nature and scale of the commodities produced by Irish farmers have altered with both social and economic implications. The reduction in the number of dairy farms and the EU-fostered intensification of beef and pig production has facilitated the dominance of the agricultural industry by large producers. This economic adaptational pressure has impacted significantly on the social structures of rural Ireland, particularly its demography, and has influenced the thrust of Ireland's Rural Development National Plans which seek to redress the impact of intensification. REPS is also changing commodity patterns as the implementation of SPS is linked to cross-compliance measures, leading to restrictions on intensive production despite the protests of larger Irish farmers. The welfarist nature of Irish agricultural policy has endured as is evident in the continued emphasis on income supports, the level of consumer subsidies and the political significance accorded to agriculture. The net budget effect of EU transfers for 2006 was over one billion (DAF, 2007), a significant influence on the country's finances.

The composition of the Irish farm population and their sources of income have also changed. In 1973, 70 per cent of income was earned from farming in farming households (Crowley, 2006: 52) whereas in 2005 'income from farming accounts for 45 per cent of gross household income, thirty six per cent is from other employment and sixteen per cent from state transfers' (DAF, 2006a: 16). In 2004 over 62 per cent of farms were part-time and on 47 per cent of the farms classified as full-time, the farmer and/or spouse had off-farm employment (DAF, 2006a: 14). From the early days of Ireland's membership, the benefits of the CAP have been unevenly distributed and scalar and wealth distribution problems persist. Benefits have tended to favour the larger, wealthier farms in the east and mid-west, thereby exacerbating the regional inequalities that existed prior to EEC membership and failing to address the problems of scale caused by small and fractured land holdings, particularly in the west. The intensification promoted by the CAP requires increased scales of production but higher land prices mean that those farmers who can afford to purchase additional milk quotas, for example, are unable to access the extra land required. Such problems hasten the exodus from the land.

The content, determination and implementation of Ireland's agricultural policy have all been affected by Europeanisation but also increasingly by global developments and domestic change. The move from protectionist policies through policies aimed at intensification and commercialisation to consumer friendly agri-environmental policy reflects changes in Ireland and the EU. The emphasis on market responsiveness and the realities of trade liberalisation have caused a fundamental change in focus. For many years subsidies from the CAP allowed Irish policy-makers to avoid taking a long-term view of the role of agriculture in the country and to delay the development of a market-focused approach (Greer 2005a; McAleese, 2000). Similarly, the lack of an emphasis on quality within the EU's headage payment regime allowed national actors to ignore this dimension resulting in a deterioration of 'the overall quality of the Irish livestock herd' (Daly, 2002: 533). However, the new century has seen a shift in emphasis from the protection of producers to responsiveness to market and consumer demands and is fostering a more long-term approach. The action plan for *Agrivision 2015* highlights competitiveness, innovation and consumer-focus as the way forward and reflects the changing domestic and European priorities.

The time-scale and policy parameters within the sphere are directly affected by EU obligations and opportunities. This is particularly evident in the conformity of successive NDPs with the EU's funding regime and the development of policy documents such as the Rural Development Plans, which accord with the EU processes. The broadening of agricultural policy to include a focus on food quality and safety as well as an emphasis on consumer issues, environmental considerations and sustainability was influenced by developments in Europe but also by global and domestic pressures. At the time of entry to the EEC the main focus of Ireland's agricultural policy was on protecting prices and on-farm employment. Concerns about agricultural prices, structures and commodities are still pertinent but have been augmented by issues such as organic production, food quality and consumer concerns as well as biochemical, technological and environmental dimensions which are all given prominence in DAF's recent review.

Policy-making in agriculture follows an agenda set nationally and in the EU with Laffan and Tonra asserting that 'Irish agricultural policy is almost entirely made in Brussels' (2005: 449). However, nationally agreed priorities such as balanced regional development, environmental sustainability and social inclusion frame the agricultural policy context, influence the policy content and approach and determine the actor preferences articulated during EU negotiations. As expansion of the EU agricultural policy agenda followed from growing concerns with food quality, safety and animal welfare, agriculture policy in Ireland adjusted to reflect Brussels' changing perspectives and priorities and increasing domestic concern with these issues. Similarly, as social and environmental dimensions increased in significance within the CAP, they also featured prominently on Ireland's agricultural policy agenda. The designation in *Agenda 2000* of rural development as a second pillar in the CAP reinforced the Irish agriculture policy milieu's realisation that rural Ireland could not survive on agriculture alone and needed a multi-faceted as well as a multi-functional approach. However, the Irish version of rural development is more all-encompassing, emphasising non-farm dimensions and the importance of rural communities whereas the EU-version is a more farm-based approach to rural development.

The mechanisms of the policy process have also been affected by Europeanisation and administrative and bureaucratic adaptation has taken place. The Department of Agriculture (in its varied nomenclatures) has always had a leading role in agriculture policy, particularly since World War II, when agriculture policy became less polarised along party lines (Daly, 2002). Because agriculture was given such importance in Irish politics and economics, the department has always been regarded as important and the ministry of agriculture is a prized one, usually held by someone with a background in agriculture. Membership of the European Community led to adaptation of the minister's role. Prior to membership the minister had to compete with other departments and sectors and try to satisfy the demands of farming organisations within a tight national budget. For many years the CAP accommodated the various demands from non-domestic resources, thereby reducing domestic discord over agriculture payments (Conway, 1991). However, in recent years because of changes in the focus of the CAP and the impact of global change, the domestic and EU pressures on ministers for agriculture have increased. Controversy in early 2008 over the WTO–EU trade agreement proposed by Commissioner Mandelson increased pressure on the incumbent minister to defend the CAP and Ireland's position and illustrated Ireland's preparedness to take a strong stance.

Both the role and functioning of the Department of Agriculture have changed to reflect the increasing complexity of domestic and EU agriculture policy. Until 1977 the lands function was carried out by a different department, the department had 'food' added to its title in 1987, was responsible for forestry during 1993–96 and was titled the Department of Agriculture, Food and Rural Development between 2000 and 2002 and is currently named the Department of Agriculture and Food but its core function has always been agriculture. In her study of the core executive in Ireland, Laffan ranks the Department of Agriculture as one of those departments wherein 'EU policies are central to what they do' (2005: 174). The Department of Agriculture and Food has adapted its structures and approach (as well as its name) in response to developments in Europe and Ireland. Schemes such as REPS have increased the bureaucratic burden. In the late 1960s the Department of Agriculture employed just over 3,000 people in two administrative divisions and three technical branches which had emerged in an *ad hoc* manner. Today, it is organised along four sections, agricultural payments, policy, corporate development and food safety and animal health (including a biodiversity section since 2004) and it employs over four thousand officials. In their assessment of the management of EU business in Ireland, Laffan and Tonra (2005) place the Department of Agriculture in the 'inner circle' because of its heavy involvement in EU business. But it must be remembered that because of its dealings with the UK, the department had built up expertise in international negotiations prior to EEC membership. Thus, while there has been significant administrative change there has been no institutional innovation as a result of Europeanisation. Similarly, there has been little institutional adaptation at sub-national level. Until the 1980s there was local involvement with the education and advisory dimensions of agriculture being organised at local level via County Committees of Agriculture which were linked to local government structures. Nowadays all agriculture policy is centrally determined with some elements delivered locally by decentralised units of the relevant state machinery.

It is not only changes within the EU that have led to adaptation within the administrative machinery – since the 1990s the annual reports of the department have given considerable attention to GATT/WTO. The North South Ministerial Council has identified topics such as animal and plant health policy and research and rural development as domains in which 'all-island' strategies should be developed (Greer, 2009; Coakley and O'Dowd, 2007). This has initiated further adaptation of policy processes and mechanisms.

Evaluation of delivered and planned interventions is now an important element of the Department of Agriculture and Food's work, reflecting international trends in public management reform as well as EU requirements. The system of checks and balances imposed by Brussels has led to the uncovering of cross-border headage payment scams and the imposition of fines for mal-administration in certain spheres during the 1990s (Greer, 2005a). Implementation of the SPS involves more inspections and the disclosure of the amounts paid to individual farmers, developments which met with resistance from the farming organisations. However, such developments have improved the efficiency and effectiveness of agriculture policy, a positive outcome of the adaptational pressure triggered by Europeanisation. Not all the adaptational traffic has been one-way – some Irish strategies have found their way to Brussels. Ireland had introduced tests for growth hormones in meat prior to the EEC's introduction of controls in 1988 and Taylor and Millar suggest that the European Food Safety Authority has 'the fingerprints of Irish practices all over it' (2002: 126). Reform of the rules for state aid in 2006 was influenced by Irish concerns about support for the agri-food industry and the forestry sector (DAF, 2007).

As elsewhere, the range of actors involved in the agricultural policy process has grown in Ireland. The Irish agricultural policy agenda is now being determined by a wider range of actors ranging from WTO, EU, consumer bodies, business interests and environmental organisations to the usual players such as government and farming interests. The salience of agriculture is highlighted by the establishment of cabinet committees to deal with the issues in *Agenda 2000* and the mid-term review and the frequency of parliamentary questions dealing with the CAP and structural funds (Laffan, 1996). Since 2002 a Joint Committee on Agricultural and Food brings Oireachtas members from both houses together to discuss relevant issues. Their reflections and those of the Joint and Select Committees on European Affairs and the sub-committee on European Scrutiny ensure that EU legislation and developments in the agricultural and other spheres are carefully considered and debated. Non-parliamentary structures are also used. On the *Agenda 2000* proposals, for example, the Irish Department of Agriculture set up four consultative groups on beef, milk, cereals and rural development (Greer 2005a).

Traditionally, the agricultural policy community was dominated by politicians, farming interests and public servants and this continues despite the involvement of new actors such as consumer groups and environmentalists. Ireland's small size and its clientelist political culture have allowed close organisational and personal ties to develop within the elite of the agriculture polity. The IFA which represents large farmers has been a key player in the agricultural polity since the 1960s. The EEC can be credited with bringing the IFA in from the political cold. In the 1960s it was notorious for its protests outside the corridors of power. By the mid-1970s, the IFA had become part of the agricultural policy decision-making community. Since then, with a strong presence locally and nationally and a well-organised structure in Brussels, it dominates 'the farming representation space' and has been instrumental in achieving compromises regarding environmental licensing, changes in the inspection regime for REPS and most recently in ensuring a derogation from aspects of the Nitrates Directive. However, it did not achieve the currency devaluation it demanded in the early 1980s nor succeed in preventing decoupling of payments from production in more recent negotiations. The IFA is the Irish member of COPA and is 'represented on twenty official EU Advisory Committees in addition to twenty-five COPA Committees' (Greer, 2005b: 69). The organisation has employed a range of professionals, many of whom have worked in Brussels. Their expertise has raised the profile and authority of the organisation while also ensuring that the IFA is not dependent on 'outsiders' for advice. The Irish Creamery Milk Suppliers' Association (ICMSA), which is generally associated with smaller farmers, also makes its voice heard, representing as it does about a quarter of Irish farmers. Macra na Feirme (a young farmers' association) is important and is involved in national and European negotiations. The United Farmers' Association advocates for marginal producers while the Irish Organic Farmers' and Growers Association is the main voice of the expanding organic sector. Although Adshead (1996) and Evans and Coen (2003) highlight the closed nature of the agricultural policy community in Ireland, Murphy points to the conflicts that have arisen between the IFA and the government on various occasions and asserts that 'while it might have an inside track, successful influence can never be taken for granted' (2005: 371). The growth of partnership as the dominant approach to policy-making in Ireland since the 1980s has anchored the farming bodies formally within the policy-making structures. For successive social partnership agreements, farming representatives have been included in the list of social partners. Interestingly, the other social partners were consulted by the government when a decision was being made on the level of decoupling to adopt (Greer, 2005b), illustrating the growing role of non-farming actors in determining agriculture policy. Thus, the politics of agriculture in Ireland involve a wide cast. However, unlike the regional policy sphere, the entities involved do not owe their existence to the Europeanisation processes.

The main Irish political parties tend to draw their farming members from different categories. Fine Gael attracts the larger livestock farmers while Fianna Fáil draws the smaller farmers (Greer, 2005a). Chubb points to the emergence of the farming vote in the 1980s as 'a political phenomenon of great potential significance' (1992: 94). This 'farming vote' is important to Irish politicians as the sector can influence change within the multi-member constituency system, particularly in rural areas. Greer argues that 'for both main parties, the promotion of the agri-food sector is a core priority, and neither is likely to go into an election pledged to abolish export subsidies or cut farm spending' (2005b: 63). The power of the farming lobby was illustrated in the lead up to the referendum on the Lisbon Treaty in 2008. In response to pressure from farming organisations which threatened to urge their members to vote 'No', the government agreed that it would use its veto if the Mandelson package were brought to the Commission. This stance seems a portent of change for Ireland's negotiating style in future CAP bargaining but also illustrates the might of the 'farming vote'.

In recent years the range of actors influencing agriculture policy has grown considerably. State bodies such as the Environmental Protection Agency (EPA) and the Food Safety Association of Ireland (FSAI), An Bord Bia (the food promotion agency) and An Bord Glas (the horticultural board), the National Milk Agency and Coillte (the National Forestry Board) all influence agendas, policy instruments and implementation processes. Teagasc, the farm advisory service, is prominent within the agriculture polity. Providing advice, guidance and education for farmers, carrying out research and assisting with the implementation of domestic and European policies it has been hugely influential. Expenditure by Teagasc in 2005 amounted to €174 million (DAF, 2006b). Crowley (2006) is critical of the productivist ethos they advocate while Tovey and Share (2005) draw attention to the effects of specialisation, commoditisation and scientisation on Irish agriculture, all of which have been advocated by Teagasc and reflect global rather than specifically European influences. Nevertheless, Europeanisation has led to changes in the nature of agricultural education. Many EU grants are conditional on having completed an agricultural training course, something which Crowley sees as ensuring that 'one's chances of survival [in farming] are tightly bound up with a particular agriscientific ethos' (2006: 56). Ireland's farm inheritance laws are also linked to agricultural education so there is an intertwining of domestic and European incentives to participate in agricultural education.

Resistance to developments in Brussels has been commonplace within Ireland throughout membership. Opponents of the Farm Modernisation Scheme brandished placards saying 'Go home Cromwell' when Commissioner Mansholt visited Ireland in 1970. The introduction of milk quotas in 1984 was strongly resisted while the saga of the nitrates directive saw continued intransigence from farming interests until derogations were agreed in 2006. In March 2008, 10,000 representatives of farming and agri-food interests marched in Dublin to protest against the EU stance in the WTO negotiations. This induced a government agreement to engage in the veto style politics referred to earlier.

The food industry in its many guises wields growing influence in the agriculture sector with the processing, retail and logistics sectors affecting policy developments. For many years the cooperative organisations (predominantly, dairy cooperatives) aggregated and promoted the interests of farmers and were run by powerful shareholding committees composed of farmers. Now, however, most of the cooperatives have mutated into large corporations with many non-farming shareholders, thereby reducing the influence of farmers. The new entities are multi-national corporations which are market led and consumer rather than farmer orientated, with much of their trade happening outside the EU. Other groups also affect the agriculture industry. Angling groups have pressed for implementation of the Nitrates Directive and a reduction in water pollution and were instrumental in taking a case to the European Court of Justice in order to ensure implementation of the directive. Consumer interests frequently express concerns about food quality and safety as well as about animal health and welfare and have influenced policy. A Consumer Liaison Panel, created in 2002, fosters communication between the Department of Agriculture and consumers, trade union and voluntary organisation representatives as well as nominees of major food retail outlets. This synopsis draws attention to the changed and ever-increasing range of players involved in Ireland's agriculture polity and the range of interests, expertise and experiences which they bring to the policy arena.

If the polity of Irish agriculture is multi-faceted, the politics are even more convoluted both at home and in Brussels. In spite of the changes previously highlighted, agriculture remains an important dimension of Irish politics and the political will to support agricultural development endures. This is demonstrated, for example, by the fact that 33 per cent of Ireland's state aid in 2001 went to agriculture (Greer, 2005a). Significantly, the Agri Vision Committee established by the Minister for Agriculture asserts that 'the social role of agriculture has diminished' (Agri Vision, 2004: 23). This represents a change from the emphasis on agriculture's social role articulated previously in many government declarations. Nevertheless, the socio-political aspects of agriculture are linked to its economic significance within Ireland and the government 'tries to create a broad consensus on the approach to the CAP reform and trade liberalisation' (Greer, 2005a: 163) while also promoting domestic priorities such as balanced regional development and sustainability. In the context of international negotiations, internal rancour, whether stemming from farming representatives or consumer interests, is minimised. In the Brussels arena, Irish policy actors are perceived as canny and capable. Interest groups such as the farming lobby are well-organised, sophisticated in their approach and strategic in their affiliations. Political actors are clear on their priorities, astute in their alliances and pragmatically adaptable in their negotiating stances. Ireland ceaselessly supports the continuation of the CAP and a rural development approach which underpins rural areas (Greer, 2005b; Adshead, 1996). It also resists attempts to renationalise agriculture because payment of subsidies would be a huge drain on the domestic finances. Ireland frequently allies itself with France on issues such as *Agenda 2000* or the Doha and Geneva WTO negotiations and has built alliances with other agriculturally strong states such as Poland and the Mediterranean members. In both the *Agenda 2000* negotiations and the MTR reforms, Ireland succeeded in arguing for significant abatement of the initial proposals. Ireland's political negotiators have been successful in negotiating concessions, whether for extra milk quotas in the 1980s or recent derogation from the Nitrates Directive. The threat to invoke the veto in the run-up to the referendum of 2008 was taken seriously in Brussels. The politics of agriculture policy within the EU are contorted and dynamic but, because of the strategic approach of Irish players, the outcomes for Ireland have generally been positive.

Conclusions

Ireland's agricultural policy impacts on the economic, social and political fabric of the country and the levels of adjustment and adaptation in this policy sphere during Ireland's membership of the European Community have been significant. As domestic and European agriculture policy has become more elaborate significant learning has taken place among farmers and farming groups, consumer and commodity organisations, administrators and politicians. It is not only the discourse of agriculture policy that has changed but causal institutional forces are discernible in this policy sphere. Europeanisation has been a direct catalyst for change because of the obligations and opportunities provided by membership of the EU and the significant financial contribution which the CAP has made to Ireland. Consequently, the CAP has served to frame agriculture, rural development and food policy developments in Ireland and has been one of the policy areas attracting significant public and political attention. A special Eurobarometer in early 2008 found that 63 per cent of Irish citizens were aware of the CAP whereas 53 per cent of respondents within EU27 had never heard of the CAP.

The pre-existing institutional and political structures and practices and the well developed patterns of interest intermediation in this policy sphere, facilitated adaptation to Europeanisation and mitigated the adjustment pressures. Because of the congruence of policy problems between the domestic and European levels and the frequent accord of actor preferences at the two levels the agricultural policy domain adapted more easily than other spheres except for the occasional dichotomy on specific issues such as nitrate levels or milk quotas. Thus, policy change involved impetus from Europe, an impetus which was influenced by domestic actors, institutions and structures. While skilful policy actors and strong mediating forces maximised the economic benefits of Europeanisation of Irish agriculture, the negative social impacts, the productivist philosophy and the increased bureaucratic burdens have not been deflected. Neither have the structural historic problems such as the income gaps between small and large farmers or the distribution of farm types been solved by decades of CAP. There is extensive evidence of commodity-specific change and administrative adaptation attributable to Europeanisation and also evidence of the 'uploading' of Irish policy preferences to the European level. CAP has also led to changes in state–farmer relations – from a purely political relationship to one which recognises the farming sector's technical expertise.

European vectors have not been the only agents of change and the Europeanisation thesis is insufficient to explain all the adaptation which has occurred. Domestic pressures such as changing employment, socialisation and settlement patterns as well as growing concerns about environmental and food quality/safety issues have affected policy formulation and implementation. The contribution of agriculture to Ireland's economy, while still significant, has diminished. Mechanisation, modernisation and metropolitisation have altered its social significance. The governance of Irish agriculture has become multi-level with a broad array of actors involved in horizontal, vertical and diagonal networks. Ireland's agricultural policy community has gradually changed from a homogenous, monodic entity to a polyphonic and less cohesive grouping so that agriculture policy has become a more contested domain and now seeks to reflect a wider range of concerns than those articulated by farming interests. Global influences, both economic and technological have impacted on the priorities and processes of agricultural policy, increasing the pressure to change and determining the parameters of that change. The agricultural policy content, processes, and mechanisms have changed since Ireland joined the EEC in 1973. So too have the policy discourse, the policy opportunity structures and the modes of governance in the sector. However, the causality of change can not be totally ascribed to Europeanisation since global issues dictated many of the elements of change and domestic political, institutional, cultural and social factors impelled and mediated that change.

Notes

1   European Union, DG Agriculture, speech (03/372) by Dr Franz Fischler, 'The CAP Reform: An Irish Perspective', delivered to the *Irish Farmers Journal* Conference (Dublin, 24 July 2003).
2   Defined as net value added at factor cost, adjusted for inflation, and divided by total annual work units.

9

Ireland's foreign relations

Nicholas Rees

Introduction

This chapter examines the impact of Europeanisation on the formation and development of Irish foreign policy. Ireland has traditionally been a small player on the international stage, but one that is viewed with having played a more significant role in international affairs than its size, resources and geo-strategic location might suggest (Tonra, 2007; Kennedy and Skelly, 2000; Skelly, 1997; Keatinge, 1984; 1978). The state's ability to formulate and conduct an independent foreign policy has been integrally linked with the formation of the state, Irish nationalism and the relationship with Britain. Under the leadership of Taoiseach Eamon de Valera, Ireland adopted a formal position of neutrality at the outset of World War II ('the Emergency'), although Irish neutrality had its roots in the anti-colonial discourse dating to the Boer War. Irish neutrality was also highly ambiguous, reflecting the manner in which it was utilised by Irish political leaders to achieve particular ends (Devine, 2007; Keohane, 2001; Salmon, 1989; McSweeney, 1985). Arguably, de Valera's position was more tactical than principled, as evident in the decision not to joint NATO in 1949, given the issue of Northern Ireland. In the post-war era the Irish state was not ideologically neutral, especially during the cold war when it favoured American and (west) European security concerns. Irish political elites from the 1960s onwards increasingly utilised Europeanisation to reshape and reposition Irish foreign policy in a European context (Rees, 2007; Tonra, 2001). In so doing, foreign policy-makers faced the challenge of strong domestic public attachment to neutrality, national sovereignty, antipathy to military structures and a commitment to an ethical foreign policy. As a result of EU membership, Irish foreign policy-makers have utilised the opportunities and challenges posed by the EU's growing role in international affairs to reframe Irish foreign in a European context.

The chapter starts by looking at the historical context of Ireland's involvement in the EU, the national-level institutions involved in foreign policy formation and the aspects of Irish foreign policy that traditionally made Ireland a small, 'neutral' state with a strong commitment to multi-lateral international institutions distinctive. It then considers the impact of pre-existing domestic structures and policies that have conditioned how Irish foreign policy-makers acted in Europe. The chapter examines the impact of the EU's growing role in international affairs on the making and conduct of Irish foreign policy, focusing on European adaptational pressures and the policy preferences of domestic elites. It looks at the adaptation and change that occurred in institutional structures and policy over the period since membership. Finally, the chapter assesses the sources and degree of policy learning and adaptation and the impact Europeanisation has had on Ireland's foreign policy outlook and role in international affairs.

Historical context: institutions and policy

In order to assess the relative impact of Europeanisation on Irish foreign policy, it is important to start by reviewing the pre-existing institutional and policy arrangements. In particular, foreign policy is an area in which states have sought to preserve their sovereign integrity, guarding this from external encroachments that might limit their ability to formulate and conduct an independent foreign policy. In the Irish case, the formation of the state and the distinctiveness of Irish nationalism shaped Ireland's foreign policy outlook in international affairs (see chapter 3). As Keown has noted, 'the forging of a separate foreign policy also formed part of a broader campaign of identity building' (2000: 29). Irish political leaders have also sought to balance a set of foreign policy principles, which resonate with Ireland's fight for independence and its concern over sovereignty, with a pragmatic approach to securing economic and political benefits for the state. The Free State Treaty which led to Ireland's independence left the state's relationship with Britain and its position in international affairs ambiguous, with Britain maintaining naval facilities in Ireland and with restrictions placed on the size of the Irish army (Keatinge, 1984: 13–14). Arising out of these circumstances, Ireland's relationship with Britain was a defining characteristic of early Irish foreign policy, reflecting a desire to bring about a united Ireland and the reluctance to totally break all links with Britain. Outside of this issue, Irish foreign policy in the 1930s was largely focused on the League of Nations and participation in Imperial Conferences, reflecting the continuing association with the British Commonwealth up until 1948 (Skelly, 1997).

During the 1930s, under the Fianna Fáil government led by Eamon de Valera, the state adopted a position of wanting to be neutral in international affairs (Keatinge, 1984: 14). This was no longer a position adopted as a means of expressing opposition to Britain, but one based on Ireland's involvement in the League of Nations and concerns about the general deteriorating international situation in the late 1930s. This position was reinforced in the 1938 Agreement with Britain, whereby it was agreed that Britain would relinquish its naval facilities in Ireland thereby further underpinning neutrality. The outbreak of war provided a further basis for reinforcing this position, with the public opposed to involvement in the war and the state legally obliged to observe certain behaviours in relation to the belligerents. The state was, however, not in a position to defend itself with just six thousand poorly equipped troops (O'Halpin, 1999: 153). In practice, as recent archival research has indicated, Ireland was less than impartial, providing support to Britain, especially in terms of military cooperation (Girvin and Roberts, 2000). Ireland's ambiguous political and security relationship with Britain was maintained throughout the war period, and it was only in 1948 that the Republic of Ireland Act broke the final constitutional link with Britain (Girvin and Roberts, 2000; O'Halpin, 1999).

In the post-war era Ireland was on the periphery of European events, participating in the Organisation for European Economic Cooperation (Marshall Aid through the European Recovery Programme, 1948) and the Council of Europe, but largely outside of discussions focused on the reconstruction of Europe and the restoration of state structures (Whelan, 2000; Maher, 1986). In the cold war climate Ireland's policy of neutrality was broadened and used to justify Ireland's position as a 'neutral state' in international affairs. By the mid-1950s, Irish statesmen espoused a broader set of foreign policy principles and increasingly began to play a larger role on the international stage through the United Nations, which the state joined in 1955 (Kennedy and McMahon, 2005). These principles were first articulated by Liam Cosgrave, the then Minister for External Affairs, in the Dáil in 1956 and included support for the UN charter; independence of blocs in the UN; and a commitment to preserve Christian civilisation in opposition to communism (Keatinge, 1973: 32). Frank Aiken, who succeeded Cosgrave as Minister for External Affairs (1951–54, 1957–69) placed considerable emphasis on the principle of independence in the United Nations with Ireland being a strong supporter of new states emerging from colonial rule.

As Ireland engaged on the international stage the state's politicians, economic policy-makers and diplomats increasingly focused their attention on the EEC and the economic benefits that might accrue through membership. In particular, concerns about the state of the Irish economy, unemployment and emigration in the 1950s led to domestic discussions about ways which Ireland might develop its economy. This generally reflected a view that domestic economic policy, which focused on import substitution and domestic capital development, had failed. The fundamental reorientation of Irish economic policy in the late 1950s inevitably had knock-on consequences for Irish foreign policy. The likelihood that Britain might join the EEC inevitably raised questions as to whether Ireland should also do so, given that in 1960 two-thirds of Ireland's trade was with Britain, and Ireland could not afford to remain outside of the community if Britain joined (see chapter 1). The state could not risk economic isolation and exclusion, and there was a strong domestic lobby with key sectoral interest groups in favour of membership (Murphy, 2003; Hederman-O'Brien, 1983). It was also considered important that Ireland's application be submitted ahead of that of Britain, thereby highlighting its independence. As it transpired, British membership was blocked by the French veto in 1963, effectively postponing Ireland's application, although only until 1967.

These early experiences with international affairs had a significant impact on those involved in forming and conducting Irish foreign policy. At the outset this was a relatively small group of leaders involved in the making of Irish foreign policy, reflecting the fact that it was largely executive led and dominated by the Taoiseach and Minister for External Affairs (see Table 9.1). Eamon de Valera was the key player who – by combining the roles of Taoiseach and Minister for External Affairs for sixteen years (1932–48) – defined the parameters of Irish foreign policy, emphasising independence and sovereignty; supporting Ireland's role in the League of Nations and espousing a policy of military neutrality during the war years. His successor, as Minister for External Affairs, Sean MacBride, followed a different path, being a stronger supporter of European unity, favouring both the development of the Organisation for European Economic Cooperation (OEEC) and Council of Europe (Murphy, 2003).

There was relatively little institutional development of the foreign policy machinery during this period, with a fairly modest Department of External Affairs created in 1923 and a small network of diplomatic missions established

Table 9.1 Head of Government/Minister for External Affairs, 1922–73

Head of government/Taoiseach		*Minister for External Affairs*	
William T. Cosgrave	1922–32	Desmond Fitzgerald	1922–27
		Patrick McGilligan	1927–31
Eamon de Valera	1932–48	Eamon de Valera	1931–48
John A. Costello	1948–51	Sean MacBride	1948–51
Eamon de Valera	1951–54	Frank Aiken	1951–54
John A. Costello	1954–57	Liam Cosgrave	1954–57
Eamon de Valera	1957–59	Frank Aiken	1957–69
Sean Lemass	1959–66		
Jack Lynch	1966–73	Patrick J. Hillery	1969–73

Source: Adapted from Coakley and Gallagher (2003: 375).

in strategic locations (e.g. the UK, USA, Vatican City, France, Germany, Belgium, Spain, Italy and Canada) (Holmes *et al.*, 1993). Despite Ireland's role in organisations such as the League of Nations and then the UN, the state depended on limited human and financial resources and much Irish foreign policy was ad hoc and based on chance meetings rather than a fully worked out policy positions. Ireland remained isolated from much of what went on in post-war Europe, reflecting a tendency to focus inwardly on developments within the state. This did not change until the late 1950s and 1960s, when the state began to re-orientate its domestic economic policies and as it became more involved in the UN and then interested in developments in the EEC. This provided a context in which Ireland assumed more external obligations and was required to change in response to a mix of external adaptational pressures.

Adaptational pressures: global, European and domestic

Global and EU adaptational pressures

Ireland, as a small state with an open economy, is classically characterised as vulnerable and sensitive to changes that may occur at the international level, especially in relation to international economic markets. Ireland is dependent on high levels of international trade, exports markets and foreign direct investment (see chapter 5). The discourse on globalisation has tended to reinforce this view, with Ireland considered as one of the most globalised states in the world (Tonra, 2007), reflecting perceptions of Ireland as highly open to such forces. However, some authors argue that this is not the case and suggest that the evidence does not stand up to scrutiny, highlighting Ireland's economic dependence on a limited number of markets in Europe (O'Sullivan, 2006; Smith, 2005). Much depends, of course, on how globalisation is defined, whether in narrow economic terms or more broadly as a process that involves technological, political, economic and cultural dimensions. The importance of globalisation may lie in the impact that such a discourse has on how foreign policy-makers view and think about international affairs.

Ireland has never operated in isolation in the international system and has used diplomatic, political and economic channels to pursue national economic and political objectives through a variety of fora, including international and regional organisations, such as the UN and EU, as well as bilaterally with key states such as the USA, Britain, Germany and France. By participating in the international system Ireland has been integrally involved in a web of organisations and relations that bring with it commitments and expectations. The state has to meets its obligations in organisations such as the UN, WTO and EU, which do place pressures on the state to adapt its policies. In some of these instances there is clearly a high degree of connectedness and integration with the European Union, where the state has to also meet its obligations and requirements to work together in formulating joint responses and actions to international issues and events. For example, the debate over the Lisbon Treaty referendum (2008) provided Irish farmers with an opportunity to protest about WTO proposals on agriculture and to pressurise the European Commissioner, Peter Mandelson, to take their concerns into account. This example highlights the degree of interconnectedness between global, EU and local concerns, as well as illustrating how an interest group in Ireland (along with those from other member states) can be affected by and influence international developments.

In understanding the varying impact that Europeanisation has had on Irish foreign policy, it is important to note that the degree of EU involvement in international affairs differs depending on which area of EU external relations is under examination. This reflects the EU's external involvement in matters of trade, aid, political affairs, security and defence cooperation (Hill and Smith, 2005; Nugent, 2003; Smith, 2003). It also depends how the EU as an international actor is perceived, with views varying as to its significance as an actor or presence in international affairs (Telò, 2007; Bretherton and Vogler, 2006; Hill and Smith, 2005; Smith, 2003; Hill, 1993; Allen and Smith, 1990). What is not in doubt is that the EU's role in international affairs has been growing and has had a significant impact on and shaped the way in which member states formulate and conduct their own foreign policies (Tonra, 2000). In contrast to other policy areas discussed, such as agriculture, environment and regional affairs, the EU's legal competences and role in international affairs has been far more limited and dependent on intergovernmentalism.

Since the Maastricht Treaty, the EU has developed from being considered a civilian power to becoming a political and potential military actor. The EU has considerable economic and political clout and is developing a distinctly 'European view' in international organisations, towards third countries and in relation to international events. The European Union has developed a global reach, with a wide array of relations with individual states and regional and international organisations. Enlargement has been the single biggest challenge the EU faced and fundamentally changed the character of the European Union (O'Brennan, 2006). Similarly, promoting stabilisation and reconstruction in the western Balkans has been a high priority for the EU, as has been the broader development of its European neighbourhood policy. The distinctly different types of adaptational pressures evident across the EU's external relations can be exemplified by contrasting its roles in trade and CSFP/ESDP, areas of specific concern to Ireland.

Trade
In the area of trade the EU has traditionally acted on behalf of its member states, where the Commission was empowered to do so at an early stage by

the original Treaty of Rome (e.g. common external tariff and common commercial policy). It acts on behalf of its member states in attempting to present a united front to the rest of the world, including with individual states (USA, Japan), regional organisations (Association of South East Asian Nations (ASEAN), European Free Trade Association (EFTA)) and at the international level (WTO and United Nations Conference on Trade and Development (UNCTAD)). In this context, the European Commission is empowered to develop proposals and negotiate on behalf of the Council, but within the parameter agreed with the Council (Article 133 Committee) and COREPER. The challenge for member states is to ensure that their views are articulated at European level and that the mandate from the Council to the Commission takes into account those views (national interests). It is, therefore, important to influence at an early stage European policy otherwise a state's particular national economic interests may be threatened. In Ireland, the protection of agricultural interests has traditionally been of concern in major trade negotiations in GATT (now WTO), sometimes pitting officials from the Department of Agriculture against colleagues in the Department of Foreign Affairs, who have been supporting a development agenda at odds with agricultural protectionism (see chapter 5). Trade does, therefore, represent an area in which there are likely to be stronger adaptational pressures in contrast to other areas of the EU's external relations.

CFSP/ESDP

In contrast, the adaptational pressures arising out of the EU's common foreign, security and defence policies have been considerably weaker, reflecting the fundamentally different decision-making processes and intergovernmental nature of the cooperation among member states in relation to international affairs. At the outset, European Political Cooperation (EPC) was largely reactive and dependent on agreement among member states, and usually only led to declarations (but little action). EPC was formalised and institutionalised as a part of the Single European Act (SEA), but it was not until the Maastricht Treaty (Treaty on European Union), that the CFSP was created and the EU's core objectives outlined (see Table 9.2). The member states, especially the larger ones such as Britain and France, have traditionally been reluctant to cede more powers and authority to Brussels, despite the fact that they are in strong positions to influence decisions in the Council of Ministers (General Affairs and External Relations). The ability of the member states to agree common positions and actions has been limited, with such attempts often highlighting the weakness of CFSP. For example, in a range of international crises since the 1990s, including the break-up of the former Yugoslavia, the NATO led campaign in Kosovo and the US-led coalition attack on Iraq. Such crises have highlighted the existence of continuing political divisions within the EU

Table 9.2 Principal CFSP/ESDP developments

Key event	Implications
European Political Cooperation, 1970	Member states engaged in foreign policy cooperation
Single European Act, 1986	Formalisation of European Political Cooperation (Title III), but not included in the treaties
Maastricht Treaty, 1993	Treaty basis for Common Foreign and Security Policy
Petersberg tasks (WEU 1992)	(Title V); framing of common Defence Policy (article J.4.2); joint actions and common positions
Amsterdam Treaty, 1997 (1999)	WEU's role transferred to EU (Petersberg tasks) Common strategies Defence, Article 17 Closer (enhanced) Cooperation
St Malo, December 1998	UK / French cooperation: called for a strengthening of CFSP through ESDP
Cologne European Council, June 1999	EU High Representative; Institutional structures: Political and Security Committee; Military Committee (and Military Staff) Rapid Reaction Force
Göteborg European Council, June 2001	Conflict Prevention Measures (including political priorities, early warning procedures, coordination) Committee for Civilian Aspects of Crisis Management Civilian Rapid Reaction Mechanism
Helsinki European Council, December 2001	Headline goal: creation of an EU rapid reaction b force of 50,000–60,000
Seville European Council, June 2002	Seville Declaration on the contribution of the CFSP, including the ESDP, to the fight against terrorism
Copenhagen European Council, December 2002	'Berlin Plus': EU access to NATO assets for RRF crisis management exercises
Treaty of Nice, 2001 (2003)	Formal institutionalisation of existing structures

Convention on Europe, 2003	EU Foreign Minister
Draft Constitutional Treaty, July 2003	Solidarity clause Issue of Mutual Defence External Action Service
Brussels European Council, March 2003	Declaration on EU Military Capabilities; EU capable of carrying out Petersberg tasks Involvement of Non-EU European Allies: 15+6 meetings Agency in the field of Defence Capabilities
Thessaloniki European Council, June 2003; Brussels European Council, December 2003	EU Security Strategy adopted
Treaty of Lisbon, 2007	High Representative for Foreign Affairs & Security Policy and Vice President of Commission EU External Action Service Additional Petersberg Tasks Permanent Structured Cooperation Mutual Assistance & Solidarity Clause

between Atlanticists (e.g. UK, Spain, Netherlands) and those states more willing to adopt an independent European approach (e.g. France, Germany, Italy). These crises also signify the dilemmas that neutral or non-aligned states such as Finland, Sweden, Austria and Ireland, face in the EU when dealing with other member states.

The development of a military capability to support political action, and the projection of a 'European view' of events, provides an interesting insight into how the EU is creating itself as an international security actor (Larsen, 2002: 290). Security has been redefined in the EU context, whereby the EU has a role in conflict prevention, crisis management and peace building (Commission, 2001). Notably, the Amsterdam Treaty incorporated the Petersberg tasks (of the Western European Union) into the treaty, thereby placing an onus on the EU to undertake humanitarian and rescue tasks, peace-keeping tasks and tasks of combat forces in crisis management, including peace-making. The EU's Security Strategy, *A Secure Europe in a Better World*, presented at the Thessaloniki European Council (June 2003), and later adopted by the European Council at its December meeting in Brussels (2003), outlines three strategic objectives as being: (1) to extend the zone of security around Europe (2) strengthen the international order based on multilateralism, and (3) counter the threats presented by terrorism, proliferation and failed states/ organised crime.

In practice, however, the EU's aspirations in international affairs and the realities of its actions continue to highlight the limits of the EU as an international actor and the continuing role played by individual states. Yet, there is a high degree of collaboration and cooperation among the EU member states, which provides invaluable sources of information and an opportunity to coordinate actions and positions in international affairs. In an Irish context, the involvement of high-level political leaders and their officials has placed Ireland in a position that it could not attain on its own. It has access to a sophisticated diplomatic and information network that influences Irish decision-making and its stance on international issues. It also provides an opportunity for a small state to play an influential role in international affairs, especially during the chairing of EU presidencies. In essence, the involvement in European affairs has proved invaluable for Irish officials, who have utilised such opportunities to influence European policies, as well as providing a basis for shaping Irish foreign policy (Rees, 2005; 2007).

Domestic pressures: public opinion and interests
In Ireland the formulation and conduct of foreign policy has remained in the hands of a relatively small group of politicians and senior officials, largely within the Department of Foreign Affairs, but also within other government departments, including the Taoiseach, Finance, Agriculture, Enterprise and Trade, and Labour. Under Article 28 of the Irish Constitution the authority to conduct external relations was placed in the hands of the executive. There was relatively little parliamentary involvement beyond voting on annual departmental estimates and international treaties. In the period prior to EEC membership there was no parliamentary oversight of foreign policy and limited debate on international issues. On joining the EEC, the Oireachtas did establish a new Select Committee on Secondary Legislation of the European Communities, although its role was largely limited and it lacked any real power (chapter 4). It was until the 1990s that a Joint Committee on Foreign Affairs (1993) and a Joint Committee on European Affairs (1995) were created in the Oireachtas. Similarly, there was only periodic public interest in international matters, usually only arising in response to international crises and sustained media coverage of famines, wars and natural catastrophes. Major issues were on occasion debated in the houses of the Oireachtas and the Taoiseach or relevant minister could usually be expected to answer verbal or written questions in the Dáil about contemporary international events.

By implication this left considerable discretion in the hands of those responsible for formulating policy and representing Irish interests overseas. It also meant that there was relatively limited political interest in international affairs and it was not considered a vote winner at elections. A study of Ireland's political and voting behaviour during the early referendums on Europe, highlights the limited nature of the opposition to Europe, especially among the traditional parties (Coakley *et al.*, 1993). The same study, however, highlights the persistence of opposition among various smaller parties (e.g. Sinn Féin, Socialist Party, Greens) and single interest groups (e.g. Peace and Neutrality Alliance, Anti-War Movement, AFRI: Action from Ireland) to various aspects of European integration, including concerns about Irish neutrality, EU militarisation and sovereignty. As a result while foreign matters have generally not featured highly on the political agendas of various governments, successive referendums over EU treaty reform have raised the issue of neutrality, leading during the first Nice referendum to it being obliquely written into the Constitution. This was something largely opposed by the civil service and by much of the political elite who considered this as limiting their prerogative and eroding their diplomatic flexibility.

The Irish government has periodically come under pressure from single-interest groups proactively to adopt stances and positions with regard to particular international issues, with recent examples including East Timor, Iraq, Palestine, Cuba, and in response to particular international crises such as the war in Iraq, the NATO attack on Kosovo, human rights violation in China (Tibet). All of these instances highlights the role of solidarity groups and the significance of media attention on such issues, but also illustrate the relative lack of sustained interest in international matters, which quickly diminishes once the media coverage declines. Similarly, there remains a strong lobby among development NGOs, who for the most part work in close cooperation with Irish Aid, the division of the Department of Foreign Affairs responsible for development aid. There have, of course, been exceptions, when Irish development NGOs have been critical of Irish Aid and its policies. For example, John O'Shea, the chair of GOAL (a development NGO), has been critical of the government's decision to continue funding projects in Uganda (*Irish Times*, 28 December 2005).

In general, public opinion has tended to operate as a constraint on Irish foreign policy-makers limiting their actions and positions. This is not an unusual development, and is generally supported by academic research on foreign policy analysis, which tends to characterise public involvement as a limiting factor on state action in international affairs (Holsti, 2004). In the Irish case, the largest constraint has involved a strong sentimental attachment to the idea of neutrality, despite the view by many academics that Irish neutrality has little meaning in international public law and that the post-cold war environment is very different from the cold war one which was characterised by intense superpower rivalry and military alliance systems (Tonra, 2001; Salmon, 1989). Nevertheless, with the exception of Fine Gael, the other major political parties have been reluctant to abandon the commitment to neutrality. Fianna Fáil has sought to circumvent it, by redefining it as military neutrality and have claimed that membership of PfP and participation in CFSP/ESDP has not comprised Ireland's position on neutrality. Notably, opposition to the government has tended to come from anti-war campaigners, who have, for example, focused their protests on Shannon airport, through which the US government has transported many of its troops going to and from Iraq (Rees, 2006: 158). Similarly, in the most recent referendum on the Lisbon Treaty (2008), the government sought to reassure the public that Irish military neutrality would not be compromised and that that state would not join an EU common defence policy.

There are, then, domestic pressures (including public opinion, interest groups and individuals) that limit and constrain what the state's politicians and representatives can do in the foreign policy arena, especially when it is seen as in fundamental conflict with Ireland's position on neutrality. Nevertheless, as in many other areas, Irish representatives have considerable room for manoeuvre and even within the security area there has been considerable development, with Ireland joining PfP, contributing to ESDP peace operations, being involved in ongoing discussions in the Council structure on military matters and participating in the Nordic Battlegroup. In particular, the decision to join the Partnership for Peace highlighted the domestic tensions that arose in progressively reshaping Irish foreign policy. Ireland was among one of the last European states to join the Partnership for Peace (PfP), which was associated with NATO (a military alliance structures), and it did so only after a protracted domestic debate (Rees, 2005). The then Fianna Fáil government argued that Ireland wanted to be involved in peacekeeping-type activities and that if it did not join PfP then it would be excluded from such activities (Doherty, 2002). The issue was divisive within the Fianna Fáil party, which had previously opposed joining PfP, as well as more broadly among sections of Irish society, where there remained a strong sentimental attachment of 'neutrality'. It also prompted strong opposition from peace and neutrality protect groups, who strongly opposed membership, arguing that it associated Ireland with NATO and would lead to a further militarisation of the European Union. In summary, the key point is that the interchange with Europe has clearly impacted on those involved in formulating and conducting Irish foreign policy. It has presented opportunities to broaden and deepen Ireland's role in international affairs, enabling the state's representatives to pursue a range of economic and political interests that has led to a closer alignment of Irish foreign policy with that of its European neighbours.

Impact of Europeanisation: institutional and policy change

Institutional change and policy development, 1973–86
The formative experiences prior to membership fundamentally shaped Ireland's foreign policy outlook and orientation, thereby strongly influencing

Ireland's positions and policies within the European Union up to the present day. In the lead-up to and immediately following EC membership, pressures to change the manner in which Irish foreign policy was formulated and implemented were low, reflecting the EC's limited role in international affairs. The EC remained a fledgeling political actor, with its primary roles in external affairs focused on trade negotiations (GATT) and aid to third world states (Yaounde and later Lomé). Indeed, Ireland was a key player in completing the negotiation of the first Lomé agreement during Ireland's first EC Presidency in 1975 under the leadership of Garret FitzGerald, the then Minister for Foreign Affairs.

Ireland's membership did impact both directly and indirectly on the formation and conduct of Irish foreign policy. In the most direct sense, Ireland was now part of the customs union and party to the common commercial policy. Thus, Ireland was assured access to EC markets and greater opportunities for trade, as well as finding its own traditional industries under threat from competitors. Outside of the economic sphere, European Political Cooperation was at an early stage of development and largely aimed at coordinating the foreign policy positions of the nine EC nine member states on issues such as arms control, oil, the Middle East and the third world (Nuttall, 1992). In practice, this largely depended on intergovernmental coordination through the member states' own political directors with common agreement often proving difficult to achieve on controversial issues. The limitations of the intergovernmental process were highlighted by the oil crisis in 1973, whereby states broke ranks with their EC counterparts and largely pursued their own national interests. For Ireland, EPC provided an important opportunity to participate in working parties on international issues and to gain strategic information which the state would otherwise not have had access to through its own limited diplomatic network. This was aided by regular consultative meetings between member state ambassadors in third countries and at the UN General Assembly. In addition, the establishment of a multi-lateral telex system ensured that the foreign ministries were in a strong position to exchange diplomatic information (Tonra, 2001: 143). The intergovernmental nature of the process ensured that Ireland was largely under no obligation to agree on foreign policy matters with other EC member states, although by engaging in discourse and working with other foreign ministries it could be argued that Ireland's foreign policy-makers' outlook was becoming more Europeanised. At the very least, by participating in this process, was able to supplement its limited resources in the Department of Foreign Affairs.

Irish foreign policy-makers were therefore under relatively little adaptational pressure to change policy direction. The original fear voiced during the 1972 referendum, namely that EEC membership might threaten Irish neutrality and jeopardise Ireland's independence, proved unfounded (Keatinge, 1984). In this period the only major instance in which the government claimed that Irish neutrality was compromised by EPC related to the Falklands War in 1982, in which the state refused to support Britain's actions. The government did seek to protect Irish neutrality, leading the government to impose caveats on European attempts at further cooperation in the sphere of common foreign and security policy. Notably, the government added a footnote to the report of the Ad Hoc Committee on Institutional Affairs (1985, also known as the Dooge Report), in regard to security and defence matters. In practice, EPC imposed very little by the way of constraints on Ireland, while offering up far more in the way of opportunities to Irish foreign policy-makers. The pressure for adaptation came from within the state and was largely associated with a policy elite that viewed this as an opportunity to bring Ireland in from the cold and reposition the state in Europe and international affairs.

Aside from having a direct impact on Irish foreign policy, membership also indirectly impacted on Ireland's foreign policy leading to expansion of Ireland's diplomatic network. This included the establishment of full embassies in Africa, Asia and the Middle East (e.g. Egypt, China, South Korea, Japan, Saudi Arabia, Lebanon, Iran and Iraq). In addition, the Fine Gael–Labour coalition government (1973–77), led by Liam Cosgrave, introduced Ireland's first bilateral aid programme in 1974, which focused on five developing states (four of whom were in Africa). This was largely in response to EC membership and in advance of Ireland's upcoming EC Presidency, which included the concluding stages of the new Lomé agreement (Holmes *et al.* 1993: 21). This illustrates how EC membership boosted Irish foreign policy, providing impetus to Ireland's long-standing UN commitment to supporting developing states.

Europeanisation takes hold, 1986–93
In the second period, dating from the Single European Act up to the Maastricht Treaty, the adaptational pressures on member states began to moderately increase as the EU developed as an actor. Up until the 1980s attempts at cooperation through EPC had highlighted the weaknesses of the process and the inability of member states to agree common positions. EPC was under considerable strain as a result of events in Afghanistan (1979), Iran (1979) and Poland (1980). Following a succession of reports and reform proposals, the Single European Act (1986) was agreed and provided the EU with the possibility to play an enhanced role on the international stage during this period. The Act was, of course, predominantly focused on the creation of a single European market, but it did provide for the codification of EPC procedures (Title III of the Act) and the commitment to the formation of a European foreign policy, including closer European cooperation on the political and economic aspects of security policy. From Ireland's viewpoint the objective throughout the negotiations was to protect Ireland's position on

neutrality by ensuring that any revisions would respect member states' different situations. The possibility of closer cooperation around security raised concerns in Ireland about the implication of these changes for Irish neutrality, with opponents of the Act actively campaigning against its approval. The process of ratification was blocked by a legal challenge undertaken by anti-EC campaigner Raymond Crotty, who argued that the Act required a constitutional amendment (see chapter 4). The case was rejected by the High Court, but overturned by the Supreme Court. As a result the act was delayed and a referendum was held in May 1987, where it was approved by 70 per cent of voters. The move towards increased coordination on foreign policy matters contained in title III of the Act still remained a matter for intergovernmental cooperation and there was no binding legal obligation on the member states.

The end of the Cold War in 1989 and the lead-up to the Maastricht Treaty on European Union, marked a critical phase for the Irish government, given the Irish Presidency was responsible for the early stages of the negotiations in the first six months of 1990. The Irish government's focus in the negotiations was largely on the structural funds, reflecting a desire to ensure any commitment to EMU would be offset by economic benefits. Irish negotiators did not, however, strongly oppose the provisions in the Treaty relating to a Common Foreign and Security Policy (CFSP), which sought to ensure that the states agreed on a joint EU position and action. Ireland supported this, provided that the unanimity rule was retained, and that qualified majority voting (QMV) around joint actions could only be agreed unanimously. The more controversial aspect of the Treaty concerned the provision that the EU should eventually frame a common defence policy (Article J.4). The key issue here is not whether the EU has a defence policy, which it already has, but whether this leads to common defence such as in NATO based on mutual defence obligations. Article J.4.4, however, sought to protect states such as Ireland by providing that the EU's security policy would not prejudice 'the specific character of the security and defence policy of certain member states'. The government's position was that this did not jeopardise Irish neutrality and that no commitment to defence cooperation has been entered into by Ireland. At a domestic level, the Maastricht Treaty referendum provided a focus for domestic opposition to the perceived EU's growing role in defence matters. Opponents of the Treaty (Green Party, Worker' Party plus a mix of single issue pressure groups), claimed that it would lead to a European superstate, the formation of a European army and conscription (Coakley, Holmes and Rees, 1997: 224). The major political parties (Fine Gael, Labour, Progressive Democrats and Finana Fáil), however, argued that Irish neutrality was not under any threat from the Treaty. The Treaty referendum was passed by 69.1 per cent to 30.9 per cent, with a turnout of 57 per cent.

In practice the adoption of provisions for the development of a Common Foreign and Security Policy seemed far distant from the reality of European foreign policy on the ground. Ireland's foreign policy position, especially in relation to neutrality, was becoming increasingly irrelevant in the post-cold war era. There was also a growing risk that by not participating in new initiatives, such as NATO's Partnership for Peace, Ireland could become isolated on the periphery of Europe and would be excluded from EU activities. It was not so much that there was direct pressure on Ireland to adapt to Europe, but that political reality suggested that in order for Ireland to stay involved the state needed to change its foreign policy orientation. In many ways, Ireland was already integrally involved in all other aspects of the EU's international activities. This involvement concretely impacted on Irish activities at home and overseas, including on the development of Irish trade with third countries, the delivery of humanitarian aid and in the UN General Assembly and associated bodies. Arising out of these activities, Ireland was increasingly drawn into a European nexus and this ensured that the discourse at home was often couched in European terms.

Irish foreign policy in Europe, 1993–2008

The adoption of the Maastricht Treaty in 1993, followed by the Amsterdam Treaty (1997) and the Nice Treaty (2001) further enhanced the powers and role of the EU as a political and security actor. The absorption of Petersberg Tasks (and the WEU) into Union and the explicit Treaty commitments to form a CFSP, based on the adoption of common positions and actions, as well as new articles on development cooperation, enhanced the EU's capacity to act. The establishment of new institutional structures in the military/security area, namely the political committee, military committee and military staff plus the adoption of headline goals around civilian and military capabilities significantly enhanced the potential of the EU as a security actor. The degree of change, some of which was precipitated by treaty change and some by intergovernmental agreements, was remarkable in such a short period of time given the reservations that some members had about the EU developing as a political and security actor. These changes also placed increasing pressure on member states to adapt their policies, processes and actions to support European-level policy development and to these requirements. A practical illustration of this is the way in which national military capabilities are being developed in response to EU (and NATO) force requirements, reflecting a commitment by the members to participating in European-level common actions and European Security and Defence Policy (ESDP) missions. However, while the adaptational pressures are evident, they are still largely based on the voluntary commitment of the members with states choosing whether they wish to participate in ESDP operations. There are, in fact, strong domestic adaptational pressures among policy elites that seem to favour enhanced cooperation on security matters, whereas public opinion in some member states lags behind that of the policy elite.

In Ireland the adaptational pressures arising during this period highlighted the limitations of Ireland's declared position as a military-neutral state. It also left Ireland 'sitting on the fence' in relation to security developments in Europe, adding ambiguity and uncertainty about Ireland's position on international issues, such as in regard to Bosnia and Herzegovina, as well as the NATO intervention in Kosovo (Rees, 2000). The problem for many politicians and diplomats was that the Irish public remained committed to such a policy, given that it had historically been interwoven with Irish nationalism and independence, asserted as a core value and was used to distinguish Irish foreign policy as highly moralistic. The government's white paper on Foreign Policy (1996), the first ever such paper on foreign policy, carefully restated Ireland's commitment to military neutrality, while opening up the possibility that Ireland might eventually seek to join the Partnership for Peace (Government of Ireland, 1996). The practice of neutrality, of course had been very different, with many observers suggesting that Ireland did not meet any of the international standards associated with neutrality, and that participation in the EU and then PfP had already undermined that position (Doherty, 2002; Salmon, 1989; Sharp, 1990). Indeed, senior politicians across most of the major political parties were cognisant that Irish neutrality meant very little outside of Ireland, and had in their opinion become increasingly irrelevant in the 1990s. It did, however, remain important to a range of groups and individuals opposed to further European integration, such as the Peace and Neutrality Alliance (PANA) and Afri, who argued that Irish neutrality was comprised through the EU's growing role in military matters and the state's participation in ESDP missions, Partnership for Peace (NATO) and the NATO-led mission in Afghanistan.[1]

The adaptational pressures associated with the EU's growing involvement in foreign and security affairs did not formally require that the Irish state change its position on neutrality, given that after the 1995 enlargement the EU now included Austria, Finland and Sweden, all of whom had similar orientations. These states shared with Ireland substantial and complex neutrality traditions, they did not seek to join NATO, although their position as traditional neutrals did change. Ireland's position was further augmented by the addition of Cyprus and Malta in 2004, who were also similar to Ireland in that their neutrality was ambiguous, based on ideological and nationalist concerns. In Ireland the pressures for adaptation came from within the state, where the policy preferences of the majority of the political and diplomatic elite cautiously favoured increasing Ireland's involvement in political and security affairs. At a political level Irish leaders were at times in influential positions whereby they were able to play a significant role at the international level in the EU and at the UN in shaping events. Notably, Ireland's EU Presidencies afforded Irish political leaders an opportunity to use their negotiating skills to pursue agendas that were closely linked to Ireland's early principled stance in the UN. For example, during Ireland's EU Presidency in 2004, the state was able to place African development and HIV/AIDs firmly on the EU's agenda and was heavily involved in the dialogue in support of the roadmap for peace in the Middle East. There is also some evidence to suggest that the state has been increasing its cooperation with its 'neutral' partners, including Irish troops in KFOR (Kosovo Force) operating under Finnish command and Ireland contributing 100-plus troops to the EU Nordic Battlegroup led by Sweden (with Finland).

In contrast, the military/security area has been the most problematic for the policy elite. A desire not to be excluded from participating in European operations and action, has to be balanced against traditional Irish concerns about being 'dragged' into operations to which the state is politically opposed. As a result, the state has often adopted an ambiguous position on actions such as that of NATO in Kosovo and the US-led coalition attack on Iraq. The state has continued to participate actively in UN peacekeeping operations, such as the United Nations Missions in Liberia (UNMIL), Ethiopia/Eritrean (UNMEE) and the United Nations Interim Force in Lebanon (UNIFIL), as well as having become increasingly involved in ESDP peacekeeping missions in Bosnia–Herzegovina, Kosovo and Chad. The triple-lock procedure, whereby Irish troops cannot participate in such peacekeeping missions, unless it is within the context of a UN-authorised operation and on the basis of Cabinet and Dáil approval, can be viewed as either a limitation or safeguard. On at least one occasion, namely in relation to the EU's operation in Macedonia in 2003 (Concordia), the state could not participate because of the lack of a UN mandate. Nevertheless, there has been a maturation of the Irish position, with the state's representatives participating in European discussions of military issues and in ESDP operations. The pressure for adaptation has tended to come from within the state, given that Ireland is not a significant security actor, and there has been little pressure from other European states for Ireland to participate. Ireland has tended to be in position of trying to 'catch up' with developments in this arena, given that it was slow to commit to participating in the 'battle groups' being identified by the EU's defence ministers as part of a rapid European reaction force that might be required to be deployed at short notice to address a crisis. The state has, however, chosen to participate in the Nordic battlegroup, which is led by Sweden, and has agreed to contribute personnel with an expertise in mine clearance. In order to facilitate this role, which required training outside the state, amendments to the existing Defence Act (1960) had to be made in the Oireachtas. At the same time the government took the opportunity of changing the act to allow Ireland also to send troops overseas to respond rapidly to humanitarian crises, such as the tsunami that occurred in the Indian Ocean in December 2005. All of this has ensured that Ireland's ambiguous neutrality tradition can be squared with the EU's evolving security role. However, as noted above, the triple-lock mechanism and the clarification of Ireland's neutral position may constrain and limit Ireland's foreign policy-makers and defence forces.

Assessment of change: limits of adaptation and domestic constraints

The impact of Europeanisation on the manner in which Irish foreign policy is formulated and conducted since the 1970s has been immense, reflecting the fundamental repositioning of the state inside the European Union (Keatinge, 1996). The distinction between domestic and foreign policy no longer exists, in so much as Europe impacts on all aspect of the Irish polity, politics and policy. The challenge for Irish political leaders and foreign policy officials is to try to shape the development of EU foreign policy in a way that is consistent with the underlying principles of Irish foreign policy, while ensuring that the state retains its prerogative to formulate and conduct its own distinctive foreign policy. As the above assessment of the three time periods has highlighted, the process of Europeanisation and its impact on Irish foreign policy has been a complex process. It highlights the significance of EU adaptational pressures, while at the same time signifying the importance of needing to examine the domestic setting. In the Irish case, the pre-existing domestic institutional arrangements, including Ireland's distinctive foreign policy orientation and strong domestic attachment to neutrality, have been challenged by a more activist EU in international affairs. This has tested Irish foreign policy-makers, who have had to balance Irish national interests with a commitment and obligation to support the EU in international affairs.

Political and attitudinal change

In examining Irish political and attitudinal change it is apparent that there has been a change in way Irish foreign policy is framed and understood at mass and elite levels as Ireland has engaged with Europe since the 1970s. In 1973 Ireland was joining a fledgeling economic community and there was limited political cooperation and discussion of the EU playing a more active role in international affairs. At this stage Irish representatives did recognise that membership might lead to new political and foreign policy commitments. For example, during the negotiation, the then Taoiseach Jack Lynch, stated that Ireland had no reservations about the political aspects of the Treaty of Rome (Maher, 1986: 222). This was in response to the Commission representatives in the negotiations raising the issue that Ireland's neutrality might pose a problem. Again, after joining the EC, Dr Garret Fitzgerald, then Minister for Foreign Affairs, also iterated that Ireland's neutrality was not an impediment to its participation in EPC.

The impact of successive EU treaty changes has significantly changed the EU's role in international affairs. In Ireland, there has been very little general opposition to the EU playing such a role, although on particular issues such as trade negotiations and its role in ESDP there has been more selective opposition and some public concern. In most cases, where the EU's role is seen as positively related to and in support of the principles of Irish foreign policy, then public support has tended to be quite high (e.g. peacekeeping, humanitarian aid and disaster relief). This resonates with a high level of general support in Ireland for European integration, as evident in successive Eurobarometers, where Ireland is above the EU average. In those same surveys, however, public support for CFSP and ESDP is below the EU average, with support for ESDP lower than CFSP. This is not surprising given that there remains a strong domestic attachment to neutrality and ambiguous support for the EU's security and defence policy. Most surveys of the public in Ireland suggest that anything labelled as 'military' get a negative response, whereas anything called 'peacekeeping' tends to be favoured. In general, Irish scepticism is also mirrored in other European states, including the UK and Northern Europe.

By implication this presents Irish foreign policy-makers with a dilemma, namely as the EU's role in these areas has been growing so has the pressures on Ireland to be involved in supporting the EU's activities, but public sentiment about neutrality means that politicians and officials must tread carefully in this area. In general, Irish foreign policy has been reoriented and focused on Europe and its role in the wider world, with successive governments and officials committed to supporting EU developments including security and defence policy. However, following the defeat of the first Nice referendum in Ireland (2001), the state sought in the run up to the second referendum (2002), a commitment from the EU to recognise Ireland's military neutrality. Thus, at the European Council meeting in June (2002) the heads of government accepted the so-called Seville Declaration, whereby it was stated that the Treaty of Nice posed no threat to Ireland's traditional position of military neutrality. Ireland had made clear that it would not be party to any mutual defence commitment or to plans to develop a European army. Also, based on the tripled lock of UN mandate, government decision and Dáil approval, Ireland would take its own sovereign decision as to whether to participate in humanitarian or crisis management tasks carried out by the EU. Similarly, the Lisbon Treaty, which was defeated in the Irish referendum in June 2008, also provided an opt-out or veto clause for states such as Ireland who might not wish to participate in mutual defence arrangements. The treaty recognised the 'specific character of the security and defence policy of certain member states' (Lisbon Treaty, Article 28A).

Administrative and institutional change

In examining administrative and institutional change in Ireland the pre-existing domestic structures and processes did have to be adapted and changed to manage this changing relationship with Europe (see chapter 3). The Irish approach has generally been characterised as incremental, piecemeal and pragmatic, reflecting a feeling that the existing system of public administration could handle European matters (Laffan and Tannam, 1998). There were also only limited resources of people and money available, thereby limiting any radical change that might have been made to the existing system. All of this ensured that EU affairs were often absorbed into the day-to-day activities of line departments. It did, however, place the Department of Foreign Affairs at the centre of the system thereby considerably enhancing its standing and position. The Department has the overall responsibility for coordinating the state's positions on European policies, while at the same time is responsible for the formulation and conduct of Irish foreign policy. It has, therefore, had a pivotal position in the management of EU affairs, along with the departments of Finance and the Taoiseach, with whom it shares key responsibilities.

The department gained significantly as a result of EC membership growing in size and prestige (Laffan, 2001). As a small department officials had close ties with each other, but a limited degree of specialisation, with much of the focus being on day-to-day issues as opposed to policy development. In 1967 the department was organised along the lines of three divisions, which included: administration, economics and politics. The principal division responsible for relations with EC was the economics division, which also handled all matters relating to GATT, EFTA and foreign trade. The changes brought about through EC membership did lead to some restructuring of the Department of Foreign Affairs, reflecting the need to reorganise the department's functions to cope with the demands of EC membership (Figure 9.1). Thus, by 1977 the department was structured around six divisions: administration; legal; Anglo-Irish; political; economics; and overseas development assistance. There was a significant expansion in the overall size of the department, with the number of staff based in Dublin growing from 68 in 1972 to 94 in 1977, and overseas from 85 to 120. It was largely the political and economic divisions that were charged with handling European matters. Membership clearly placed a considerable burden on the department, especially in the run-up to Ireland's first EC Presidency in 1975, and the overall increase of staff numbers was inadequate to cope with the increased workload and the complexity of dealing with EC business.

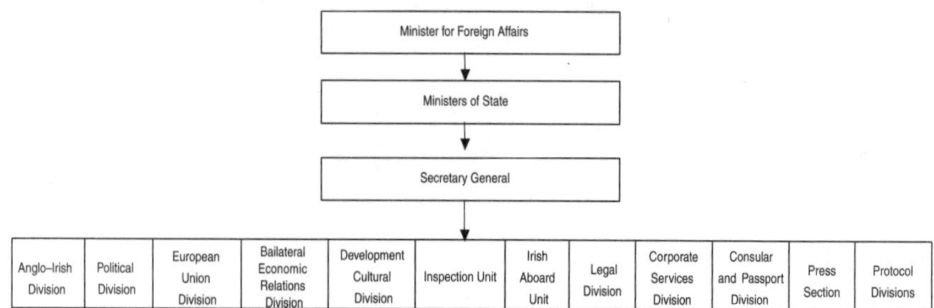

Figure 9.1 Department of Foreign Affairs structure
Source: *Administration Yearbook and Diary* (2006)

Over the course of Ireland's membership the Department has continued to play the leading role in European affairs, remaining the main conduit and interlocutor between Brussels and Dublin (Laffan, 2001). There are now more divisions and units within the Department than at membership (see Figure 9.1), although most European matters are still handled by the EU and political divisions, and while staff numbers have grown it still depends on other functional departments to initiate and develop policy, offer technical advice and provide personnel for the staffing of the Permanent Representation in Brussels. A key feature of change brought about by involvement in the EU has been the expansion of staff overseas, both within the Irish permanent mission in Brussels (Table 9.3) and in key country locations, with Ireland's diplomatic network extended since EC membership to include most of the countries of Central and Eastern Europe, all major Asian states and key Middle Eastern states.

EC membership placed Irish political leaders and diplomats at the heart of international affairs. Prior to membership, Ireland had already made its mark in the UN system by playing a leading role in supporting decolonisation, arms control and the rights of all sovereign states. It was, nevertheless, still a small state with a limited ability to influence events. As a part of the European Union, however, Irish officials are privy to a wealth of information and intelligence that has placed the state's governmental leaders and officials in a position to play an important role in world affairs. They have access to privileged information through the COREU telex network and regular working group meetings (Tonra, 2001: 257). For example, the monthly meeting of the General Affairs and External Relations Council, means that the Minister for Foreign Affairs and his European counterparts from twenty-six other EU states, have a regular opportunity to examine both internal domestic EU affairs and major international issues associated with topics as diverse as the Middle East peace

Table 9.3 The Irish Permanent Representation, 2004

Grade	*Numbers*
Permanent representative	1
Deputy permanent representative	1
Representative on PSC	1
Military representatives to EUMC/PSC	8
Deputy-Secretary General	1
Counsellors	20
Advisers	1
First Secretary	40
Third Secretary	24
Total	97

Note: Includes representatives to EU Political and Security Committee and EU Military Committee.

Source: EU Inter-institutional Directory, www.Europa.eu.int.

road map, the war in Iraq, Afghanistan, terrorism, and a myriad of other topics. At a lower level Irish officials sit on a range of Council working groups that examine these issues and try to agree EU common positions and actions in advance of ministerial meetings. Similarly, in the UN structure the EU seeks to coordinate its position on major international issues through the EU Presidency. In October 2001, following the 9/11 attacks Ireland as an elected member of the UN Security Council chaired the meetings and led the UN's response. In this role it sought to also ensure that all the other EU states were briefed on developments in the UN Security Council, and it aimed to ensure that the US response to these events took place within a UN context. Irish leaders, therefore, have access to world leaders, international organisations and multi-level talks, which places the state in a position to pursue and advance its own foreign policy objectives.

Europeanisation has also impacted on the legislature in Ireland. In contrast to the role of the executive, the legislature in Ireland has traditionally had a limited role in foreign policy. However, Europeanisation has provided a particular catalyst for change in this area. At the outset, when Ireland joined the EC, the European Communities Act (1972) provided the Oireachtas with a limited role in relation to the European Communities, principally through the monitoring of EC legislation (see chapter 4). The government was required on a twice-yearly basis (section 5, EC Act) to submit to both houses reports on developments within the European Community.[2] In the mid-1990s the government decided to establish a new Joint Committee on Foreign Affairs (1993), along with a Joint Committee on European Affairs (1995), reflecting a growing interest in debating foreign and European affairs in the Oireachtas, given the EU's own growing role in international affairs. The existence of the two committees, both of which have been renewed following elections, provided the Oireachtas with a greater opportunity to debate and examine international and European matters. They also offered a forum in which outside experts, professionals and interested parties, could give evidence and contribute to discussion on topical issues of concern to the Oireachtas. On an annual basis the two committees have published a small number of reports on topical issues, such as on Turkish accession to the EU (2004), the crisis in Uganda (2004) and the Lisbon Strategy (2005), which contributed to members understanding of foreign affairs.

However, despite these developments, there was limited interest in ensuring that the Dáil and Seanad scrutinised or in any way played a role in relation to European matters up until the outcome of the first Nice Treaty referendum in June 2001 (Laffan, 2005). The outcome of the Nice referendum in which a narrow majority of voters opposed the adoption of the treaty in Ireland prompted a far-reaching reappraisal by the government of the manner in which EU matters were debated and communicated in Ireland (Laffan, 2005; O'Mahony, 2001).[3] It was strongly felt that the Irish public were detached from developments in the European Union, with EU business, and more generally European affairs, having slipped down the agenda. Similarly, many Irish officials felt that Ireland had become complacent and was not in tune with developments in Europe, perhaps focusing inwardly on its own economic and social developments, and absorbed by a number of domestic scandals. Even prior to the result the government had decided to convene a National Forum on Europe (2001) to stimulate debate and discussion regarding Ireland's relationship with Europe and to look at the future of Europe in light of the upcoming European Convention.[4] However, in light of the referendum result, and in a context where a further referendum was likely, the Taoiseach and Minister for Foreign Affairs placed Europe centre stage on the government's agenda. Thus, the National Forum on Europe took on added prominence, with the government ensuring a continuing presence of senior ministers and officials at its meetings.

The government also sought to improve the Oireachtas role in the process by establishing under the Select Committee on European Affairs a Sub-committee on European Scrutiny (EU Scrutiny Act, 2002). The sub-committee, which comprises 11 members, has a broad remit to scrutinise all aspects of EU affairs, across the principal EU and Irish institutions.[5] In recent years the Taoiseach, the Minister for Foreign Affairs and other ministers have briefed the Oireachtas on European-level developments, especially on the out-come of European Council meetings, Treaty reform proposals and major international events, such as the crises in the Middle East peace process (see chapter 4). These developments have ensured that the Oireachtas's involvement in examining European proposals has grown and may, on occasion, even be able to influence policy outcomes. It has also brought the Oireachtas closer to Europe, improving the members understanding and knowledge of Europe and its role in international affairs.

Policy change

A key issue in terms of Europeanisation is the extent to which Europe has impacted on the important elements of Irish foreign policy. In foreign policy, Ireland had established itself as a reasonably principled actor in international affairs prior to accession. Primarily through its work in the UN, it acquired a reputation for supporting a range of 'progressive' policies in areas such as nuclear disarmament and arms control, decolonisation, peaceful resolution of disputes and a broad commitment to international economic justice. These did not disappear as a part of Irish foreign policy on joining the EU. Indeed, Sharp (1990: 239) suggests that successive Irish governments 'maintained a distinctive approach to arms control, disarmament and peacekeeping, and extended the projection of an Irish role into the issues of development assistance and a Middle Eastern peace settlement'. EU membership, however, did involve a significant broadening of the range of issues under consideration by Irish diplomats and required in some areas the formation of policy positions on a range of issues which Irish foreign policy-makers had previously had little knowledge of or involvement with. EC membership gave a significant boost to Irish foreign policy, both leading the state to broaden its involvement in international affairs and slowly expand its diplomatic representation. Another noteworthy development was the establishment of a bilateral aid programme, thereby ensuring that Ireland had moved from being a recipient of funds to one which provided support and assistance to a group of the least developed and poorest developing states (Holmes *et al.*, 1993).

Irish foreign policy-makers have had to balance Ireland's principled stance in international affairs against its pragmatic political and economic interests in Europe. It has also to meet the challenge of making its voice heard in a union in which the larger states, such as Britain, Germany and France can dominate EU forums and decision-making. Irish political leaders and diplomats have proved to be skilled at defending Irish interests in key negotiations while supporting more general common European policies and positions in international affairs. This was particularly notable in the various rounds of GATT negotiations, where the Commission was charged with leading the negotiations on behalf of its member states, but in which its negotiating mandate was subject to the control of those same states. In the case of

Ireland, the issue of agricultural policy was always of major concern in such negotiations, given the sensitivity of the issue in Ireland. Irish negotiators were usually strongly allied with states such as France and the Mediterranean countries, who were opposed to liberalising the market and making concessions to developing states. The dilemma for Irish negotiators was that the pursuit of Irish economic interests was not always consistent with Ireland's principled approach to development issues and support for developing states. Similarly, in relation to climate negotiations over CO_2 emissions Irish government policy was supportive of a reduction in emissions, which was in line with EU policy, but at a practical level the government was reluctant to put in place a carbon tax that might have adversely affected Irish economic competitiveness (see chapter 7).

Ireland has also retained and restated its commitment to military neutrality, leading to a certain refinement and clarification as to what is meant by the term. Successive referendums have had the effect of placing the issue on the agenda and ensuring that public concerns are listened to by the political elite. Ireland's position on neutrality has also provided the state with an escape clause whereby Ireland decides on those areas in ESDP in which it wants to engage with Europe. At a practical level, Irish military personnel are involved in EU institutions, such as the EU Military Committee and Military Staff, as well as in authorised EU ESDP operations. Ireland has also joined the Nordic Battlegroup and its troops have engaged in joint training exercises alongside troops from other EU states. In order to enable the government to make this happen, the Defence Act had to be changed to allow Irish troops to go overseas on training exercises with their European counterparts. Similarly, Ireland has provided troops in support of the EUFOR peace operation in Chad (with the mission under the command of an Irish Lieutenant General at the Operational HQ in Paris), despite some domestic concerns over whether this was an appropriate mission to become involved in given the nature of the Chadian political regime and concerns that the EU (especially the French military forces) might not be seen as impartial. In all of this, the triple-lock mechanism discussed earlier remains in place and public opinion remains an important constraint on Ireland's role in such European-level developments.

Irish governments have also been cautious in adopting clear positions on major crises such as in Kosovo, 9/11, Afghanistan and Iraq (see Table 9.4). As the following table indicates they have tended to avoid taking a position, especially in cases where they might offend particular states or organisations, usually supporting the EU stand, but preferring to sit on the fence or await further developments. In most cases, where a crisis has occurred the state has reaffirmed its commitment to supporting the UN and its approach to the crisis and has provided humanitarian aid, often through the UN and/or EU agencies.

Table 9.4 Ireland and EU positions on selected international crises

Crisis	EU position	Irish position
Kosovo, 1999	EU remained united and supportive of NATO actions	Ireland sat on the fence, avoided criticism of US/NATO, but eventually supportive of military action
9/11 and Afghanistan, 2001–2002	EU supportive of America; EU action on terrorism; supported a broad coalition against terrorism under the remit of the UN Security Council	Ireland supportive of a measured response and involvement of the UN
Iraq, 2003	EU divided over the American-led attack and unable to maintain a common position; France, Germany critical; US supported by UK, Spain, Italy, Denmark, Poland	Ireland supported UN Security Council resolution 1441, avoid war, but US allowed to use Shannon airport

Source: Adapted from Rees (2006: 182–3; 2007).

The impact of Europeanisation on Irish foreign policy has been largely positive ensuring that the state is in a position to shape and participate in EU foreign policy actions. At a policy level this means that Irish officials and politicians are now embedded and involved in international relations in a way that is very different from the 1950s and 1960s. Ireland, as an EU member state has a much stronger voice in international affairs, especially on those occasions when it speaks for Europe during the Presidency. It has played a critical role in international negotiations ranging from concluding the early Lomé agreements on European aid to developing countries, to negotiation in the Middle East peace process and conflict resolution in Africa. It has also become involved in EU ESDP peace operations, deploying military and police, as well as civilians, in support of such operations. Ireland has, nevertheless, been able to maintain an independent foreign policy. For example, the state has through the Irish Aid programme provided aid to a number of bilateral partners largely in Africa. It has also been able to use its position in Europe, such as during the Irish Presidency in 2004, to prioritise Africa on the EU's agenda. Ireland's role in Europe has matured and this is reflected in the ability of the state to change its foreign policy outlook, largely dropping references to neutrality, while positively accentuating its commitment to using its defence forces for humanitarian and peace operations.

Summary of adaptation and learning

Irish politicians and officials involved in foreign policy-making and development welcomed EU membership seeing it as both an opportunity for the state and for Irish foreign policy. Europeanisation was used as means of adapting and changing the state's foreign policy in order to meet the needs of a progressively modernising state. At all times foreign policy-makers were aware of the key issues for Ireland inside Europe, whether they related to EU treaty negotiations or more general international affairs. In some ways the development and maturation of EU foreign policy over a lengthy period suited Ireland, given that early concerns around neutrality and economic interests influenced everything that the state did inside Europe. Ireland was, by any standard, cautious about supporting and playing a part in a more developed European foreign and security policy. On any issues related to defence and security matters there was deep reluctance to engage at an early stage with Europe, given that domestic public sentiment continued to favour neutrality. There was also a concern about the role of large states, who were perceived as reluctant to take on board the concerns of small states.

The state's participation in Europe, and the development of elements of a European foreign policy, afforded many opportunities to Ireland that would not have been available previously and Irish foreign policy matured and has managed to adapt to the post-cold war environment. Ireland is still a small player on the international stage, but the state's foreign policy-makers are better informed and in a much stronger position to play a meaningful part on that stage. This is reflected in the manner in which Ireland is valued as a partner in peace operations and is a strong supporter of UN reform. This suggests that there remains a strong consistent thread in Irish foreign policy thinking, dating back to principles enunciated at the UN in the 1950s, although adapted to take account of Ireland's position in Europe. The state has extended its diplomatic network across the globe and has focused its activities on developing trade links in Central and Eastern Europe, India and Asia. It has also maintained a strong focus on aid to poor states, supported initiatives on HIV/AIDS, and provided support to meet humanitarian crises as and when they arise. The key point in all of this is that Ireland's place in Europe has assured it a stronger role in international affairs. There are, of course, times when Irish foreign policy-makers have found themselves at odds with their European counterparts, but for the most part this has been minimised and Irish politicians and officials have usually been able to play the European game to its advantage.

In this case the learning that has occurred has been largely driven from within the Irish foreign policy elite, who have striven to change and shape Irish foreign policy in light of the changing international environment (Rees and Holmes, 2002). Nevertheless, the underlying principles that have guided Irish foreign policy since the 1950s, and which were reiterated in the 1996 white paper on Foreign Policy, are still evident in the formulation and conduct of Irish foreign policy. For example, the renewed commitment in the 2006 white paper on Development Aid, leading to a number of new policy developments and initiatives in this arena, reflects Ireland's fundamental support for developing states, especially the least developed ones. Ireland remains strongly committed to international peacekeeping, as evident in its commitment of troops in UN missions in Liberia and Lebanon, as well as in EU ESDP missions to places such as Kosovo and Chad. At times Irish foreign policy was slow to adapt to Europe, given domestic political concerns around neutrality, but this no longer seems as relevant today as in the cold war era. Irish foreign policy is firmly embedded in European foreign policy, but is still distinctive, reflecting core underlying Irish foreign policy principles, with the states having gained immensely from coordination and cooperation with other EU states in the foreign and security policy arena.

Notes

1   See Dorris, M. (2007), *The Militarisation of Ireland's Foreign and Defence Policy: A Decade of Betrayal and the Challenge of Renewal* (Dublin: Afri); Maguire, J. (2002), *Defending Peace: Ireland's Role in a Changing Europe* (Cork: Cork University Press).
2   Following enactment of the 2002 European Scrutiny Act the twice-yearly reports were changed to a yearly report.
3   See the *Sixth Progress Report: The Referendum*, the All-Party Oireachtas Committee on the Constitution, Government of Ireland (2001), for a review of the factors leading to a 'No' vote.
4   The National Forum on Europe, which is chaired by Senator Maurice Hayes, comprises representatives of all the Oireachtas parties, as well as an observer group made up of representatives of civil society. See reports of the chairman of the Forum on Europe accessible at www.forumoneurope.ie.
5   For terms of reference for the Sub-committee on European Scrutiny, see www.irl.gov.ie/oireachtas/committees.

10

Conclusions: institutional learning and adaptation to Europe

Nicholas Rees, Bríd Quinn and Bernadette Connaughton

Introduction

This study contributes to the literature on Europeanisation and its impact on patterns of governance through an examination of the Irish case. At the outset, the study drew on the definition of Europeanisation developed by Radaelli, namely, 'the processes of (a) construction (b) diffusion, and (c) institutionalisation of formal and informal rules, procedures, policy paradigms, styles, "ways of doing things" and shared beliefs and norms which are first defined and consolidated in the making of EU decisions and then incorporated in the logic of domestic discourse, identities and political structures, and public policies' (2003: 30). Europeanisation was interpreted as the process whereby European integration and policy-making affect domestic structures and the processes by which domestic structures (polity, politics and policy) adapt to European integration. The transformations and effects impelled by Europeanisation are investigated by exploring a number of policy areas in Ireland – some of which were well established prior to EU membership, such as economic, agricultural and foreign policies, and others, regional and environmental policies, which have been developed in recent years, partly in response to European and global pressures. There are, however, limitations regarding the usefulness of Europeanisation as a concept in helping to explain change and learning given the complexity and nature of EU and domestic policy-making, which involves a range of actors at different levels with varying interests.

The evidence across the case studies suggests that *Europeanisation has had an uneven impact on Ireland's polity, politics and policies.* The uneven impact of Europeanisation may be explained on a number of levels. First, the nature of European integration and the EU's varying involvement in different policy areas, reflecting its legal competence. Second, the essential features of the pre-existing domestic arrangements which shaped the state's responses to external pressures for change. Third, the manner in which change was mediated by the domestic actors and their own policy preferences. This suggests that Europeanisation is a much more complex process than is sometimes suggested in the models and approaches discussed in chapter 2. Our study stresses the need to understand the historical, political, cultural and institutional setting in a member state and then to place any consideration of Europeanisation in the context of understanding its impact on domestic polity, politics and polices. There is evidence that thick institutionalism – including the existence of strong pre-existing domestic structures – played a significant part in shaping Ireland's adaptation to Europe. The history of the Irish state, including its complex relationship with Britain, has ensured that the state has guarded and retained a strong attachment to national sovereignty and its distinctive identity. Yet, it has also pragmatically adapted its public administration system in response to European requirements, while simultaneously pursuing national interests as defined by the political and policy elite.

In chapter 2, which examined the various approaches adopted to studying Europeanisation, we suggested that the work of social constructivism and sociological institutionalism provided valuable insights that could be usefully used to understand the Irish case. The evidence in the case studies does suggest that domestic actors have been socialised by European norms and practices, especially through participation in a European discourse and experience of other state practices, reflecting a process of learning and adaptation. This is affirmed by evidence from the study, which suggests that the policy discourse in Ireland has changed through involvement in European institutions, forums and dialogues. The state has also formally been required to comply with European directives by transposing these into national law. In cases where this has not happened, as was illustrated in the environmental chapter, the state has been subjected to European legal challenges and fines. However, in understanding policy change it is evident that it is important to understand the domestic polity, politics and policy. The existence of past problems, policy legacies, and policy preferences, as well as the very nature of the institutional machinery, mean that any change in policy direction is a complex process requiring an understanding of the domestic context. Many of the explanations that focus on EU policy development and implementation in the member states simply do not readily understand the intricacies of the domestic polity, politics and policy.

In what follows we draw together the evidence from the case studies by focusing first on the changing nature of the EU and its role in the policy process, moving on to then consider how this relates to the domestic polity, politics and policy in Ireland. The concluding section considers the impact Europeanisation has had on Ireland and whether there is any evidence that this has led to new patterns of governance emerging across the state.

The changing nature of the EU and its policy process

In drawing conclusions from the case studies presented in this book it is important to note that the very nature of the European Union has changed during the period being examined, from 1973 to the current period. It has successfully grown in size from a Union which comprised nine member states in 1973 to one of 27 states in 2008, with a population of 495 million people. In enlarging in this manner, it has also deepened, with its policy competences now significantly expanded to include a range of new areas in which the EU had no involvement in 1973. Hix has observed in a historical comparison of EU and US policy competences that in the EU, policy centralisation was very rapid during the 1990s, with most regulatory and monetary policies decided at EU level with the member states retaining authority over expenditure, citizen and foreign policies (Hix, 2005: 19). In effect, the critical juncture in the EU's policy development was the creation of the Single European Market and the consequent development of Economic and Monetary Union at the time of the Maastricht Treaty. The European Union has an exclusive competence to form and develop policies in a limited, but significant number of areas, as indicated in Table 10.1. The EU does, however, share competence with the member states in a large number of areas, which have grown significantly since the Maastricht Treaty (1992). There is, then, a complex system of multi-level governance at play in which Europeanisation significantly influences politics, polity and policy in the member states.

Table 10.1 EU policy competences

Exclusive competence The EU has exclusive competence in the following areas:	• customs union; • competition rules necessary for the internal market; • monetary policy (for the member states whose currency is the Euro); • common commercial policy; • international agreements.
Shared competence The EU has shared competence with the Member States in a wide range of areas:	• internal market; • social policy; • economic, social and territorial cohesion; • agriculture and fisheries • environment; • consumer protection; • transport; • trans-European networks; • area of freedom, security and justice.

By implication, the European Union and the member states are integrally involved in working together in the formation and development of policy across all types of areas (i.e. joint policy-making). But while the EU has accumulated policy competences, as documented by Pollack, it is less clear whether this represents the type of trend evident in the US federal system (2000: 522). The evidence in this study suggests that national politics and policy-making remains a distinctive process in many areas. There are, of course, interesting comparisons here with other developed states, such as the USA, Canada and Australia. Irish political leaders and civil servants have retained significant independence and latitude to formulate and implement policies appropriate to the Irish context. Our study argues that national policy elites have been extremely adept at managing the policy process to ensure compliance with EU requirements, while retaining the national prerogative to develop and implement policies in accordance with domestic structures. In this they have been aided by both a backlash against over-regulation from Brussels (including a commitment to subsidiarity) and new EU methods and approaches to policy-making. For example, the utilisation of the open-method of coordination in some key policy areas, such as economic policy and the Lisbon Strategy, ensured that member states were required to coordinate their economic policies with a view to achieving certain outcomes.

In the selected policy areas examined in this book the trend towards greater EU involvement in the formulation of policy process was evident (Table 10.2). The following table provides a very general guide to how the EU policy competences changed in the areas under examination over the period since Irish membership.

The EU's competence in most of these policy areas has grown and it is also evident that the Irish government (as with the other member states) retains the prerogative in many key domestic policy areas, such as economic and taxation policies, foreign relations and defence. The picture is, of course, far more complex than this table suggests as even in areas where the EU has

Table 10.2 EU involvement in selective policy areas

Degree of EU involvement in policy sphere	*EEC enlargement, 1973*	*SEA, 1986*	*Maastricht, 1992*	*Treaty of Amsterdam, 1997*	*Treaty of Nice 2001*
Agriculture	High	High	High	High	High
Regional	Low	Medium	Medium-high	Medium	Medium
Economy	Low	Low-medium	Medium	Medium	Medium
Environment	Low	Medium	Medium	Medium	Medium
Foreign relations	Low	Low	Medium	Medium	Medium

the dominant policy prerogative, such as agriculture, the member states still have considerable room for manoeuvre and interpretation of EU policy. The manner in which the state adapts to meet European requirements ensures the continuance of much discretion, with the government and officials being able to decide how and in what ways to make policy and implement it.

Domestic polity, politics and policy in Ireland

Ireland's historical development and political culture have been significant in shaping the State's response to Europeanisation. In the Irish case, national identity and state formation are important factors in understanding Ireland's relationship with the European Union. A turbulent early history linked to an ambiguous relationship to Britain, meant that Europe offered an opportunity to assert Irish identity and develop new relationships inside the EU. The focus on Europe was overwhelmingly economic with limited consideration given to what impact the EU might have on Ireland's domestic polity, politics and policy (see chapter 1). The evidence presented in this study suggests that the impact of Europeanisation has been highly differentiated, making generalisation difficult. Nevertheless, there are some trends of domestic change evident across all the case studies.

First, in terms of the polity, there has been moderate domestic change in terms of state institutions, structures and relationships. At the outset of membership, the core institutions of government – including the executive, departmental structures and the legislature – were not significantly changed as a result of membership.[1] There were alterations to national administrative structures and intergovernmental relations, whereby EU business and requirements have been incorporated as a part of the policy process (chapter 4). Reform of the political-administrative system and efforts to introduce new institutional repertoires have not, however, been wholly attributable to the EU but have, rather, been bound up with wider modernisation pressures stimulated by new public management and wider reforms influenced in particular by New Zealand and the UK. It may be argued that EU membership has led to incremental, piecemeal change whereby the state has striven to demonstrate that it has complied with demands for change from Brussels. This has been most noticeable with regard to the environment and regional policies where new national and regional institutions were created and have become part of the policy process. In addition, there is also evidence of new patterns of governance emerging in these two policy areas, reflecting changes in the way in which public and private actors work together (Rees *et al.*, 2006). In contrast, there is less evidence of significant institutional innovation in agriculture, economic and foreign policy, although in all three areas administrative structures were adjusted, supplemented and new divisions created to manage

European affairs. It is interesting to note that it took a significant shock to the political system – namely the failure to ratify the Treaty of Nice during the first referendum in 2001 – to change government–parliamentary relations (see chapter 4). Irish political elites had taken developments in the EU and Irish public support too much for granted, failing to recognise that events in Europe were distant from everyday concerns of Irish people and there was limited understanding of the EU decision-making process and European developments generally. These circumstances have been further compounded by the No result (53.4 per cent) in the Lisbon Treaty referendum on 12 June 2008, with a high turnout of 53.1 per cent.

In relation to intergovernmental relations, Ireland remains extremely centralised. For example, regional structures have been fluid and pragmatic rather than an intrinsic part of the institutional machinery. Unlike the situation in some other European states, there has not been a distinct regionalist movement in Ireland, with most political pressures being highly localised reflecting the clientelist nature of the Irish political system. Although there is little public affinity with regions in Ireland, key government documents in recent years, such as the National Spatial Strategy 2002–20, have articulated the need for balanced regional development. Despite the rhetoric, adequate resources have not been designated in order to achieve these aspirations or give optimal effect to new sub-national structures. Recent reforms at both national and local levels underscore the dominant role of the centre and the importance of the county/city as the unit of functional local governance while little emphasis has been placed on the region as a meaningful political or economic entity. It is unlikely that the Regional Authorities and Regional Assemblies would have been created if they had not been prompted by the requirements for EU regional policy.

Second, this point raises interesting questions about the nature of politics in Ireland and the impact Europeanisation had on party politics, interest intermediation, patterns of contestation and public opinion. In the Irish case, party politics have not been directly affected by Europeanisation, in so much as no new parties have emerged and the major political parties (e.g. Fianna Fáil and Fine Gael) have been overwhelmingly supportive of Europe and adopted very similar positions on EU issues. There have been some differences between the smaller political parties. The Labour Party changed its position from one of opposition to EEC membership to being supportive of the European Union. The Labour party has been the one most focused on social and labour issues; the Progressive Democrats more pro-business and supportive of a strong EU in the world; while the Green Party and Sinn Féin have been more critical of the European Union and opposed to key EU policy developments. The differences between the parties on Europe do on occasion emerge at election time, although during most national elections EU issues are not prominent.

It is more likely that differences on Europe will surface either during European Parliament elections or referendums on EU treaty reform. There are, of course, other links with Europe, both through Irish MEPs and Irish party membership of European party groupings, which provide important opportunities for dialogue and influence. All of this may influence party platforms and, ultimately, the programme of government adopted by the victorious party or parties who come to form the government of the day.

In addition to political parties, organised interest groups such as the Irish Business and Employers Confederation (IBEC), the Irish Farmers Association (IFA) and the Irish Congress of Trade Unions (ICTU) have played a significant role as mediating structures in relation to EU politics. As mediating structures they sought to influence and shape EU policies that impacted on their members. On joining the EEC, both the IFA and IBEC established offices in Brussels, thereby providing their members with key listening posts and an opportunity to lobby national representatives, Council and Commission officials and parliamentarians (Brennan, 2008). Officials in these organisations were usually able to relay information on Commission proposals back to Dublin, as quickly, if not quicker, than anything being transmitted by the Permanent Representation to government departments. These organisations were also critical players on the national stage, where they were usually included in official discussions with regard to implementation of EU regulations, directives and guidelines. In many instances their support or opposition had a direct influence on the ability of government departments and agencies to implement policy. Thus, in areas where EU policies brought direct financial benefits, including EU regional and agricultural policies, it was most likely that the government needed their support and cooperation to ensure that Ireland could maximise its receipts. This also increased their influence over the shape and manner in which policy was influenced. In the environmental area, there was a higher level of opposition to EU-level developments, given that groups like the IFA and IBEC were concerned that new environmental standards and requirements might detrimentally impact on their members. Also, the growth of new policy instruments and the role of private industry contributed to the growth of single-issue protest groups around the country in opposition to particular projects (e.g. private waste contractors and the development of incinerators). In a very different area, foreign policy, there also emerged over the course of the last thirty years a group of single-interest groups whose members have been critical of the EU's role in international affairs, especially CFSP. The emergence of groups such as PANA and AFri, who have often been critical of the Irish role in CFSP, highlights the continuing persistence of opposition to Europe in Ireland. Despite these developments it should be noted that the Irish public have overwhelmingly been supportive of EU membership and the benefits it brings to Ireland, although these same people have a limited knowledge about the European Union and have tended to view it as a distant entity (see chapter 3).

Third, there has been significant domestic change to the Irish policy process with EC membership reflecting the modernisation of the public administration system and the adoption of new ways and approaches to public policy. Involvement in EU affairs both required and prompted change at the domestic level, although change was also a product of domestic pressures including new government thinking about the public sector, the adoption of new ideas about public management and a growing professionalisation of the delivery of government services. This reflected new thinking in Ireland and Europe, the USA, Australia and New Zealand about the role of the state and the provision of services. There was a focus on ensuring wider consultation of both the public and organised interest groups in the development and implementation of policy, reflecting pressure from Brussels to be more inclusive. This was particularly evident at the national level, through the social partnership process and various fora, as well as at local and regional levels, through consultative mechanisms. This was underpinned by a tripartite partnership between government, industry and the trade unions which ensured a stable environment (see chapter 5). There was a notable growth in the range of new policy instruments used by the government, including the adopting of public–private partnerships and increasing recourse to private sector solutions, to address what were traditional government problems and areas in which it delivered public services.

The impact of Europeanisation and new patterns of governance

In the Irish case, Europeanisation has shaped institutions, discourse, norms and political action. The policy case studies confirm both singularly and collectively that Europeanisation matters and has fomented change in polity, politics and policies. However, the level of change in discourse, policy paradigms, procedures and the degree of institutionalisation of European norms varied. Such variation cannot be simply explained by differences in policy ranking, stage of development or content. Rather, the evidence of change results from the distinctive fusion of domestic, European and global elements in each policy area. As a result, it is challenging to determine the precise role Europeanisation plays as a variable in distinction from other factors inducing change. Even when reviewing the European dimension in isolation, considerable variation in adaptational pressures can be delineated, reflecting the evolutionary nature of the EU's policies and processes. The asymmetry of impact was sharpened by the permutations of the Irish policy process in each sphere, given long established traditions and ways of doing things. This suggests the limits of Europeanisation as an explanation and highlights the continuing value of traditional public policy analysis.

In the first case study, Europeanisation did progressively impact on Ireland's economic and monetary policies, reflecting the EU's growing involvement in economic and monetary policy. The state benefited significantly from EU financial transfers arising out of EU agricultural and structural policies, which directly contributed to Ireland's economic growth (Mattila 2006). It also ensured that the core infrastructure (physical and human resources) necessary to attract and keep large MNCs was in place. However, while the EU supported and underpinned Ireland's economic success, the key driver remained the state and successive governments who were able to take advantage of the precipitous economic conditions to promote growth. Ireland was supportive of the EU's Lisbon Agenda, which sought to promote competitiveness, economic growth and employment. At a European level, this required that the government provide regular updates to the Commission on Ireland's economic progress, although the actual EU policy process was based on the open method of coordination, thereby adaptational pressures from Europe were low-medium (see Table 10.3). This was in marked contrast to monetary policy, whereby participation in EMU and the single currency ensured that the state no longer had discretionary control over interest rates (medium to high adaptational pressures). This meant that interest rates were set at the European level by the ECB and that monetary policy was determined at a European level by the ECB and member state finance ministers. Nevertheless, even in this area, member states, including Ireland, have breached the Growth and Stability Pact requirements.

The second case study – environmental policy – highlights the strength of EU and global adaptational pressures and illustrates the difficulty that Ireland had in adapting to the European regulatory framework. As Ireland's economic growth accelerated, environmental issues became more important, reflecting the impact of economic development and a growing awareness that Ireland's environment has been increasingly threatened. This sphere illustrates the tension between national economic priorities and environmental concerns as well as the problems encountered in trying to comply with EU demands. It also highlights an area in which there was little policy development and administrative expertise prior to EU involvement. The need to comply with new EU standards, however, has proven problematic for domestic administrative and political reasons reflecting a lack of understanding of how to cope with EU requirements and at times sectoral opposition to those requirements. As public authorities in Ireland have sought to grapple with the problems of compliance and address environmental issues, they have increasingly sought the involvement of the private sector in areas such as waste management and incineration with new patterns of governance emerging to address public policy problems (see Table 10.4).

Table 10.3 Adaptational pressures and change

Policy sphere	Adaptational pressure			Degree of change			Indicators of change
	EU	Global	Domestic	Policy	Politics	Polity	
Economy	Low-medium	Medium	Medium	Medium-high	Low	Low	Economic coordination with EU Partnership Programmes (1987+) National Development Plans (1988+)
Environment	High	Medium	Low	High	Medium	Medium	Environmental Protection Agency (1992) Public Private Partnerships Policy content and legislation
Regional	High	Low	Medium	High	Medium	Medium	Regional authorities and assemblies (1994, 1999) Enterprise Boards (1993) Partnerships (1991–96) Regional Tourism Authorities (1991) Regional dimension of national policies (1988+) LEADER groups (1994–)
Agriculture	High	High	High	High	Medium	Low	Structure and composition
Foreign relations	Low-medium	Low	Medium	Medium	Low	Low	Administrative adaptation NGO forum White paper on Development (2006) New partnerships with business (2006)

Table 10.4 New patterns of governance in Ireland

Key indicators	New actors	New policy instruments	Networks	Forums for dialogue	Institutional development	Outputs/new patterns of governance
Economy	High	Medium	Low-medium	Medium-high	Medium	Medium
Environment	High	Medium-high	Medium	Medium-high	Medium	Medium
Regional	High	Medium	Medium	High	Medium-high	Medium
Agriculture	Medium	Medium	Medium	Medium	Low	Low
Foreign relations	Low	Low-medium	Low-medium	Medium	Medium	Low

The third case study of regional policy provides a good illustration of the ability of the state to change in a pragmatic manner in response to high EU adaptational pressures. This was helped by the availability of significant financial incentives to adapt existing domestic administrative structures and policies to meet with EU requirements and expectations. As a result, this is the area in which there is considerable evidence of change to polity, politics and policy (Table 10.2). There were also domestic pressures for change, given that economic prosperity challenged the state to address regional disparities, especially in areas that have not benefited economically from the 'celtic tiger', leading to new attempts at local and regional innovation, spatial planning and institution building. In this arena, new patterns of governance have emerged that engage not only public actors, but also private and civil society actors, and there have been attempts to forge a range of sub-national partnerships (see Table 10.4). Nevertheless, the creation of new structures and the development of new ways of promoting local and regional development have not led to the development of strong regional identities or even the vesting of political authority at this level.

The fourth area examined – agriculture – has traditionally been the cornerstone of Ireland's economic development. The change from an agrarian to a post-modern industrialised society has been affected by developments within the EU and Ireland. In this area, EU and global adaptational pressures have been high, as they have been at the domestic level. This is a sensitive political area, and while Ireland has changed and become a more urban society, agricultural interests still exert considerable political influence, especially with the larger political parties. Such organised interests have exerted strong influence during negotiations of EU agricultural policy, at the WTO talks and during referenda over EU treaty reform. This policy sphere illustrates the changing adaptational pressures as domestic and European circumstances and priorities have altered. It is also an area where there are signs of some new patterns of governance beginning to emerge to address the problems of rural development and ensure the future of this aspect of Irish life.

Finally, Ireland's distinctive foreign policy approach, with its strong attachment to neutrality, has been both adapted and enhanced as a result of Europeanisation. In this area EU adaptational pressures were initially weak, given the early focus on intergovernmental cooperation, although this has been changing since the 1990s. Arising out of the Maastricht Treaty, the development of the EU's CFSP, European Security and Defence Policy (ESDP) and Commercial Policy required Irish foreign policy-makers to question and refocus Ireland's role in international relations. Irish foreign policy has been firmly located in a European context, where there exist considerable opportunities for the state to play a significant role in international affairs. Nevertheless, neutrality has remained as a key aspect of Irish foreign policy, possibly even reinvigorated and clarified as a result of EU referendums and media discussion. Ireland remains a distinctive actor in international affairs with a foreign policy that is reflective of its commitment to international justice, multilateral institutions and support for developing states. The domestic mechanisms whereby foreign policy is formed have changed in response to both European and domestic pressures with a much greater emphasis on 'democratisation' of the process and incorporation of a broader array of institutional (e.g. the Oireachtas and its committees) and non-governmental actors (development NGOs, the public, the private sector and academic institutions) into the policy process (see Table 10.4). This case study also illustrates varying dimensions of Europeanisation, highlighting the challenges of policy adaptation and the impact on Ireland's foreign policy outlook and focus. It also provides a good example of how Europeanisation was used by domestic elites to reshape Irish foreign policy, making it more relevant to Europe, despite the persistence of some domestic opposition to EU-level developments especially around ESDP.

In summing up, there is evidence of institutional and policy adaptation in each of the case-study areas, although to varying degrees, reflecting the different adaptational pressures and existing domestic structures in the various spheres. In examining the degree of domestic change, learning and adaptation of the domestic polity, politics and policy to Europeanisation, we conclude that EU adaptational pressures were insufficient to account for domestic change in Ireland. We believe that the pre-existing domestic structures and patterns of governance are an integral part of the explanation. The evidence also points to the need to understand the decisions made by Irish political leaders and officials and the premises supporting their policy preferences. The study does highlight evidence of policy learning in response to Europeanisation, but also the significance of domestic opposition to change and the need to understand domestic patterns of political behaviour. In the Irish case, there is evidence that Europeanisation has supported and in some cases prompted the emergence of new patterns of governance to address public policy issues.

Note

1   The 1972 referendum did alter the relationship between the executive through inclusion of the legislature in the law making process leading to the establishment of the Joint Committee on Secondary Legislation (1974).

Bibliography

Adshead, M., 'Beyond Clientelism: Agricultural Networks in Ireland and the EU', *West European Politics*, 19: 3 (1996), 583–608.

Adshead, M., 'Europeanisation and Changing Patterns of Governance in Ireland', *Public Administration*, 83: 1 (2005), 159–78.

Adshead, M. and Millar, M. (eds), *Public Administration and Public Policy in Ireland: Theory and Methods* (London: Routledge, 2003), pp. 1–29.

AFCON Management Consultants, *Ex Ante Evaluation of the National Rural Development Plan* (Dublin: AFCON, 2006).

Agri Food 2010 Committee, *Main Report* (Dublin: The Stationery Office, 2000).

Agri Vision 2015 Committee, *Report* (Dublin: The Stationery Office, 2004).

Ahern, B., 'Fianna Fáil Proud of Achievements on Range of Green Issues', *Irish Times* (23 March 2007), p. 16.

Allen, D. and Smith, M., 'Western Europe's Presence in the Contemporary International Arena', *Review of International Studies*, 16: 1 (1990), 135–54.

Allen, K., *The Celtic Tiger: The Myth of Social Partnership in Ireland* (Manchester: Manchester University Press, 2000).

Anderson, J., 'Europeanisation and the Transformation of the Democratic Polity, 1945–2000', *Journal of Common Market Studies*, 40: 5 (2002), 793–822.

Bache, I., *The Politics of European Regional Policy: Multi-level Governance or Flexible Gatekeeping?* (Sheffield: Sheffield Academic Press, 1998).

Bache, I. and Jordan, A., *The Europeanisation of British Politics* (Basingstoke: Palgrave, 2006).

Bache, I. and Flinders, M. (eds), *Multi-level Governance* (Oxford: Oxford University Press, 2004).

Bachtler, J. and Wrcn, C., 'Evaluation of EU Cohesion Policy: Research Questions and Policy Challenges', *Regional Studies*, 40: 2 (2006), 143–53.

Bachtler, J. and F. Wishlade, F., *From Building Blocks to Negotiating Boxes: The Reform of EU Cohesion Policy*, European Policies Research papers, no. 57 (Glasgow: European Policies Research Centre, University of Strathclyde, 2005).

Bannon, M. J., 'Development Planning and the Neglect of the Critical Regional Dimension' in M. J. Bannon (ed.) *Planning: The Irish Experience* (Dublin: Wolfhound, 1989), pp. 122–57.

Bannon, M. J., 'Environment and Planning Policies in the 1980s' in M. J. Bannon, J. Hendry and K. Mawhinney (eds), *Planning: The Irish Experience 1920–1988* (Dublin: Wolfhound, 1997), pp. 157–73.

Bannon, M. J., and Lombard, M. 'Evolution of Regional Policy in Ireland', in Shannon Development, *Regional Policy, A Report by a Regional Policy: Advisory Group* (Shannon: Shannon Development, 1996), pp. 57–83.

Barrett, G., 'The European Union and the Oireachtas' in M. Callanan (ed.), *Foundations of an Ever Closer Union: An Irish Perspective on the Fifty Years since the Treaty of Rome* (Dublin: Institute of Public Administration, 2007), pp. 195–214.

Barrington, R. and Cooney, J., *Inside the EU* (Dublin: O'Brien Press, 1984).

Barrington, T. J., *The Irish Administrative System* (Dublin: Institute of Public Administration, 1980).

Barrington, T. J., 'Whatever Happened to Irish Government?' in F. Litton (ed.), *Unequal Achievement: The Irish Experience 1957–1982* (Dublin: Institute of Public Administration, 1982) pp. 89–114.

Barry, F. (ed.), *Understanding Ireland's Economic Growth* (Basingstoke: Macmillan, 1999).

Barry, F., Bradley, J. and Hannon, A. (2001), 'The Single Market, the Structural Funds and Ireland's Recent Economic Growth', *Journal of Common Market Studies*, 39: 2, 537–52.

Bartley, B. and Kitchin, R. (eds), *Understanding Contemporary Ireland* (London: Pluto Press, 2007).

Bomberg, E., 'Adapting Form to Function?: From Economic to Sustainable Development Governance in the European Union', in W. M. Lafferty (ed.), *Governance for Sustainable Development: The Challenge of Adapting Form to Function* (Aldershot: Edward Elgar, 2004), pp. 61–94.

Börzel, T. A., 'Towards Convergence in Europe? Institutional Adaptation to Europeanisation in Germany and Spain', *Journal of Common Market Studies*, 39: 4 (1999), 573–96.

Börzel, T. A., 'Improving Compliance through Domestic Mobilisation? New Instruments and the Effectiveness of Implementation in Spain', in C. Knill and A. Lenschow (eds), *Implementing EU Environmental Policy: New Directions and Old Problems* (Manchester: Manchester University Press, 2000), pp. 222–50.

Börzel, T., 'Europeanisation and Territorial Institutional Change: Towards Cooperative Regionalism', in M. G. Cowles, J. Caporaso and T. Risse (eds), *Transforming Europe: Europeanisation and Domestic Change* (Ithaca, Cornell University Press 2001) pp. 137–80.

Börzel, T. A., 'Member State Responses to Europeanisation', *Journal of Common Market Studies*, 40: 3 (2002a), 193–214.

Börzel, T. A., 'Pace-setting, Foot-dragging and Fence-sitting: Member States' Responses to Europeanisation', *Journal of Common Market Studies*, 40: 2 (2002b), 193–214.

Börzel, T. A., 'How the European Union Interacts with its Member States', in S. Bulmer and C. Lequesne (eds) *Member States and the European Union* (Oxford: Oxford University Press, 2005), pp. 45–76.

Börzel, T. A. and Risse, T., 'When Europe Hits Home: Europeanisation and Domestic Change', *European Integration on Line Papers*, 4: 15 (2000), www.eiop.or.at/eiop/texte/2000–05.htm.

Börzel, T. A. and Risse, T., 'Conceptualising the Domestic Impact of Europe', in K. Featherstone and C. Radaelli (eds) *The Politics of Europeanisation* (Oxford: Oxford University Press, 2003), pp. 57–80.

Breen, R., Hannan, D. F., Rottman, D. B. and Whelan, C. T., *Understanding Contemporary Ireland: State, Class and Development in the Republic of Ireland* (Basingstoke: Macmillan, 1990).

Brennan, P., *Negotiating Behind Closed Doors* (Dublin: Blackhall Publishing, 2008).

Bugdahn, S., 'Of Europeanisation and Domestication: The Implementation of the Environmental Information Directive in Ireland, Great Britain and Germany', *Journal of European Public Policy*, 12: 1 (2005), 177–99.

Bulmer, S. J., 'Domestic Politics and EC Policy-making', *Journal of Common Market Studies*, 21: 4 (1983), 261–80.

Bulmer, S. J., 'Theorising Europeanisation' in P. Graziano and M. Vink (eds), *Europeanisation: New Research Agendas* (Basingstoke: Palgrave, 2007), pp. 46–58.

Bulmer, S. J. and Burch, M., 'Organising for Europe: Whitehall, the British State and the EU', *Public Administration*, 76: 4 (1998), 601–28.

Bulmer, S. J. and Burch, M., 'The Europeanisation of Central Government: the UK and Germany in Historical Institutional Perspective', in M. Aspinwall and G. Schneider (eds) *The Rules of Integration* (Manchester: Manchester University Press, 2000), pp. 73–96.

Bulmer, S. J. and Burch, M., 'Central Government' in I. Bache and A. Jordan (eds), *The Europeanisation of British Politics* (Basingstoke: Palgrave Macmillan, 2006), pp. 37–51.

Bulmer, S. J. and Lequesne, C. (eds), *The Member States of the European Union* (Oxford: Oxford University Press, 2005).

Bulmer, S. J. and Radaelli, C. M., 'The Europeanisation of National Policy' in S. J. Bulmer and C. Lequesne (eds), *The Member States of the European Union* (Oxford: Oxford University Press, 2005), pp. 338–60.

Burns, B. and Salmon, T., 'Policy-making Coordination in Ireland on European Community Issues', *Journal of Common Market Studies*, 15: 4 (1977), 272–87.

Bretherton, C. and Vogler, J., *The European Union as a Global Actor* (London: Routledge, 2006).

Callanan, M., 'Local Government and the European Union' in M. Callanan and J. F. Keogan (eds), *Local Government in Ireland Inside Out* (Dublin: Institute of Public Administration, 2003), pp. 404–28.

Callanan, M., 'Local and Regional Government in Transition' in N. Collins and T. Cradden (eds), *Political Issues in Ireland Today*, third edition (Manchester: Manchester University Press, 2004), pp. 56–78.

Caporaso, J., 'The European Union and Forms of State: Westphalian Regulatory or Post-modern', *Journal of Common Market Studies*, 34: 1 (1996), 29–52.

Caporaso, J., 'The Three Worlds of Regional Integration Theory' in P. Graziano and M. Vink (eds), *Europeanisation: New Research Agendas* (Basingstoke: Palgrave, 2007), pp. 23–34.

Cassells, P., 'Recasting the European Social Model' in R. O'Donnell (ed.) *Europe: The Irish Experience* (Dublin: Institute of European Affairs, 2000), pp. 69–78.

Central Statistics Office (CSO), Census 2006: Commentary (Dublin: Central Statistics Office, 2006).

Central Statistics Office (CSO), *Measuring Ireland's Progress, 2006* (Dublin: Central Statistics Office, 2007).

Central Statistics Office (CSO), *Equality in Ireland 2007* (Dublin: Central Statistics Office, 2008).

Checkel, J., 'Social Construction and Integration', *Journal of European Public Policy*, 6: 4 (1999), 545–60.

Checkel, J., 'Constructing European institutions', in G. Schneider and M. Aspinwall (eds), *The Rules of Integration: Institutionalist Approaches to the Study of Europe* (Manchester: Manchester University Press, 2001a), pp. 19–39.

Checkel, J., 'Social Construction and European Integration', in T. Christiansen, E. Jorgensen and A. Wiener (eds), *The Social Construction of Europe* (London: Sage Publications (2001b), pp. 50–84.

Chubb, B., *The Government and Politics of Ireland*, third edition (London: Longman, 1992).

Cichowski, R., 'Sustaining Democracy: A Study of Authoritarianism and Personalism in Irish Political Culture', *CSD papers* (2000), www.democ.uci.edu/papers/Rachel.htm.

Clinch, P., Convery, F. and Walsh, B., *After the Celtic Tiger: Challenges Abroad* (Dublin: O'Brien Press, 2002).

Coakley, J., 'Society and Political Culture', in J. Coakley and M. Gallagher (eds), *Politics in the Republic of Ireland*, fourth edition (London: Routledge in association with PSAI Press, 2005a), pp. 36–71.

Coakley, J., 'Irish Public Opinion and the New Europe', in M. Holmes (ed.), *Ireland and the European Union: Nice Enlargement and the Future of Europe* (Manchester: Manchester University Press, 2005b), pp. 94–113.

Coakley, J. and Gallagher, M. (eds), *Politics in the Republic of Ireland*, fourth edition (London: Routledge in association with PSAI Press, 2005).

Coakley, J. and O'Dowd, L. (eds), *Crossing the Border* (Dublin: Irish Academic Press, 2007).

Coakley, J., Holmes, M. and Rees, N., 'The Irish Response to European Integration: Explaining the Persistence of Opposition', in A. W. Cafruny and C. Lankowski (eds), *Europe's Ambiguous Unity: conflict and consensus in the Post-Maastricht Era* (Boulder: Lynne Riener, 1993), pp. 209–38.

Collins, N. and Cradden, T., *Irish Politics Today*, second edition (Manchester: Manchester University Press, 1991).

Collins, N. and Cradden, T. (ed.), *Political Issues in Ireland Today* (Manchester: Manchester University Press, 2004).

Collins, N., Cradden, T. and Butler, P., *Modernising Irish Government* (Dublin: Gill & Macmillan, 2007).

Commins, P., 'The EC and the Irish Rural Economy', in P. Clancy, S. Drudy, K. Lynch and L. O'Dowd (eds) *Irish Society: Sociological Perspectives* (Dublin, Institute of Public Administration, 1995), pp. 178–204.

Commins, P. and O'Hara, P., 'Starts and Stops in Rural Development' in S. Healy and B. Reynolds (eds), *Rural Development Policy* (Dublin, Conference of Major Religious Superiors, 1991), pp. 9–41.

Commission of the European Communities (CEC), *Taking European Environment Policy Seriously* (Brussels: Commission of the European Communities, 1996).

Commission of the European Communities (CEC), *Communication on Conflict Prevention*, Com (2001) 211 final (Brussels: European Commission, 11 April 2001).

Commission of the European Communities (CEC), *Perceptions of the EU: A Qualitative Study of the Public's Attitudes and Expectations of the EU in the Fifteen Member States and in Nine Candidate Countries* (Brussels: European Commission and OPTEMSALL, 2001).

Commission of the European Communities, *Eurobarometer 68* (Brussels: European Commission, 2008).

Conlan, P., 'Ireland: Enhanced Parliamentary Scrutiny of European Affairs', in J. O'Brennan and T. Raunio (eds), *National Parliaments within the Enlarged EU: From Victims of Integration to Competitive Actors?* (London: Routledge, 2007), pp. 178–200.

Connaughton, B., 'The Impact of Coalition Government on Politico-administrative Relations in Ireland 1981–2002' in B. Guy Peters, T. Verheijen and L. Vass (eds), *Coalitions of the Unwilling? Politicians and Civil Servants in Coalition Governments* (Bratislava: Network of Institutes and Schools of Public Administration in Central and Eastern Europe (NISPAcee), 2005a), pp. 247–74.

Connaughton, B., 'EU environmental policy and Ireland', in M. Holmes (ed.), *Ireland and the European Union: Nice, Enlargement and the Future of Europe* (Manchester: Manchester University Press, 2005b), pp. 36–54.

Connaughton, B., 'Reform of Politico-administrative Relations in the Irish System: Clarifying or Complicating the Doctrine of Ministerial Responsibility?', *Irish Political Studies*, 21: 3 (2006), 257–76.

Connaughton, B., 'Ireland: Modernisation as Opposed to Radical Reform', in J. Killian and N. Eklund (eds), *Handbook of Administrative Reform: An International Perspective* (Boca Raton: CRC Press, 2008), pp. 95–113.

Connaughton, B., Quinn, B. and Rees, N., 'The Europeanisation of Irish Environmental Policy: The EU as the Engine of Domestic Policy Change', *Administration*, 54: 4 (2007), 77–93.

Connaughton, B., Quinn, B. and Rees, N., 'Rhetoric or Reality? Responding to the Challenge of Sustainable Development and New Governance Patterns in Ireland', in S. Baker and K. Eckerberg (eds), *In Pursuit of Sustainable Development: New Governance Practices at the Subnational Level in Europe* (London: Routledge, 2008).

Conway, A., 'Agricultural Policy' in P. Keatinge (ed.) *Ireland and EC Membership Evaluated* (London, Pinter Publishers, 1991), pp. 42–59.

Coulter, C. and Coleman, S. (eds), *The End of Irish History? Critical approaches to the Celtic Tiger* (Manchester: Manchester University Press, 2002).

Cowles, M. G., Caporaso, J. and Risse, T. (eds), *Transforming Europe: Europeanisation and Domestic Change* (Ithaca, NY: Cornell University Press, 2001).

Cox, P., 'The Governance of an Enlarged Europe' in D. de Buitléir, D. Ruane and F. Ruane (eds), *Governance and Policy in Ireland* (Dublin: Institute of Public Administration, 2003), pp. 17–28.

Coyle, C., 'Administrative Capacity and the Implementation of EU Environmental Policy in Ireland', in S. Baker (ed.), *Protecting the Periphery: Environmental Policy in Peripheral Regions of the European Union* (Frank Cass, 1994), pp. 62–80.

Crowley, E., *Land Matters* (Dublin: Liliput Press, 2006).

Daly, M., *The First Department* (Dublin, Institute of Public Administration, 2002).

Department of Agriculture and Food, *Annual Report 2005* (Dublin: The Stationery Office, 2006a).

Department of Agriculture and Food, *Agri Vision 2015 Action Plan* (Dublin: The Stationery Office, 2006b).

Department of Agriculture and Food, *Annual Review and Outlook for Agriculture and Food 2006–7* (Dublin: The Stationery Office, 2007).

Department of Environment, Heritage and Local Government (DoEHLG), *Waste Management: Changing Our Ways* (Dublin: DoELG, 1998).

Department of Environment, Heritage and Local Government, *Attitudes and Actions 2003: A National Survey on the Environment* (Dublin: DoEHLG, 2003).

Department of Environment, Heritage and Local Government, *National Climate Change Strategy 2007–2012* (Dublin: DoEHLG, 2007).

Department of Environment and Local Government, *Sustainable Development: A Strategy for Ireland* (Dublin: DoEHLG, 1997).

Devine, K., 'Deconstructing Concepts of Irish Neutrality', in *Irish Studies in International Affairs*, 17 (2007), 115–40.

Dimitrova, A. and Steunenberg, B., 'The Search for Convergence of National Policies in the European Union: An Impossible Quest?', *European Union Politics* 1: 2 (2000), 201–26.

Doherty, R., *Ireland, Neutrality and European Security Integration* (Aldershot: Ashgate, 2002).

Dooge, J. and Barrington, R. (eds), *A Vital National Interest: Ireland in Europe, 1973–1998* (Dublin: Institute of Public Administration, 1999).

Dooney, S. and O'Toole, J., *Irish Government Today*, second edition (Dublin: Gill and Macmillan, 1998).

Doyle, A., 'Employment Equality since Accession to the EU', in G. Kiely A. O'Donnell, P. Kennedy and S. Quinn (eds), *Irish Social Policy in Context* (Dublin: University College Dublin Press, 1999), pp. 114–38.

Drudy, P., 'The regional implications of EEC Policies in Ireland', in P. Drudy and D. McAleese (eds), *Ireland and the European Community* (Cambridge: Cambridge University Press, 1984), pp. 191–214.

Dunkerley, J., *Americana: The Americas in the World around 1850* (London: Verso, 2000).

Dyson, K.,'Economic Policy' in P. Graziano and M. Vink (eds), *Europeanisation: New Research Agendas* (Basingstoke: Palgrave, 2007), pp. 281–94.

Economic and Social Research Institute, *Quarterly Economic Commentary: Summer 2007* (Dublin: Economic and Social Research Institute, 2007).

Economic and Social Research Institute, *Irish Economy* (2008), accessed at www.esri./ irish_economy.

Elgie, R. and Fitzgerald, P., 'The President and the Taoiseach' in J. Coakley and M. Gallagher (eds), *Politics in the Republic of Ireland* (London: Routledge/ PSAI Press, 2005), pp. 305–27.

Elgie, R. and Stapleton, J., 'The Parliamentary Activity of the Head of Government in Ireland (1923–2000) in Comparative Perspective', *Journal of Legislative Studies* 9: 1 (2003), 37–56.

Environmental Protection Agency (EPA), *Ireland's Environment 2004* (Wexford: EPA, 2005).

Environmental Protection Agency (EPA), 2020 *Vision: Protecting and Improving Ireland's Environment* (Wexford: EPA, 2007).

European Council, *Conclusions* (Brussels: European Council, March 2000).

European Court of Justice (ECJ), *Commission of the European Communities v Ireland* C-494/01: ECJ (2004).

Evans, M. and Coen, L., 'Elitism and agri-environmental policy in Ireland', in M. Adshead and M. Millar (eds), *Public Administration and Public Policy in Ireland: Theory and Methods* (London: Routledge, 2003), pp. 1–29.

Fabbrini, S. and Dona, A., 'Europeanisation as Strengthening of Domestic Executive Power?', *Journal of European Integration*, 25: 1 (2003), 31–50.

Fagan, H., *Grounding Waste: Towards a Sociology of Waste Networks*, NIRSA Working Paper Series No. 18 (Maynooth: NIRSA, 2002).

Fagan, H., O'Hearn, D., McCann, G. and Murray, M., *Waste Management Strategy: A Cross-border Perspective*, NIRSA Working Papers, Series no. 2 (Maynooth: NIRSA, 2001).

Fahey, T., Hayes, B. and Sinnott, R., *Conflict and Consensus* (Dublin: IPA, Institute of Public Administration, 2005).

Falkner, G., 'Comparing Europeanisation Effects: From Metaphor to Operational-isation', *European Integration on-line Papers*, 7 (2003), www.eiop.or.at/eiop/ texte/2003.

Falkner, G. and Laffan, B., 'The Europeanisation of Austria and Ireland: Small Can Be Difficult?', in S. Bulmer and C. Lequesne (eds), *The Member States of the European Union* (Oxford: Oxford University Press, 2005), pp. 209–28.

Falkner, G., Treib, O., Hartlapp, M. and Leiber, S., *Complying with Europe: EU Harmonisation and Soft Law in the Member States* (Cambridge: Cambridge University Press, 2005).

Fahey, T., Hayes, B. and Sinnott, R., *Conflict and Consensus* (Dublin: Institute of Public Administration, 2005).

Fahey, T., Russell, H. and Whelan, C. T. (eds), *Best of Times? The Social Impact of the Celtic Tiger* (Dublin: Institute of Public Administration, 2007).

Fanning, R., *Irish Department of Finance, 1922–58* (Dublin: Institute of Public Administration, 1978).

Farrell, D., 'Ireland: A Party System Transformed', in D. Broughton and M. Donovan (eds), *Changing Party Systems in Western Europe* (London: Pinter, 1999), pp. 30–47.

Featherstone, K., 'Introduction: In the Name of 'Europe', in K. Featherstone and C. Radaelli (eds), *The Politics of Europeanisation* (Oxford: Oxford University Press, 2003), pp. 3–26.

Featherstone, K. and Radaelli, C. M. (eds), *The Politics of Europeanisation* (Oxford: Oxford University Press, 2003).

Finnegan, R. B., 'Ireland: Brussels and the Celtic Tiger', in E. E. Zeff and E. B. Pirro (eds), *The European Union and the Member States: Cooperation, Coordination and Compromise* (London: Lynne Rienner, 2001), pp. 175–90.

FitzGerald, J., 'The Story of Ireland's Failure: and Belated Success', in B. Nolan, P. J. O'Connell and C. T. Whelan (eds), *Understanding Ireland's Economic Growth* (Dublin: Institute of Public Administration, 2000).

Fitzpatrick Associates, *CSF 2000–2006 Update Evaluation* (Dublin: Fitzpatrick Associates, 2005).

Forfás, *Key Waste Management Issues in Ireland* (Dublin: Forfás, 2001).

Flynn, B., 'Ireland: The Triumph of Policy Style over Substance', in A. Jordan and D. Liefferink (eds), *Environmental Policy in Europe: The Europeanization of National Environmental Policy* (London: Routledge, 2004), pp. 118–35.

Flynn, B., *The Blame Game: Rethinking Ireland's Sustainable Development and Economic Performance* (Dublin: Irish Academic Press, 2007).

Fouilleux, E., 'The Common Agricultural Policy' in M. Cini (ed.), *European Union Politics*, second edition (Oxford: Oxford University Press, 2007) pp. 340–55.

Gallagher, M., 'Parliament' in J. Coakley and M. Gallagher (eds), *Politics in the Republic of Ireland* (London: Routledge/PSAI Press, 2005), pp. 211–41.

Gallup, *Citizens' Perceptions of EU regional policy*, Flash Eurobarometer, no. 234 (Brussels: DG Regional Policy, 2008).

Garvin, T., *Preventing the Future: Why Was Ireland Poor for So Long?* (Dublin: Gill and Macmillan, 2004).

Garvin, T., *The Birth of Irish Democracy* (Dublin: Gill and Macmillan, 1996).

Gilland Lutz, K., 'Irish Party Competition in the New Millennium: Change, or Plus ca Change?', *Irish Political Studies,* 18: 2 (2003), 40–59.

Gilland, K., 'Ireland's (First) Referendum on the Treaty of Nice', *Journal of Common Market Studies,* 40 (2002), 527–35.

Girvin, B., *From Union to Union* (Dublin: Gill & Macmillan, 2002).

Girvin, B., *The Emergency: Neutral Ireland, 1939–45* (London: Pan Macmillan, 2006).

Girvin, B. and Roberts, G. (eds), *Ireland and the Second World War: Politics, Society and Remembrance* (Dublin: Four Courts Press, 2000).

Giuliani, E., *Multi-level Governance and Institutional Change: The Europeanisation of Regional Policy in Italy* (Aldershot: Ashgate, 2004).

Giuliani, M., 'Europeanisation in Comparative Perspective: Institutional Fit and National Adaptation' in K. Featherstone and C. Radaelli (eds) *The Politics of Europeanisation* (Oxford: Oxford University Press, 2003), pp. 134–58.

Goetz, K. and Hix, S. (eds), 'European Integration and National Executives: A Cause in Search of Effect?', *Special Edition of West European Politics* 23: 4 (2000), 211–31.

Goetz, K. and Hix, S. (eds), *Europeanised Politics? European Integration and National Political Systems* (London: Frank Cass, 2001).

Government of Ireland, *National Development Plan 1994–1999* (Dublin Stationery Office, 1993).

Government of Ireland, *Challenges and Opportunities Abroad: White Paper on Foreign Policy* (Dublin: Department of Foreign Affairs, 1996a).

Government of Ireland, *Delivering Better Government: A Programme of Change for the Irish Civil Service, Second Report of the Coordinating Group of Secretaries* (Dublin: Stationery Office, 1996b).

Government of Ireland, *National Development Plan 2000–2006* (Dublin Stationery Office, 1999).

Government of Ireland, *National Development Plan 2007–2013* (Dublin Stationery Office, 2007a).

Government of Ireland, *National Strategic Reference Framework* (Dublin Stationery Office, 2007b).

Gowland, D., Dunphy, R. and Lythe, C., *The European Mosaic* (Harlow: Prentice Hall, 2006).

Graziano, P. and Vink, M. (eds), *Europeanisation: New Research Agendas* (Basingstoke: Palgrave, 2007).

Greer, A., *Agricultural Policy in Europe* (Manchester: Manchester University Press 2005a).

Greer, A., 'Farm Interest Groups in Ireland: Adaptation, Partnership and Resilience', in D. Halpin (ed.), *Surviving Global Change: Agricultural Interest Groups in Comparative Perspective* (Aldershot: Ashgate, 2005b), pp. 51–70.

Greer, A., 'Agriculture', in M. Adshead and M. Millar (eds), *Governance and Public Policy in Ireland* (Dublin: Irish Academic Press, 2009).

Haas, E. B., *The Uniting of Europe: Political, Social and Economic Forces, 1950–57* (Stanford, Ca: Stanford University Press, 1958).

Halligan, B., 'The Political Perspective in 1972' in R. O'Donnell (ed.), *Europe: The Irish Experience* (Dublin: Institute of European Affairs, 2000), pp. 18–34.

Hardiman, N., 'From Conflict to Coordination: Economic Governance and Political Innovation in Ireland', *West European Politics* 25: 4 (2002), 1–24.

Harmsen, R., 'The Europeanisation of National Administrations: A Comparative Study of France and the Netherlands', *Governance*, 12: 1 (1999), 81–113.

Hart, J., 'The European Regional Development Fund and the Republic of Ireland', in M. Keating and B. Jones (eds), *Regions in the European Community* (Oxford: Clarendon Press, 1985).

Hart, J. and Laffan, B., 'Consequences of the Community's Regional and Social Policies' in D. Coombes (ed.), *Ireland and the European Communities: Ten Years of Membership* (Dublin: Gill and Macmillan,1983), pp. 133–57.

Haslam, R., 'The Origins of Irish Local Government' in M. Callanan and J. F. Keogan (eds), *Local Government in Ireland Inside Out* (Dublin: Institute of Public Administration, 2003), pp. 14–40.

Hastings, T., Sheelan, B. and Yeates, P. *Saving the Future: How Social Partnership Shaped Ireland's Economic Success* (Dublin: Blackhall Publishing, 2007).

Haughton, J., 'The Dynamics of Economic Change', in W. Crotty and D. E. Schmitt (eds), *Ireland and the Politics of Change* (London: Longman, 1998), pp. 27–50.

Haverland, M., 'National Adaptation to European Integration: The Importance of National Veto Points', *Journal of European Public Policy*, 20: 1 (2000), 83–103.

Haverland, M., 'The Impact of the European Union on National Environmental Policies', in K. Featherstone and C. M. Radailli (eds), *The Politics of Europeanisation* (Oxford: Oxford University Press, 2003), pp. 203–21.

Haverland, M., 'Does the EU *Cause* Domestic Development? Improvising Case Selection in European Research', *West European Politics*, 29: 1 (2006), 134–46.

Hayward, K., '"If at first You Don't Succeed" . . . The Second Referendum on the Treaty of Nice 2002', *Irish Political Studies*, 18: 1 (2003), 120–32.

Hayward, K., 'A Marriage of Convenience? Ireland's Regionalisation and EU Integration', paper presented to the PSAI conference, Cork, 13–15 October 2006.

Hayward, K., 'Building on the EU's legacy: Cross-border Cooperation in Ireland', *European Administration*, 55: 3 (2007a), 53–74.

Hayward, K. and MacCarthaigh, M. (eds), *Recycling the State* (Dublin: Irish Academic Press, 2007b).

Hay, C. and Rosamond, B., 'Globalisation, European Integration and the Discursive Construction of Economic Imperatives', *Journal of European Public Policy*, 9: 2 (2002), 147–67.

Hederman-O'Brien, M., *The Road to Europe: Irish Attitudes, 1948–1961* (Dublin: Institute of Public Administration, 1983).

Hennis, M., 'Europeanisation and Globalization', *Journal of Common Market Studies*, 39: 5 (2001), 829–50.

Héritier, A., 'Differential Europe: National Administrative Responses to Community Policy' in M. Cowles, J. Caporaso and T. Risse (eds), *Transforming Europe: Europeanization and Domestic Change* (Ithaca NY: Cornell University Press, 2001), pp. 44–59.

Héritier, A. and Knill, C., 'Differential Responses to European Policies: A Comparison', in A. Hértier *et al.* (eds), *Differential Europe: The European Union Impact on National Policy-Making* (Lanham, MD: Rowman and Littlefield, 2001), pp. 257–94.

Héritier, A., Kerwer, D., Knill, C., Lehmkuhl, D., Teutsch, M., Douillet, A. (eds), *Differential Europe: The European Union Impact on National Policy-making* (Lanham, MD: Rowman and Littlefield, 2001).

Hildebrand, P., 'The European Community's Environmental Policy, 1957 to "1992": from incidental measures to an international regime?' *Environmental Politics*, 1: 4 (1993), 13–44.

Hill, C., 'The Capability–Expectations Gap, or Conceptualising Europe's International Role', *Journal of Common Market Studies*, 31: 3 (1993), pp. 305–25.

Hill, C. and Smith, M. (eds), *International Relations and the European Union* (Oxford: Oxford University Press, 2005).

Hix, S. (ed.), National Integration and National Political Systems, *West European Politics*, 23: 4 (2000), 27–51.

Hix, S., *The Political System of the European Union* second edition (London: Palgrave Macmillan, 2005).

Hix, S. and Goetz, K., 'Introduction: European Integration and National Political Systems', *West European Politics*, special issue, 23: 4 (2000), 1–26.

Hoffmann, S., 'Reflections on the Nation State in Western Europe', *Journal of Common Market Studies*, 20: 1 (1982), 29–37.

Holmes, M., 'The Development of Opposition to European Integration in Ireland', in M. Holmes (ed.), *Ireland and the European Union: Nice Enlargement and the Future of Europe* (Manchester: Manchester University Press, 2005), pp. 75–93.

Holmes, M. (ed.), *Ireland and the European Union: Nice Enlargement and the Future of Europe* (Manchester: Manchester University Press, 2005).

Holmes, M. and Rees, N., 'Regions within a Region: The Paradox of the Republic of Ireland', in B. Jones and M. Keating (eds), *The European Union and the Regions* (Oxford: Clarendon Press, 1995), 231–48.

Holmes, M. and Rees, N., 'Capacity, Perceptions and Principles: Ireland's Changing Place in Europe', *Current Politics and Economics of Europe*, special edition, 11: 1: (2002), 49–60.

Holmes, M., Rees, N. and Whelan, B., *The Poor Relation: Irish Foreign Policy and the Third World* (Dublin: Trocaire/Gill and Macmillan, 1993).

Holsti, O., *Public Opinion and American Foreign Policy* (Michigan: University of Michigan Press, 2004).

Hooghe, L. and Marks, G., *Multi-level Governance and European Integration* (New York: Rowman and Littlefield, 2001).

Hooghe, L. and Marks, G., 'Unravelling the Central State: But How?', *American Political Science Review*, 97: 2 (2003), 233–4.

Honohan, P. and Walsh, B., 'Catching up with the Leaders: the Irish Hare' *Brookings Papers on Economic Activity* (Washington, DC: Brookings Institution, 2002).

Hourihane, J. (ed.), *Ireland and the European Union: The First Thirty Years, 1973–2002* (Dublin: Lilliput Press, 2004).

House, J. D. and McGrath, K., 'Innovative Governance and Development in the New Ireland: Social Partnership and the Integrated Approach', *Governance: An International Journal of Policy, Administration, and Institutions*, 17: 1 (2004), 29–58.

Hughes, I., Clancy, P., Harris, C. and Beetham, D., *Power to the People?: Assessing Democracy in Ireland* (Dublin: TASC, 2007).

Humphreys, P., *The Fifth Irish Presidency: Some Management Lessons, CPMR Discussion Paper 2* (Dublin: Institute of Public Administration, 1997).

Industrial Policy Review Group, *A Time for Change: Industrial Policy for the 1990s* (Dublin: The Stationery Office, 1992).

International Social Survey Programme, *National Identity: International Data 1994–1996* (ISSP Study no. 0028, 1995), www.issp.org/.

Jordan, A., 'Introduction: European Union Environmental Policy – Actors, Institutions and Policy Process', in A. Jordan (ed.) *Environmental Policy in the European Union: Actors, Institutions and Processes*, second edition (London: Earthscan, 2005), pp. 1–18.

Jordan, A. and Liefferink, D. (eds), *Environmental Policy in Europe: The Europeanisation of National Environmental Policy* (London: Routledge, 2004).

Jordan, A., Wurzel, R. and Zito, A., 'The Rise of "New" Policy Instruments in Comparative Perspective: Has Governance Eclipsed Government?', *Political Studies*, 53: 3 (2005), 477–96.

Jordana, J., Levi-Faur, D. and Puig, P., 'The Limits of Europeanisation: Telecommunications and Electricity Liberalisation in Spain and Portugal', *Governance*, 19: 3 (2006), 437–64.

Kassim, H., 'Conclusion', in H. Kassim, A. Mennon, B. G. Peters and V. Wright (eds), *The National Coordination of EU Policy: The Domestic Level* (Oxford: Oxford University Press, 2000) pp. 235–64.

Kassim, H., 'Meeting the Demands of EU Membership: The Europeanisation of National Administrative Systems', in K. Featherstone and C. M. Radaelli (eds), *The Politics of Europeanisation* (Oxford: Oxford University Press, 2003), pp. 83–111.

Kassim, H., 'Member States Institutions and the European Union: Impact and Interaction', in S. Bulmer and C. Lequesne (eds), *The Member States and the EU* (Oxford: Oxford University Press, 2005), pp. 285–316.

Kassim, H., Mennon, A., Peters, B. G. and Wright, V. (eds), *The National Coordination of EU Policy: The European Level* (Oxford: Oxford University Press, 2000).

Keatinge, P., *The Formulation of Irish Foreign Policy* (Dublin: Institute of Public Administration, 1973).

Keatinge, P., *A Place Among the Nations: Issues of Irish Foreign Policy* (Dublin: Institute of Public Administration, 1978).

Keatinge, P., *A Singular Stance: Irish Neutrality in the 1980s* (Dublin: Institute of Public Administration, 1984).

Keatinge, P., *European Security: Ireland's Choices* (Dublin: Institute of European Affairs, 1996).

Kelly, M. and Rolston, B., 'Broadcasting in Ireland' in P. Clancy *et al.* (eds), *Irish Society: Sociological Perspectives* (Dublin: Institute of Public Administration, 1995).

Kennedy, K. and Dowling, B., *Economic Growth in Ireland: The Experience since 1957* (Dublin: Gill and Macmillan, 1975).

Kennedy, M. and McMahon, D. (eds), *Obligations and Responsibilities: Ireland and the United Nations, 1955–2005* (Dublin: Institute of Public Administration, 2005).

Kennedy, M. and Skelly, J. (eds), *Irish Foreign Policy, 1919–1966* (Dublin: Four Courts Press, 2000).

Keogan, J. F., 'Reform in Irish Local Government', in M. Callanan and J. F. Keogan (eds), *Local Government in Ireland Inside Out* (Dublin: Institute of Public Administration, 2003), pp. 82–96.

Keohane, D., 'Realigning Neutrality: Irish Defence Policy and the EU', Occasional Paper 24 (Paris: EU Institute for Security Studies, March 2001).

Keown, G., 'Creating an Irish Foreign Policy in the 1920s', in M. Kennedy and J. Skelly (eds), *Irish Foreign Policy, 1919–1966* (Dublin: Four Courts Press, 2000), pp. 25–43.

Kirby, P., *Poverty Amid Plenty: World and Irish Development Reconsidered* (Dublin: Gill and Macmillan, 1997).

Kirby, P., *The Celtic Tiger in Distress: Growth with Inequality in Ireland* (Basingstoke: Palgrave, 2002).

Kirby, P., Jacobson, D. and Ó Broin, D. (eds), *Taming the Tiger: Social Exclusion in a Globalised Ireland* (Dublin: New Island Press, 2006).

Kitchin, R. and Bartley, B., 'Ireland in the Twenty First Century', in B. Bartley and R. Kitchin (eds), *Understanding Contemporary Ireland* (London: Pluto Press, 2007), pp. 1–26.

Knill, C., 'European Policies: The Impact of National Administrative Traditions', *Journal of Public Policy*, 18: 1 (1998), 1–28.

Knill, C., *The Europeanisation of National Administrations: Administrative Patterns of Institutional Change and Persistence* (Cambridge: Cambridge University Press, 2001).

Knill, C., 'Environmental Policy', in B. G. Peters and J. Pierre (eds), *The Handbook of Public Policy* (London: Sage, 2006), pp. 249–64.

Knill, C. and Lehmkuhl, D., 'How Europe Matters: Different Mechanism of Europeanisation', *European Integration Papers on Line*, 3: 7 (1999), www.eiop.or.st/eiop/texte/1999–007.htm.

Knill, C. and Lehmkuhl, D. 'The National Impact of European Union Regulatory Policy: Three Europeanisation Mechanisms', European Journal of Political Research 41: 2 (2002), 255–80.

Knill, C. and Lenschow, A., 'Coping with Europe: The Impact of British and German Administrations on the Implementation of Environmental Policy, *Journal of European Public Policy*, 5: 4 (1998), 595–615.

Knill, C. and Lenschow, A. (eds), *Implementing EU Environmental Policy: New Directions and Old Problems* (Manchester: Manchester University Press, 2000).

Knill, C. and Liefferink, D., *Environmental Politics in the European Union* (Manchester: Manchester University Press, 2007).

Kohler-Koch, B., 'Catching Up with Change: the Transformation of Governance in the European Union', *Journal of European Public Policy*, 3: 3 (1996), 359–80.

Kohler-Koch, B. and Eisling, R. (eds), *The Transformation of Governance* (London: Routledge, 2000).

Ladrech, R., 'Europeanisation of Domestic Politics and Institutions: The Case of France', *Journal of Common Market Studies*, 32: 1 (1994), 69–88.

Ladrech, R., 'Europeanisation and Political Parties Towards a Framework for Analysis', *Party Politics*, 8: 4 (2002), 389–403.

Laffan, B., 'Ireland', in D. Rometsch and W. Wessels (eds), *The European Union and Member States: Towards Institutional Fusion?* (Manchester, Manchester University Press,1996a), pp. 291–312.

Laffan, B., 'Ireland: A Region without Regions – the Odd Man Out', in L. Hooghe (ed.) *Cohesion Policy and European Integration* (Oxford: Oxford University Press, 1996b), pp. 320–41.

Laffan, B., 'Rapid Adaptation and Light Co-ordination' in R. O'Donnell (ed.), *Europe: The Irish Experience* (Dublin: Institute of European Affairs, 2000), pp. 125–47.

Laffan, B., *Organising for a Changing Europe: Irish Central Government and the European Union* (Dublin: Policy Institute, Trinity College Dublin, 2001).

Laffan, B., 'Ireland and the European Union', in W. Crotty and D. Schmitt (eds), *Ireland on the World Stage* (London: Longman, 2002), pp. 83–94.

Laffan, B., 'Ireland: modernisation via Europeanisation', in W. Wessels, A. Maurer and J. Mittag (eds), *Fifteen into One? The European Union and Its Member States* (Manchester: Manchester University Press, 2003), pp. 248–70.

Laffan, B., 'Irish Government and European Governance', in T. Garvin, M. Manning and R. Sinnott (eds) *Dissecting Irish Politics: Essays in Honour of Brian Farrell* (Dublin: University College Dublin Press, 2004), pp. 116–33.

Laffan, B., 'The Impact of Nice on Public Administration, in Michael Holmes (eds) *Ireland and the European Union: Nice, Enlargement and the Future of Europe* (Manchester: Manchester University Press, 2005a) pp. 171–88.

Laffan, B., 'Ireland's Management of EU Business: The Impact of Nice' in M. Holmes (ed.), *Ireland and the European Union: Nice, Enlargement and the Future of Europe* (Manchester: Manchester University Press, 2005b), pp. 171–88.

Laffan, B., 'Managing Europe from Home in Dublin, Athens and Helsinki: A Comparative Analysis', *West European Politics*, 29: 4 (2006), 687–708.

Laffan, B., 'Managing European Dossiers in the Irish Civil Service: Living with the EU System?', in M. Callanan (ed.), *Foundations of an Ever Closer Union: An Irish Perspective on the Fifty Years since the Treaty of Rome* (Dublin: Institute of Public Administration, 2007), pp. 175–94.

Laffan, B. and O'Donnell, R., 'Ireland and the Growth of International Governance', in W. Crotty and D. E. Schmitt (eds), *Ireland and the Politics of Change* (London: Longman, 1998), pp. 156–77.

Laffan, B. and O'Mahony, J., *Managing Europe from Home: the Europeanisation of the Core Executive*, Occasional Paper, 1.1 (Dublin: Dublin European Institute, 2003).

Laffan, B. and O'Mahony, J., 'Mis-fit, Politicisation and Europeanisation: The Implementation of the Habitats Directive in Ireland', *OEUE Occasional Paper* (Dublin: OEUE, 2004).

Laffan, B. and O'Mahony, J., 'Managing Europe from an Irish Perspective: Critical Junctures and the Increasing Formalisation of the Core Executive in Ireland', *Public Administration*, 85: 1 (2007) 167–88.

Laffan, B. and Tannam, E., 'Ireland: The Rewards of Pragmatism', in K. Hanf and B. Soetendorp (eds) *Adapting to European Integration: Small States and the European Union* (London: Longman, 1998), pp. 69–83.

Laffan, B. and Tonra, B., 'Europe and the International Dimension', in J. Coakley and M. Gallagher (eds), *Politics in the Republic of Ireland*, fourth edition (London: Routledge in association with PSAI Press, 2005), pp. 430–61.

Lafferty, W. and Meadowcroft, J. (eds), *Implementing Sustainable Development: Strategies and Initiatives in High Consumption Societies* (Oxford: Oxford University Press, 2000).

Larsen, H., 'The EU: A Global Military Actor?', *Cooperation and Conflict*, 37: 3 (2002), 283–302.

Laver, M. and Hunt, W. B., *Party and Party Competition* (London: Routledge, 1992).

Leddin, A. and Walsh, B., *The Macroeconomy of the Eurozone: An Irish Perspective* (Dublin: Gill and Macmillan, 2003).

Lee, J. J., *Reflections on Ireland in the EEC* (Dublin Irish Council for the European Movement, 1984).

Lee, J. J., *Ireland 1912–1985: Politics and Society* (Cambridge: Cambridge University Press, 1989).

Lee, J. J., 'From Empire to Europe: The Irish State, 1922–73', in M. Adshead, P. Kirby and M. Millar (eds), *Contesting the State: Lessons from the Irish Case* (Manchester: Manchester University Press, 2008), pp. 25–49.

Lemass, S., Statement to Ministers of the Member States of the European Economic Community, Brussels, 18 January in Maher, D., *The Tortuous Path* (Dublin: Institute of Public Administration, 1986), pp. 375–85.

Lenschow, A., 'Transformation in European Environmental Governance', in B. Kohler-Koch and R. Eising, R. (eds), *The Transformation of Governance in the European Union* (London: Routledge, 1999), pp. 39–60.

Lenschow, A., 'Europeanisation of Public Policy' in J. Richardson (ed.), *European Union: Power and Policy-making*, third edition (London: Routledge, 2006), pp. 55–72.

Leonard, L., *Green Nation: The Irish Environmental Movement from Carnsore Point to the Rossport Five* (Drogheda: Choice Publishing, 2006).

Lijphart, A., *Patterns of Democracy: Government Forms and Performance in Thirty Six Countries* (New Haven, CT and London: Yale University Press, 1999).

Lynch, B., *EMU: Ireland's Dream Start* (Dublin: Institute of European Affairs, 2008).

MacCarthaigh, M., *Accountability in Irish Parliamentary Politics* (Dublin: Institute of Public Administration, 2005).

MacCarthaigh, M., *The Corporate Governance of Regional and Local Public Service Bodies in Ireland CPMR Research Report 8* (Dublin: IPA, 2007).

Mac Sharry, R., 'Changes in the Common Agricultural Policy and Its Implications for Regional Development', in M. Cuddy and T. A. Boylan (eds), *The Future of Regional Policy in the European Communities* (Galway: Social Sciences Research Centre, 1987), pp. 41–8.

Mac Sharry, R., 'Reform of the CAP', in J. Dooge and R. Barrington (eds), *A Vital National Interest: Ireland in Europe* (Dublin: IPA, 1999), pp. 295–311.

Mac Sharry, R., 'Achieving Convergence and Cohesion within the EU' in R. Mac Sharry and P. White (eds), *The Making of the Celtic Tiger* (Cork: Mercier Press, 2000), pp. 162–77.

Mac Sharry, R. and White, P., *The Making of The Celtic Tiger: The Inside Story of Ireland's Boom Economy* (Dublin: Mercier Press, 2000).

Maher, D. J., *The Tortuous Path: The Course of Ireland's Entry into the EEC, 1948–73* (Dublin: Institute of Public Administration, 1986).

Mair, P., 'The Limited Impact of Europe on National Party Systems', in K. H. Goetz and S. Hix (eds), *Europeanised Politics? European Integration and National Political Systems* (London: Frank Cass, 2001), pp. 27–51.

Mair, P. and Weeks, L., 'The Party System' in J. Coakley and M. Gallagher (eds), *Politics in the Republic of Ireland*, fourth edition (London: Routledge in association with PSAI Press, 2005), pp. 135–59.

Majone, G., *Regulating Europe* (London: Routledge, 1996).

Malone, M., 'Empowering Parliaments? The 2004 Constitution for Europe and the Evolving Role of National Parliaments in the European Union', in M. Mulreany and T. McNamara (eds) *Governance Issues in the Irish Public Sector, Administration 55*: 1 (2007), 117–48.

March, J. and Olsen, J., *Rediscovering Institutions: The Organisational Basis of Politics* (New York: Free Press, 1989).

Marks, G., 'Structural Policy and Multilevel Governance in the EC', in A. W. Cafruny and G. G. Rosenthal (eds), *The State of the European Community: The Maastricht Debates and Beyond*, vol. 2 (Boulder, CO: Lynne Rienner, 1993) pp. 391–411.

Marks, G., 'An Actor-centered Approach to Multi-level Governance', in C. Jeffery (ed.), *The Regional Dimension of the European Union: Towards a Third Level in Europe* (London: Frank Cass, 1996), pp. 20–40.

Marks, G., Hooghe, L. and Blank, K., 'European Integration from the 1980s: State Centric v Multi-level Governance', *Journal of Common Market Studies*, 34: 3 (1996), 341–78.

Mastenbroek, E. and van Keulen, M., 'Beyond the Goodness of Fit: A Preference Based Account of Europeanisation', in R. Holzhacker and M. Haverland (eds), *European Research Reloaded: Cooperation and Integration Among Europeanised States* (New York: Springer, 2006), pp. 19–42.

Matthews, A., 'The Economic Consequences of EEC Membership for Ireland', in D. Coombes (ed.), *Ireland and the EEC* (Dublin: Gill and MacMillan, 1983), pp. 110–98.

Mattila, M., 'Fiscal Transfers and Redistribution in the European Union: Do Smaller States Get More Than Their Share?', *Journal of European Public Policy*, 13: 1 (2006), 34–51.

Mawhinney, K., 'Environmental Conservation: Concern and Action, 1920–1970', in M. J. Bannon, J. Hendry and K. Mawhinney (eds), *Planning: The Irish Experience 1920–1988* (Dublin: Wolfhound, 1989), pp. 86–104.

Mbaye, H., 'Why National States Comply with Supranational Law: Explaining Implementation Infringements in the European Union, 1972–1993', *European Union Politics*, 2: 3 (2001), 259–82.

McAleese, D., 'Ireland the European Community: The Changing Pattern of Trade', in P. J. Drudy and D. McAleese (eds), *Ireland and the European Community* (Cambridge: Cambridge University Press, 1984), 145–72.

McAleese, D., 'Twenty-five Years a Growing', in R. O'Donnell, *Europe: The Irish Experience* (Dublin: Institute of European Affairs, 2000), pp. 79–111.

McCarthy, E. and Yearley, S., 'The Irish Environmental Protection Agency: The Early Years – Profile', *Environmental Politics*, 4: 4 (1995), 258–64.

McDonagh, J., *Renegotiating Rural Development in Ireland* (Aldershot: Ashgate, 2001).

McDonald, F., 'Report Shows up Grim Reality of Ireland's Greenhouse Gas Record', *Irish Times* (16 February 2007).

McGowan, L. and Murphy, M., 'Europeanisation and the Irish Experience', in Adshead, M. and Millar, M. (eds), *Public Administration and Public Policy in Ireland* (London: Routledge, 2005), pp. 182–200.

McSweeney, B., *Ireland and the Threat of Nuclear War: The Question of Irish Neutrality* (Dublin, Dominican Publications, 1985).

Meny, Y., Muller, P. and Quermonne, J. L., *Adjusting to Europe: The Impact of the European Union on National Institutions and Policies* (London: Routledge, 1996).

Milward, A. S., *The European Rescue of the Nation-State* (London: Routledge, 1992).

Moravcsik, A., 'Negotiating the Single European Act: National Interests and Conventional Statecraft in the European Community', *International Organization*, 45: 1 (1991), 19–56.

Motherway, B., Kelly, M., Faughan, P. and Tovey, H., *Trends in Irish Environmental Attitudes between 1993 and 2002: A Report from the Research Programme on Environmental Attitudes, Values and Behaviour in Ireland* (Dublin: Social Science Research Centre, UCD, 2003).

Mullally, G., 'Relocating Protest: Globalization and the Institutionalization of Organized Environmentalism in Ireland?', in L. Connolly and N, Hourigan (eds), *Social Movements in Ireland* (Manchester: Manchester University Press, 2006), pp. 145–67.

Mulreanny, M., Foley, A. and Malone, M., 'The Single Market: Constantly Evolving and Adapting', in M. Callanan (ed.), *Foundations of an Ever Closer Union: An Irish Perspective on the Fifty Years since the Treaty of Rome* (Dublin: Institute of Public Administration, 2007), pp. 57–76.

Murphy, G., *Economic Realignment and the Politics of EEC Entry: Ireland 1948–72* (Bethesda Academic Press, 2003a).

Murphy, G., 'Towards a Corporate State? Sean Lemass and the Realignment of Interest Groups in the Policy Process 1948–1964', *Administration*, 51: 1–2 (2003b), 105–18.

Murphy, G., 'Interest Groups in the Policy-making Process', in J. Coakley and M. Gallagher (eds), *Politics in the Republic of Ireland*, fourth edition (London: Routledge in association with PSAI Press, 2005), pp. 352–83.

National Competitiveness Council, *Annual Competitiveness Report, 2007*, vols 1 and 2 (Dublin: Forfas/National Competitivenees Council, 2007).

National Economic and Social Council, *Ireland in the European Community: Performance, Prospects and Strategy*, no. 89 (Dublin: National Economic and Social Council, 1989).

National Economic and Social Council, *The Developmental Welfare State* (Dublin: National Economic & Social Council, 2005).

Norton, P. (ed.), *Parliaments and Governments in Western Europe* (London: Frank Cass, 1998).

Nugent, N., *The Government and Politics of the European Union* (Basingstoke: Palgrave Macmillan, 2003).

Niedemeyer, O. and Sinnott, R. (eds), *Public Opinion and Institutionalised Governance* (Oxford: Oxford University Press, 1995).

Nuttall, S., *European Political Cooperation* (Oxford: Oxford University Press, 1992).

Oberreuter, H. (ed.), *Parlamentärische Opposition: Ein Internationaler Vergleich* (Hamburg: Hoffman and Campe, 1975).

Office of the First Minister and Deputy First Minister *Taking Our Place in Europe: Northern Ireland's European Strategy* (Belfast: OFMDFM, 2006).

Organisation for Economic Cooperation and Development (OECD), *Environmental Performance Reviews: Ireland* (Paris: Organisation for Economic Cooperation and Development, 2000).

Organisation for Economic Cooperation and Development (OECD), *Modernising Government: The Way Forward* (Paris: OECD, 2005).

Organisation for Economic Cooperation and Development (OECD), *Ireland: Towards an Integrated Public Service* (Paris: OECD, 2008).

Olsen, J. P., 'Europeanisation and the Nation-state Dynamics', in S. Gutsavsson and L. Lewin (eds), *The Future of the Nation State* (Stockholm: Nerenius and Santeurus, 1996).

Olsen, J. P., 'The Many Faces of Europeanisation', *Journal of Common Market Studies*, 40: 5 (2002), 921–52.

O'Brennan, J., 'Ireland's European Discourse and the National Forum on Europe', in M. Holmes (ed.), *Ireland and the European Union: Nice, Enlargement and the Future of Europe* (Manchester: Manchester University Press, 2005), pp. 114–32.

O'Brennan, J., *The Eastern Enlargement of the European Union* (London: Routledge, 2006).

Ó'Broin, D., 'Democratising Local Governance in Ireland', in D. Jacobsen, P. Kirby and D. Ó'Broin (eds), *Taming the Tiger: Social Exclusion in a Globalised World* (Dublin: New Island, 2006), pp. 154–79.

O'Carroll, J. P., 'Culture Lag and Democratic Deficit in Ireland: Or, Dat's Outside the Terms of D'agreement', *Community Development Journal*, 37: 1 (2002), 10–19.

O'Donnell, R. (ed.), *Economic and Monetary Union*, Studies in European Union, no. 2 (Dublin: Institute of European Affairs, 1991a).

O'Donnell, R., 'Environmental Policy', in P. Keatinge (ed.), *Ireland and EC Membership Evaluated* (London: Pinter Publishers, 1991b), pp. 118–25.

O'Donnell, R., *Europe: The Irish Experience* (Dublin: Institute of European Affairs, 2000a).

O'Donnell, R., 'The New Ireland in the New Europe', in R. O'Donnell (ed.) *Europe: The Irish Experience* (Dublin: Institute of European Affairs, 2000b), pp. 161–214.

O'Donnell, R., 'The Celtic Tiger', paper presented to the Re-imagining Ireland Conference, University of Virginia, USA, May, 2003.

O'Donnell, R., 'The Partnership State: Building the Ship at Sea', in M. Adshead, P. Kirby and M. Millar (eds), *Contesting the State: Lessons from the Irish Case* (Manchester: Manchester University Press, 2008), pp. 73–99.

O'Donnell, R. and Walsh, J., 'Ireland: Region and State in the European Union', in M. Rhodes (ed.), *The Regions and the New Europe* (Manchester: Manchester University Press, 1995).

Ó Gráda, C., *A Rocky Road: the Irish Economy since the 1920s* (Manchester: Manchester University Press, 1997).

Ó Grada, C., *Ireland: A New Economic History, 1780–1939* (Oxford: Oxford University Press, 1995).

O'Hagan, J. and Newman, C., *The Economy of Ireland: National and Sectoral Policy Issues* (Dublin: Gill and Macmillan, 2005).

O'Halpin, E., *Defending Ireland: The Irish State and Its Enemies since 1922* (Oxford: Oxford University Press, 1999).

O'Hearn, D., 'Macroeconomic Policy in the Celtic Tiger: A Critical Assessment', in C. Coulter and S. Coleman (eds), *The End of Irish History? Critical Reflections on the Celtic Tiger* (Manchester: Manchester University Press, 2003), pp. 34–55.

O'Kennedy, M., 'The Evolution of Economic and Budgetary Policy, 1973–83', in J. Dooge and R. Barrington (eds), *A Vital National Interest: Ireland in Europe, 1973–1998* (Dublin: Institute of Public Administration, 1999), 267–81.

O'Mahony, J., '"Not So Nice": the Treaty of Nice, the International Criminal Court and the Abolition of the Death Penalty: The 2001 referendum experience', *Irish Political Studies*, 16 (2001), 201–13.

O'Mahony, J., 'Europeanisation as Implementation': The Impact of the European Union on Environmental Policy Making in Ireland', *Irish Political Studies*, 22: 3 (2007), 265–86.

O'Riain, S., 'The Flexible Development State: Globalization, Information Technology and the "Celtic Tiger"', *Politics and Society*, 28: 3 (2000): 3–37.

O'Sullivan, M. J., *Ireland and the Global Question* (Cork: Cork University Press, 2006).

Ó Tuathaigh, M. A. G., 'The Regional Dimension' in K. Kennedy (ed.), *Ireland in Transition* (Cork: Mercier Press, 1986), pp. 120–32.

PA Consulting Group, *Evaluation of the Strategic Management Initiative* (Dublin: PA Consulting, 2002).

Page, E. and Wouters, L., 'The Europeanisation of National Bureaucracies', in J. Pierre (ed.), *Bureaucracy in the Modern State: An Introduction to Comparative Public Administration* (Aldershot: Edward Elgar, 1995), pp. 185–204.

Paraskevopoulos, C., 'Social Capital, Institutional Learning and European Regional Policy: Evidence from Greece', *Regional and Federal Studies*, 8: 3 (1998), 31–64.

Paraskevopoulos, C., 'EU Enlargement and Multi-level Governance in European Public Policy-making: Actors, Institutions and Learning', in C. Paraskevopoulos, P. Getmis and N. Rees (eds), *Adapting to EU Multi-level Governance: Regional and Environmental Policies in Cohesion and CEE Countries* (Aldershot: Ashgate, 2006), pp. 3–24.

Paraskevopoulos, C., Getmis, P. and Rees, N. (eds), *Adapting to EU Multi-level Governance: Regional and Environmental Policies in Cohesion and CEE Countries* (Aldershot: Ashgate, 2006).

Peters, G. 'Agenda Setting in the European Community', *Journal of European Public Policy*, 1: (1994), 9–26.

Pierre, J. (ed.), *Debating Governance: Authority, Steering and Democracy* (Oxford: Oxford University Press, 2000).

Pike, A., Rodriguez-Posi, A. and Tomaney, J., *Local and Regional Development* (London: Routledge, 2006).

Pollack, M., 'The End of Creeping Competence? EU Policy-making Since Maastricht', *Journal of Common Market Studies*, 38: 3 (2000), 519–38.

Pollitt, C. and Bouckaert, G., *Public Management Reform: A Comparative Analysis*, second edition (Oxford: Oxford University Press, 2004).

Potter, C. and Tilzey, M., 'Agricultural Policy Discourses in the European Post-Fordist Tradition: Neoliberalism, Neomercantilism and Multifunctionality', *Human Geography*, 29: 5 (2005), 581–600.

Quinn, B., 'Irish Local Government in a Comparative Context', in M. Callanan and J. F. Keogan (eds), *Local Government in Ireland Inside Out* (Dublin: Institute of Public Administration, 2003), pp. 447–59.

Radaelli, C. M., 'How Does Europeanisation Produce Domestic Change?', *Comparative European Politics*, 30: 5 (1997), 553–75.

Radaelli, C. M., 'Whither Europeanisation? Concept Stretching and Substantive Change', *European Integration Online Papers*, 4: 8 (2000), http://eoip.or.at/eiop/text/2000–008a.htm.

Radaelli, C. M., 'The Europeanisation of Public Policy', in K. Featherstone and C. M. Radaelli (eds), *The Politics of Europeanisation* (Oxford: Oxford University Press, 2003), pp. 27–56.

Radaelli, C. M., 'Europeanisation: Solution or Problem?' *European Integration Online Papers*, 8: 16 (2004), http://eiop.or.at/eoip/texte/2004–06.

Radaelli, C. M., 'Europeanisation: Solution or Problem?', in M. Cini and A. K. Bourne (eds), *European Union Studies* (Basingstoke: Palgrave, 2006), pp. 56–76.

Rees, N., 'The Kosovo Crisis, the International Response and Ireland', *Irish Studies in International Affairs*, 11 (2000), 55–70.

Rees, N., 'Europe and Ireland's Changing Security Policy', in M. Holmes (ed.), *Ireland and the European Union: Nice Enlargement and the Future of Europe* (Manchester: Manchester University Press, 2005), pp. 55–74.

Rees, N., 'Ireland's Foreign Relations in 2005', *Irish Studies in International Affairs*, 17 (2006), 151–82.

Rees, N., 'The Adaptation of Irish Foreign Policy to Europe', in M. Callanan (ed.), *Foundations of an Ever Closer Union: An Irish Perspective on the Fifty Years since the Treaty of Rome* (Dublin: Institute of Public Administration, 2007), pp. 121–42.

Rees, N. and Holmes, M., 'Capacity, Perceptions and Principles: Ireland's Changing Place in Europe', *Current Politics and Economics of Europe*, special edition, 11: 1 (2002), 49–60.

Rees, N., Quinn, B. and Connaughton, B., 'Adapting Irish Public Policy to European Integration', *Regional and Federal Studies*, 14: 3 (2004), 379–404.

Rees, N., Quinn, B. and Connaughton, B., 'The Challenge of Multi-level Governance and Europeanization in Ireland', in C. J. Paraskevopoulos, G. Panagiotis and N. Rees (eds), *Adapting to EU Multi-level Governance: Regional and Environmental Policies in Cohesion and CEE Countries* (Aldershot: Ashgate, 2006), pp. 53–78.

Reeves, E. and Palcic, D., 'Privatisation Policy and Enterprise Performance: The Case of Ireland', *Annals of Public and Cooperative Economics*, 75: 4 (2004), 525–48.

Risse, T., Cowles, M. G. and Caporaso, J., 'Europeanisation and Domestic Change: Introduction' in M. G. Cowles, J. Caporaso and T. Risse (eds), *Transforming Europe: Europeanisation and Domestic Change* (Ithaca, NY: Cornell University Press, 2001), pp. 1–20.

Robinson, M., 'Irish Parliamentary Scrutiny of European Community Legislation', *Common Market Law Review*, 16: 1, 9–30.

Rometsch, D. and Wessels, W., *The European Union and Member States: Towards Institutional Fusion* (Manchester: Manchester University Press, 1996).

Ruane, F., 'Chapter Four', in P. M. Sweeney (ed.), *Ireland's Economic Success: Reasons and Prospects* (Dublin: New Island, 2008), pp. 41–59.

Ryan, L., 'Strengthening Irish Identity through Openness' in R. O'Donnell (ed.), *Europe: The Irish Experience* (Dublin: Institute of European Affairs, 2000), pp. 55–68.

Salmon, T., *Unneutral Ireland: An Ambivalent and Unique Security Policy* (Oxford: Clarendon Press, 1989).

Sandholtz, W., 'Membership Matters: Limits of the Functional Approach to European Institutions', *Journal of Common Market Studies*, 34: 3 (1996), 403–29.

Sandholtz, W. and Sweet, A. S. (eds), *European Integration and Supranational Governance* (Oxford: Oxford University Press, 1998).

Scannell, Y., *The Law and Practice relating to Pollution Control in Ireland* (London: Graham and Trotman, 1982).

Scharpf, F., *Governing in Europe: Effective and Democratic?* (Oxford: Oxford University Press, 1999).

Schmidt, V., 'European Federalism and its Encroachments on National Institutions', *Publius*, 29: 1 (1999), 19–44.

Schmidt, V., 'Europeanisation and the Dynamics and Mechanics of Economic Policy Adjustment', *Journal of European Public Policy*, 9: 6 (2002), 894–912.

Schmidt, V., 'The Europeanisation of National Economies?', in S. Bulmer and C. Lequesne (eds), *The Member States of the European Union* (Oxford: Oxford University Pres, 2005), pp. 360–87.

Schmidt, V., 'Procedural Democracy in the EU: The Europeanisation of National and Sectoral Policy-making Processes', *Journal of European Public Policy*, 13: 3 (2006), 670–91.

Schmidt, V. and Radaelli, C., 'Conceptual and Methodological Issues in Policy Change', in C. Radaelli and V. Schmidt (eds), 'Policy, Change and Discourse in Europe', *West European Politics*, 27: 4 (2004), 1–28.

Schneider, V., 'Institutional Reform in Telecommunications: The European Union in Transnational Policy Diffusion', in M. G. Cowles, J. Caporaso and T. Risse (eds), *Transforming Europe: Europeanisation and Domestic Change* (Ithaca, NY: Cornell University Press, 2001), pp. 60–78.

Scott, D., *Ireland's Contribution to the European Union*, Occasional Paper, no. 4 (Dublin: Institute of European Affairs, 1994).

Sharp, P., *Irish Foreign Policy and the European Community: A Study of the Impact of Interdependence on the Foreign Policy of a Small State* (Aldershot: Dartmouth, 1990).

Sheehy, S., 'Towards Free Trade for Agriculture', in F. O'Muircheartaigh (ed.), *Ireland in the Coming Times* (Dublin, Institute of Public Administration, 1997), pp. 285–98.

Sheehy, S., 'Agricultural Policy', in J. Dooge and R. Barrington (eds) *A Vital National Interest: Ireland in Europe, 1973–1998* (Dublin: Institute of Public Administration, 1999), pp. 944–56.

Skelly, J., *Irish Diplomacy at the United Nations, 1945–1965* (Dublin: Irish Academic Press, 1997).

Smith, K. E., *European Union Foreign Policy in a Changing World* (Cambridge: Polity Press, 2003).

Smith, N. J.-A., *Showcasing Globalisation: The Political Economy of the Irish Republic* (Manchester: Manchester University Press, 2005).

Sverdrup, U., 'Compliance and Styles of Conflict Management', *Arena Working Paper 08/3* (Oslo: University of Oslo, 2003).

Sweeney, P., *The Celtic Tiger: Ireland's Continuing Economic Miracle* (Dublin: Oak Tree Press, 1999).

Sweeney, P., *Ireland's Economic Success: Reasons and Lessons* (Dublin: New Island, 2008).

TASC, *Public Perspectives on Democracy in Ireland, Topline Results* (Dublin: TASC, June 2005).

Tansey, P., *The Economic Consequences of Maastricht*, Occasional Paper no. 2 (Dublin: Institute of European Affairs, 1992).

Taylor, G., 'Conserving the Emerald Tiger: The Politics of Environmental Regulation in Ireland', *Environmental Politics*, 7: 4 (1998), 53–74.

Taylor, G., *Conserving the Emerald Tiger: The Politics of Environmental Regulation in Ireland* (Galway: Arlen House, 2001).

Taylor, G., *Negotiated Governance and Public Policy in Ireland* (Manchester: Manchester University Press, 2005).

Taylor, G. and Horan, A., 'From Cats, Dogs and Playgrounds to IPC Licensing: Policy Learning and the Evolution of Environmental Policy in Ireland', *British Journal of Politics and International Relations*, 3: 3 (2001), 369–92.

Taylor, G. and Millar, M., 'The Appliance of Science: The Politics of European food Regulation and Reform', in *Public Policy and Administration*, 17: 2 (2002), 125–46.

Telò, M., *Europe: A Civilian Power? European Union, Global Governance, Word Order* (Basingstoke: Palgrave Macmillan, 2007).

Thatcher, M., 'Winners and Losers in Europeanisation: Reforming the National Regulation of Telecommunications', *West European Politics*, 27: 2 (2004), 284–309.

Tonra, B., 'Denmark and Ireland' in I. Manners and R. Whitman (eds), *The Foreign Policies of European Union Members* (Manchester: Manchester University Press, 2000), pp. 224–42.

Tonra, B., *The Europeanisation of National Foreign Policy: Dutch, Danish and Irish Foreign Policy in the European Union* (Aldershot: Ashgate, 2001).

Tonra, B., *Global Citizen and European Republic: Irish Foreign Policy in Transition* (Manchester: Manchester University Press, 2007).

Toonen, T., 'Europe of the Administrations: The Challenge of 1992 (and beyond)', *Public Administration Review*, 52: 2 (1992), 108–15.

Tovey, H. and Share, P., *A Sociology of Ireland*, second edition (Dublin: Gill & Macmillan, 2005).

Wallace, H., Wallace, W. and Webb, C. (eds), *Policy-making in the European Communities* (London: John Wiley and Sons, 1977).

Wallace, H., Wallace, W. and Webb, C. (eds), *Policy-making in the European Communities* (London: John Wiley and Sons, 1983).

Walsh, J., 'EC Structural Funds and Economic Development in the Republic of Ireland', in P. Shirlow (ed.), *Development Ireland: Contemporary Issues* (London: Pluto Press, 1995), pp. 54–68.

Walsh, J. A., 'Regional Development', in B. Bartley and R. Kitchin (eds), *Understanding Contemporary Ireland* (London: Pluto Press, 2007).

Wessels, W., Maurer, A. and Mittag, J. (eds), *Fifteen into One? The European Union and Its Member States* (Manchester: Manchester University Press, 2003), pp. 248–70.

Whelan, B., *Ireland and the Marshall Plan, 1947–1957* (Dublin: Four Courts Press, 2000).

Whelan, P., T. Arnold, T., Aylward, A., Doyle, M., Lacey, B., Loftus, L., McLoughlin, N., Molloy, E., Payne, J., Pine, M., *Cross Departmental Challenges: A Whole of*

Government Approach for the Twenty-first Century (Dublin: Institute of Public Administration, 2003).

Whitaker, T. K., *Economic Development* (Dublin: Department of Finance/The Stationery Office, 1958).

Whitaker, T. K., 'Ireland's New Economic Strategy and the Beginnings of European Integration', in M. Callanan (ed.), *Foundations of an Ever Closer Union: An Irish Perspective on the Fifty Years since the Treaty of Rome* (Dublin: Institute of Public Administration, 2007), pp. 51–6.

Wright, V., 'Reshaping the State: The Implications for Public Administration', *West European Politics*, 17: 3 (1994), 102–37.

Yearley, S., 'The Social Shaping of the Irish Environmental Movement', in P. Clancy, M. Kelly, R. Zoltaniecki and J. Wiatr (eds), *Irish Society: Sociological Perspectives* (Dublin: Institute of Public Administration, 1995), pp. 652–74.

Young, H. and Rees, N., 'EU Voting in the UN General Assembly', *Irish Studies in International Affairs*, 16 (2005) 193–08.

<h1 style="text-align:center">Index</h1>